Fodor's InFocus

VIRGIN
ISLANDS

Where to Stay and Eat
for All Budgets

Must-See Sights
and Local Secrets

Ratings You Can Trust

Fodor's Travel Publications New York, Toronto, London, Sydney, Auckland
www.fodors.com

FODOR'S VIRGIN ISLANDS 2008

Series Editor: Douglas Stallings

Editor: Mark Sullivan

Editorial Production: Astrid deRidder

Editorial Contributors: Carol M. Bareuther, Lynda Lohr

Maps & Illustrations: Bob Blake and Rebecca Baer, *map editors*

Design: Fabrizio LaRocca, *creative director*; Guido Caroti, Siobhan O'Hare, *art directors*; Ann McBride, *designers*; Melanie Marin, *senior picture editor*

Photography:

Cover Photo: (Deadman's Bay, Peter Islands, British Virgin Islands): Karl Weatherly/Photographer's Choice/Getty Images

Production/Manufacturing: Matthew Struble

COPYRIGHT

ISBN 978-1-4000-1931-1

ISSN 1940-3305

SPECIAL SALES

This book is available for special discounts for bulk purchases for sales promotions or premiums. Special editions, including personalized covers, excerpts of existing books, and corporate imprints, can be created in large quantities for special needs. For more information, write to Special Markets/Premium Sales, 1745 Broadway, MD 6-2, New York, New York, NY 10019, or e-mail specialmarkets@randomhouse.com.

AN IMPORTANT TIP & AN INVITATION

Although all prices, opening times, and other details in this book are based on information supplied to us at press time, changes occur all the time in the travel world, and Fodor's cannot accept responsibility for facts that become outdated or for inadvertent errors or omissions. **So always confirm information when it matters,** especially if you're making a detour to visit a specific place. Your experiences—positive and negative—matter to us. If we have missed or misstated something, **please write to us.** We follow up on all suggestions. Contact the Virgin Islands editor at editors@fodors.com or c/o Fodor's at 1745 Broadway, New York, NY 10019.

PRINTED IN THE UNITED STATES OF AMERICA

10 9 8 7 6 5 4 3 2 1

Be a Fodor's Correspondent

Your opinion matters. It matters to us. It matters to your fellow Fodor's travelers, too. And we'd like to hear it. In fact, we *need* to hear it. When you share your experiences and opinions, you become an active member of the Fodor's community. Here's how you can help improve Fodor's for all of us.

Tell us when we're right. We rely on local writers to give you an insider's perspective. But our writers and staff editors also depend on you. Your positive feedback is a vote to renew our recommendations for the next edition.

Tell us when we're wrong. We update most of our guides every year. But things change. If any of our descriptions are inaccurate or inadequate, we'll incorporate your changes in the next edition and will correct factual errors at fodors.com *immediately*.

Tell us what to include. You probably have had fantastic travel experiences that aren't yet in Fodor's. Why not share them with a community of like-minded travelers? Share your discoveries and experiences with everyone directly at fodors.com. Your input may lead us to add a new listing or a higher recommendation.

Give us your opinion instantly at our feedback center at www.fodors.com/feedback. You may also e-mail editors@fodors.com with the subject line "Virgin Islands Editor." Or send your nominations, comments, and complaints by mail to Virgin Islands Editor, Fodor's, 1745 Broadway, New York, NY 10019.

Happy Traveling!

Tim Jarrell, Publisher

CONTENTS

ABOUT THIS BOOK

Our Ratings

We wouldn't recommend a place that wasn't worth your time, but sometimes a place is so experiential that superlatives don't do it justice: you just have to be there to know. These sights, properties, and experiences get our highest rating, **Fodor's Choice** indicated by orange stars throughout this book. Black stars highlight sights and properties we deem **Highly Recommended** places that our writers, editors, and readers praise again and again.

Credit Cards

Want to pay with plastic? **AE, D, DC, MC, V** following restaurant and hotel listings indicate whether American Express, Discover, Diners Club, MasterCard, and Visa are accepted.

Restaurants

Unless we state otherwise, restaurants serve both lunch and dinner daily. We mention dress only when there's a specific requirement and reservations only when they're essential or not accepted—it's always best to book ahead.

Hotels

Unless we tell you otherwise, you can assume that the hotels have private bath, phone, TV, and air-conditioning. We always list facilities but not whether you'll be charged an extra fee to use them, so when pricing accommodations, find out what's included.

Many Listings

★	Fodor's Choice
★	Highly recommended
⊠	Physical address
⊹	Directions
⑅	Mailing address
☎	Telephone
🖷	Fax
⊕	On the Web
✎	E-mail
🖾	Admission fee
☉	Open/closed times
Ⓜ	Metro stations
▭	Credit cards

Hotels & Restaurants

🏨	Hotel
⟲	Number of rooms
⌂	Facilities
⑂	Meal plans
✕	Restaurant
☙	Reservations
⟍	Smoking
🍷	BYOB
✕🏨	Hotel with restaurant that warrants a visit

Outdoors

⛳	Golf
⛺	Camping

Other

☾	Family-friendly
⇨	See also
⊠	Branch address
☞	Take note

The Virgin Islands

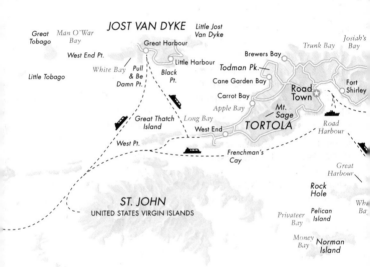

JOST VAN DYKE

Great Tobago

Man O'War Bay

Little Jost Van Dyke

Great Harbour

West End Pt.

White Bay

Little Tobago

Pull & Be Damn Pt.

Little Harbour

Black Pt.

Brewers Bay

Todman Pk.

Cane Garden Bay

Carrot Bay

Apple Bay

Trunk Bay

Josiah's Bay

Road Town

Mt. Sage

TORTOLA

Fort Shirley

Great Thatch Island

Long Bay

West End

Frenchman's Cay

Road Harbour

West Pt.

Great Harbour

Rock Hole

ST. JOHN
UNITED STATES VIRGIN ISLANDS

Privateer Bay

Pelican Island

Money Bay

Norman Island

Wh Ba

Long P

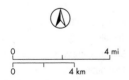

0   4 mi
0   4 km

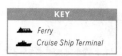

KEY

🛥 *Ferry*
🚢 *Cruise Ship Terminal*

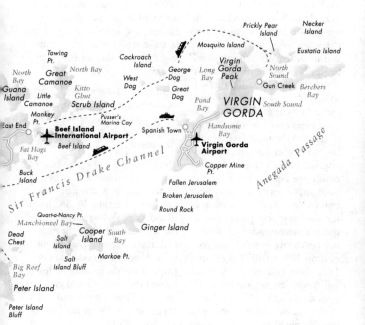

Towing Pt.
North Bay
Great Camanoe
North Bay
Cockroach Island
West Dog
George Dog
Long Bay
Virgin Gorda Peak
North Sound
Prickly Pear Island
Necker Island
Eustatia Island

North Bay
Guana Island
Kitto Ghut
Little Camanoe
Scrub Island
Great Dog
Pond Bay
Gun Creek
Berchers Bay
South Sound

VIRGIN GORDA

Monkey Pt.
Pusser's Marina Cay
East End
Beef Island International Airport
Spanish Town
Handsome Bay
Virgin Gorda Airport

Fat Hogs Bay
Beef Island

Buck Island
Copper Mine Pt.

Sir Francis Drake Channel

Fallen Jerusalem

Anegada Passage

Broken Jerusalem

Round Rock

Quart-o-Nancy Pt.
Manchioneel Bay
Dead Chest
Cooper Island
South Bay
Salt Island
Ginger Island

Big Reef Bay
Salt Island Bluff
Markoe Pt.

Peter Island

Peter Island Bluff

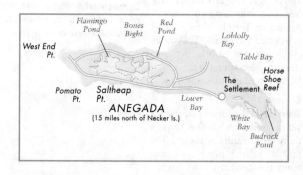

Flamingo Pond
Bones Bight
Red Pond
Loblolly Bay

West End Pt.
Table Bay

Horse Shoe Reef

Pomato Pt.
Saltheap Pt.
ANEGADA
(15 miles north of Necker Is.)
Lower Bay
The Settlement

White Bay

Budrock Pond

WHEN TO GO

The high season in the Virgin Islands is traditionally winter—from December 15 to the week after the St. Thomas Carnival, usually the last week in April—when northern weather is at its worst. During this season, you're guaranteed the most entertainment at resorts and the most people with whom to enjoy it. It's also the most fashionable, the most expensive, and the most popular time to visit—and most hotels are heavily booked. You must make reservations at least two or three months in advance for the very best places (sometimes a year in advance for the most exclusive spots). Hotel prices drop 20% to 50% after April 15; airfares and cruise prices also fall. Saving money isn't the only reason to visit the Virgin Islands during the off-season. Summer is usually one of the prettiest times of the year; the sea is even calmer, and things move at a slower pace (except for the first two weeks of August on Tortola when the BVI celebrates Carnival). The water is clearer for snorkeling and smoother for sailing in the Virgin Islands in May, June, and July.

Climate

Weather in the Virgin Islands is a year-round wonder. The average daily temperature is about 80°F, and there isn't much variation from the coolest to the warmest months. Rainfall averages 40 to 44 inches per year. But in the tropics, rainstorms tend to be sudden and brief, often erupting early in the morning and at dusk.

In May and June what's known as the Sahara Dust sometimes moves through, making for hazy spring days and spectacular sunsets.

Toward the end of summer, of course, hurricane season begins in earnest, with the first tropical wave passing by in June. Islanders pay close attention to the tropical waves as they form and travel across the Atlantic from Africa. In an odd paradox, tropical storms passing by leave behind the sunniest and clearest days you'll ever see. (And that's saying something in the land of zero air pollution.)

Information **Weather Channel Connection** (☎ *900/932–8437 95¢ per minute from a Touch-T one phone* ⊕ *www.weather.com*).

St. Thomas

"Now for the 'must sees'—that's tough. [On St. Thomas that means] snorkeling at Secret Harbour or the more touristy and popular Coki Beach. A couple-hour island tour with one of the tour guides with stops at Mountain Top, Drake's Seat, etc. Paradise Tramway. Shopping in Charlotte Amalie or Havensight (where the cruise ships dock) or the new Yacht Haven. Checking out the historical buildings in Charlotte Amalie. Kayak[ing in] the mangroves."

—beachplum

Updated
By
Carol M.
Bareuther

If you fly to the 32-square-mi (83-square-km) island of St. Thomas, you land at its western end; if you arrive by cruise ship, you come into one of the world's most beautiful harbors. Either way, one of your first sights is the town of Charlotte Amalie. From the harbor you see an idyllic-looking village that spreads into the lower hills. If you were expecting a quiet hamlet with its inhabitants hanging out under palm trees, you've missed that era by about 300 years. Although other islands in the USVI developed plantation economies, St. Thomas cultivated its harbor, and it became a thriving seaport soon after it was settled by the Danish in the 1600s.

The success of the naturally perfect harbor was enhanced by the fact that the Danes—who ruled St. Thomas with only a couple of short interruptions from 1666 to 1917—avoided involvement in some 100 years' worth of European wars. Denmark was the only European country with colonies in the Caribbean to stay neutral during the War of the Spanish Succession in the early 1700s. Thus, products of the Dutch, English, and French islands—sugar, cotton, and indigo—were traded through Charlotte Amalie, along with the regular shipments of slaves. When the Spanish wars ended, trade fell off, but by the end of the 1700s Europe was at war again, Denmark again remained neutral, and St. Thomas continued to prosper. Even into the 1800s, while the economies of St. Croix and St. John foundered with the market for sugarcane, St. Thomas's economy remained vigorous. This prosperity led to the development of shipyards, a well-organized banking system, and a large merchant class. In 1845 Charlotte Amalie had 101 large importing houses owned by the English, French, Germans, Haitians, Spaniards, Americans, Sephardim, and Danes.

Charlotte Amalie is still one of the world's most active cruise-ship ports. On almost any day at least one and sometimes as many as eight cruise ships are tied to the dock or anchored outside the harbor. Gently rocking in the shadows of these giant floating hotels are just about every other kind of vessel imaginable: sleek sailing mono- and multihulls that will take you on a sunset cruise complete with rum punch and a Jimmy Buffett soundtrack, private megayachts that spirit busy executives away, and barnacle-bottom sloops—with laundry draped over the lifelines—that are home to world-cruising gypsies. Huge container ships pull up in Sub Base, west of the harbor, bringing in everything from breakfast cereals to tires. Anchored right along the waterfront are down-island barges that ply the waters between the Greater Antilles and the Leeward Islands, transporting goods like refrigerators, VCRs, and disposable diapers.

The waterfront road through Charlotte Amalie was once part of the harbor. Before it was filled in to build the highway, the beach came up to the back door of the warehouses that now line the thoroughfare. Two hundred years ago those warehouses were filled with indigo, tobacco, and cotton. Today the stone buildings house silk, crystal, linens, and leather. Exotic fragrances are still traded, but by island beauty queens in air-conditioned perfume palaces instead of through open market stalls. The pirates of old used St. Thomas as a base from which to raid merchant ships of every nation, though they were particularly fond of the gold- and silver-laden treasure ships heading to Spain. Pirates are still around, but today's versions use St. Thomas as a drop-off for their contraband: illegal immigrants and drugs.

EXPLORING ST. THOMAS

St. Thomas is 13 mi (21 km) long and less than 4 mi (6½ km) wide, but it's extremely hilly, and even an 8- or 10-mi (13- or 16-km) trip could take well over an hour. Don't let that discourage you, though; the mountain ridge that runs east to west through the middle and separates the island's Caribbean and Atlantic sides has spectacular vistas.

ABOUT THE RESTAURANTS

The beauty of St. Thomas and its sister islands has attracted a cadre of professionally trained chefs who know their way around fresh fish and local fruits. You can dine on everything from terrific cheap local dishes such as goat water (a spicy stew) and fungi (a cornmeal polentalike side dish) to imports such as hot pastrami sandwiches and raspberries in crème fraîche.

If your accommodations have a kitchen and you plan to cook, there's good variety in St. Thomas's mainland-style supermarkets. Just be prepared for grocery prices that are about 20% higher than those in the United States. As for drinking, outside the hotels a beer in a bar will cost between $2 and $3 and a piña colada $5 or more.

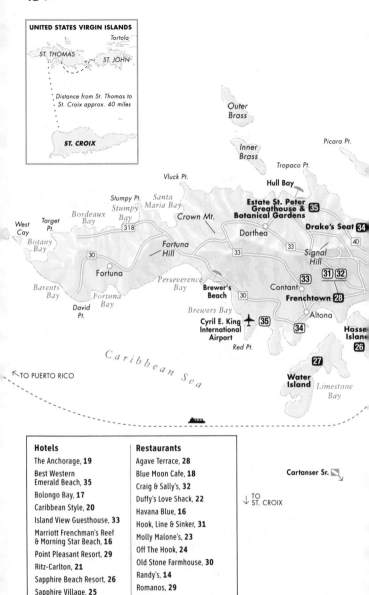

UNITED STATES VIRGIN ISLANDS

Tortola

ST. THOMAS   ST. JOHN

Distance from St. Thomas to
St. Croix approx. 40 miles

ST. CROIX

Outer
Brass

Picara Pt.

Inner
Brass

Tropaco Pt.

Vluck Pt.

Hull Bay

Stumpy Pt.   Santa
Stumpy   Maria Bay
Bay

Crown Mt.

**Estate St. Peter
Greathouse &
Botanical Gardens** 35

Bordeaux
Bay

West   Target
Cay   Pt.

Botany
Bay

Dorthea

Drake's Seat 34

40

318

Fortuna
Hill

33   33

Signal
Hill

30

33   31 32

Fortuna

Perseverence
Bay

Contant

Barents
Bay

Fortuna
Bay

**Brewer's
Beach**

Frenchtown 28

David
Pt.

30

Altona

Brewers Bay

Cyril E. King ✈ 35
International
Airport

34

Hasse
Island

Red Pt.

26

27

Caribbean Sea

Water
Island

Limestone
Bay

← TO PUERTO RICO

🚢

Cartanser Sr. ◥

↓ TO
  ST. CROIX

Hotels	**Restaurants**
The Anchorage, **19**	Agave Terrace, **28**
Best Western Emerald Beach, **35**	Blue Moon Cafe, **18**
Bolongo Bay, **17**	Craig & Sally's, **32**
Caribbean Style, **20**	Duffy's Love Shack, **22**
Island View Guesthouse, **33**	Havana Blue, **16**
Marriott Frenchman's Reef & Morning Star Beach, **16**	Hook, Line & Sinker, **31**
Point Pleasant Resort, **29**	Molly Malone's, **23**
Ritz-Carlton, **21**	Off The Hook, **24**
Sapphire Beach Resort, **26**	Old Stone Farmhouse, **30**
Sapphire Village, **25**	Randy's, **14**
Secret Harbour, **18**	Romanos, **29**
Wyndham Sugar Bay, **27**	Tickle's, **34**
	W!kked, **15**

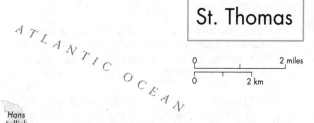

St. Thomas

1

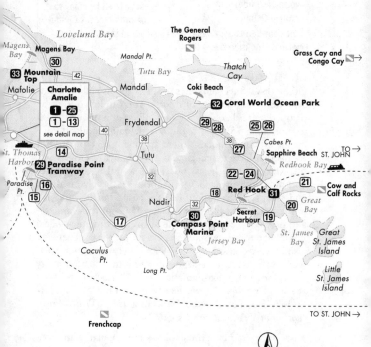

ATLANTIC OCEAN

Hans Lollick

Lovelund Bay

Magens Bay

Magens Bay **30**

33 Mountain Top

Mafolie

Charlotte Amalie
1-**25**
1-**13**
see detail map

The General Rogers

Mandal Pt.

Tutu Bay

Thatch Cay

Grass Cay and Congo Cay →

Coki Beach

32 Coral World Ocean Park

Mandal

42

Frydendal

40

29 **28**

38

25 **26**

Cabes Pt.

27 Sapphire Beach

TO ST. JOHN →

St. Thomas Harbor **29** Paradise Point Tramway **14**

38

Tutu

32

Redhook Bay

22-**24**

Paradise Pt. **15**

16

Nadir

32

18 Red Hook **31**

21

20

Cow and Calf Rocks

Great Bay

17

Compass Point Marina **30**

Secret Harbour **19**

Jersey Bay

St. James Bay

Great St. James Island

Coculus Pt.

Long Pt.

Little St. James Island

Frenchcap

TO ST. JOHN →

KEY	
〰	Beaches
◳	Dive Sites
⛴	Cruise Ship Terminal
1	Exploring Sights
1	Hotels & Restaurants

ST. THOMAS TOP 5

Shop 'til you drop: Find great deals on duty-free jewelry, timepieces, and electronics along Charlotte Amalie's Main Street.

Tell Fish Stories: Go in search of magnificent blue marlins and other trophy-worthy fish from June through October.

Get Your Sea Legs: Cruise between the islands any time of year or join the International Rolex Regatta in March.

Hit the Links: Play through the "Devil's Triangle," an intimidating cliffside trio of holes at Mahogany Run Golf Course.

Take a Dip: Swim at Magens Bay, considered by many to be one of the most beautiful beaches in the world.

ABOUT THE HOTELS

Of the USVI, St. Thomas has the most rooms and the greatest number and variety of resorts. You can let yourself be pampered at a luxurious resort—albeit at a price of $300 to more than $500 per night, not including meals. If your means are more modest, there are fine hotels (often with rooms that have a kitchen and a living area) in lovely settings throughout the island. There are also guesthouses and inns with great views (if not a beach at your door) and great service at about half the cost of what you'll pay at the beachfront pleasure palaces. Many of these are east and north of Charlotte Amalie or overlooking hills—ideal if you plan to get out and mingle with the locals. There are also inexpensive lodgings (most right in town) that are perfect if you just want a clean room to return to after a day of exploring or beach-bumming. You can learn more about the smaller properties on the island from the **St. Thomas–St. John Hotel & Tourism Association** *(see ⇨ Visitor Information in Virgin Islands Essentials).*

East-end condominium complexes are popular with families. Although condos are pricey (winter rates average $350 per night for a two-bedroom unit, which usually sleeps six), they have full kitchens, and you can definitely save money by cooking for yourself—especially if you bring some of your own nonperishable foodstuffs. (Virtually everything on St. Thomas is imported, and restaurants and shops pass shipping costs on to you.) Though you may spend some time laboring in the kitchen, many condos ease your burden with daily maid service and on-site restaurants; a few also have resort amenities, including pools and tennis courts. The east end is convenient to St. John, and it's a hub for the boating crowd, with some good restaurants. The prices below reflect rates in high season, which runs from December 15 to April 15. Rates are 25% to 50% lower the rest of the year.

WHAT IT COSTS IN DOLLARS				
$$$$	$$$	$$	$	¢
RESTAURANTS				
OVER $30	$20–$30	$12–$20	$8–$12	UNDER $8
HOTELS				
* OVER $350	$250–$350	$150–$250	$80–$150	UNDER $80
** OVER $450	$350–$450	$250–$350	$125–$250	UNDER $125

*EP, BP, CP; **AI, FAP, MAP; Restaurant prices are for a main course at dinner, excluding tip. Hotel prices are for two people in a double room during high season, excluding 8% tax, service charge and energy surcharges (which can vary significantly), and meal plans (except for all-inclusives).

TIMING

April is a great time to visit St. Thomas, as the island comes alive for Carnival. The celebrations—steel-drum music, colorful costumes, and dancing in the streets—culminate the last weekend of the month.

CHARLOTTE AMALIE

Look beyond the pricey shops, T-shirt vendors, and bustling crowds for a glimpse of the island's history. The city served as the capital of Denmark's outpost in the Caribbean until 1917, an aspect of the island often lost in the glitz of the shopping district.

Emancipation Gardens, right next to the fort, is a good place to start a walking tour. Tackle the hilly part of town first: head north up Government Hill to the historic buildings that house government offices and have incredible views. Several regal churches line the route that runs west back to the town proper and the old-time market. Virtually all the alleyways that intersect Main Street lead to eateries that serve frosty drinks, sandwiches, and West Indian fare. There are public rest rooms in this area, too. Allow an hour for a quick view of the sights.

A note about the street names: In deference to the island's heritage, the streets downtown are labeled by their Danish names. Locals will use both the Danish name and the English name (such as Dronningens Gade and Norre Gade for Main Street), but most people refer to things by their location ("a block toward the Waterfront off Main Street" or "next to the Little Switzerland Shop"). You may find it more useful if you ask for directions by shop names or landmarks.

Numbers in the margin correspond to points of interest on the Charlotte Amalie map.

WHAT TO SEE

㉒ All Saints Anglican Church. Built in 1848 from stone quarried on the island, the church has thick, arched window frames lined with the yellow brick that came to the islands as ballast aboard ships. Merchants left the brick on the waterfront when they filled their boats with molasses, sugar, mahogany, and rum for the return voyage. The church was built in celebration of the end of slavery in the USVI. ✉*Domini Gade* ☎*340/774–0217* ⊘*Mon.–Sat. 9–3.*

㉔ Cathedral of St. Peter & St. Paul. This building was consecrated as a parish church in 1848 and serves as the seat of the territory's Roman Catholic diocese. The ceiling and walls are covered with murals painted in 1899 by two Belgian artists, Father Leo Servais and Brother Ildephonsus. The San Juan–marble altar and side walls were added in the 1960s. ✉*Lower Main St.* ☎*340/774–0201* ⊘*Mon.–Sat. 8–5.*

㉓ Danish Consulate Building. Built in 1830, this structure once housed the Danish Consulate. Although the Danish Consul General, Soøren Blak, has an office in Charlotte Amalie, the Danish Consulate is now in the Scandinavian Center in Havensight Mall. This building is not open to the public. ✉*Take stairs north at corner of Bjerge Gade and Crystal Gade to Denmark Hill.*

⑪ Dutch Reformed Church. This church has an austere loveliness that's amazing considering all it's been through. Founded in 1744, it's been rebuilt twice following fires and hurricanes. The unembellished cream-color hall gives you a sense of peace—albeit monochromatically. The only other color is the forest green of the shutters and the carpet. Call ahead if you wish to visit at a particular time, as the doors are some-

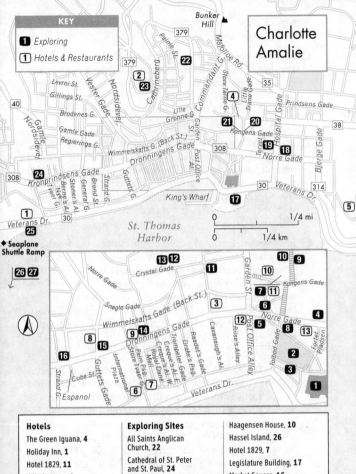

KEY

1 Exploring

1 Hotels & Restaurants

Charlotte Amalie

Bunker Hill

379
Palme St.
379
22
Levroi St.
2
Gillings St.
23
Nordsidevej
Vester Gade
Cathrineberg
Little Gronne G.
Brodenes G.
Gamle Nordsidevej
Gamle Gade
Regierings G.
Wimmelskafts G. (Back St.)
Drohningens Gade
Guttets G.
Strand G.
Brand St.
General G.
Stoner's Al.
Berne's Al.
Nye G.
Kronprindsens Gade
24
308
308
King's Wharf
17
Veterans Dr.
1
25
Seaplane Shuttle Ramp
26 27

Matloroe Rd.
35
Store Tårne G.
Little Trane Gade
Garden St.
Post Office Al.
4
21
20
Kongens Gade
19
18
Norre Gade
308
30
Veterans Dr.
Hospital Gade
Prindsens Gade
38
Bjerge Gade
314
5

Torvet

St. Thomas Harbor

0   1/4 mi
0   1/4 km

Norre Gade
Crystal Gade
13 12
11
Snegle Gade
3
Wimmelskafts Gade (Back St.)
9 14
Drohningens Gade
Trompeter Gade
Creque's Al. E.
Creque's Al. W.
Royal Dane
Palm Psg.
Store Tvaer Gade
6
8
15
16
International Plaza
Strand G.
Cuba St.
Espanol
Gutteths Gade
7
Veterans Dr.

Garden St.
10 9
10
7 11
6
Norre Gade
5
12
Cavanaugh's Al.
Raadet's Gade
Drake's Psg.
Riise's Alley
Post Office Alley
8
2
3
4
13
Tolbod Gade
Fortet Pladsen
1

Hotels

The Green Iguana, **4**
Holiday Inn, **1**
Hotel 1829, **11**
Villa Santana, **2**

Restaurants

Banana Tree Grille, **5**
Café Amici, **12**
Cuzzin's Caribbean
Restaurant & Bar, **3**
Gladys' Cafe, **7**
Greenhouse, **6**
Hervé, **10**
Jen's Gourmet, **13**
Meson Amalia, **8**
Virgilio's, **9**

Exploring Sites

All Saints Anglican
Church, **22**
Cathedral of St. Peter
and St. Paul, **24**
Danish Consulate
Building, **23**
Dutch Reformed Church, **11**
Educators Park, **6**
Edward Wilmouth
Blyden Marine Terminal, **25**
Emancipation Garden, **2**
Enid M. Baa Public Library, **15**
Fort Christian, **1**
Frederick Lutheran Church, **4**
Government House, **21**
Grand Hotel, **8**

Haagensen House, **10**
Hassel Island, **26**
Hotel 1829, **7**
Legislature Building, **17**
Market Square, **16**
Memorial Moravian
Church, **18**
00 Steps, **9**
Pissarro Building, **14**
Roosevelt Park, **19**
Seven Arches Museum, **20**
Synagogue, **12**
U.S. Post Office, **5**
Vendors Plaza, **3**
Water Island, **27**
Weibel Museum, **13**

times locked. ✉*Nye Gade and Crystal Gade* ☎*340/776–8255* ⏱*Weekdays 9–5.*

❻ Educators Park. A peaceful place amid the town's hustle and bustle, the park has memorials to three famous Virgin Islanders: educator Edith Williams, J. Antonio Jarvis (a founder of the *Daily News*), and educator and author Rothschild Francis. The last gave many speeches here. ✉*Main St., across from post office.*

㉕ Edward Wilmoth Blyden Marine Terminal. Locally called Tortola Wharf, it's where you can catch the *Native Son* and other ferries to the BVI. The restaurant upstairs is a good place to watch the Charlotte Amalie harbor traffic and sip an iced tea. Next door is the ramp for the *Seaborne Airlines* seaplane, which offers commuter service to St. Croix, the BVI, and Puerto Rico. ✉*Waterfront Hwy.*

❷ Emancipation Garden. Built to commemorate the freeing of ⏱ slaves in 1848, the garden was the site of a 150th anniversary celebration of emancipation. A bronze bust of a freed slave blowing a symbolic conch shell commemorates this anniversary. The gazebo here is used for official ceremonies. Two other monuments show the island's Danish-American connection—a bust of Denmark's King Christian and a scaled-down model of the U.S. Liberty Bell. ✉*Between Tolbod Gade and Fort Christian.*

⓯ Enid M. Baa Public Library. Like so many other structures on ⏱ the north side of Main Street, this large pink building is a typical 18th-century town house. The library was once the home of merchant and landowner Baron von Bretton. He and other merchants built their houses (stores downstairs, living quarters above) across from the brick warehouses on the south side of the street. This is the island's first recorded fireproof building, meaning it was built of ballast brick instead of wood. Its interior of high ceilings and cool stone floors is the perfect refuge from the afternoon sun. You can browse through historic papers or just sit in the breeze by an open window reading the paper. ✉*Main St.* ☎*340/774–0630* ⏱*Weekdays 9–5, Sat. 10–3.*

❶ Fort Christian. St. Thomas's oldest standing structure, this ⏱ monument was built between 1672 and 1680 and now has U.S. National Landmark status. The clock tower was added in the 19th century. This remarkable building has, over time, been used as a jail, governor's residence, town hall, courthouse, and church. Closed for renovations since

1

2005, the fort is scheduled to reopen in 2008. It will then house the **Virgin Islands Museum,** where you can see exhibits on the fascinating history of the region. The gift shop, which sells local crafts, books, and other souvenirs, will reopen at the same time. ✉ *Waterfront Hwy., east of shopping district* ☎ *340/776–4566.*

❹ **Frederick Lutheran Church.** This historic church has a massive mahogany altar, and its pews—each with their own door—were once rented to families of the congregation. Lutheranism is the state religion of Denmark, and when the territory was without a minister, the governor—who had his own elevated pew—filled in. ✉ *Norre Gade* ☎ *340/776–1315* ☉ *Mon.–Sat. 9–4.*

㉑ **Government House.** Built in 1867, this neoclassical white brick-and-wood structure houses the offices of the governor of the Virgin Islands. Inside, the staircases are of native mahogany, as are the plaques hand-lettered in gold with the names of the governors appointed and, since 1970, elected. Brochures detailing the history of the building are available, but you may have to ask for them. ✉ *Government Hill* ☎ *340/774–0294* 🎟 *Free* ☉ *Weekdays 8–5.*

❽ **Grand Hotel.** This imposing building stands at the head of Main Street. Once the island's premier hotel, it has been converted into offices and shops. ✉ *Tolbod Gade at Norre Gade* ☎ *340/774–7282* ☉ *Weekdays 8–5, Sat. 9–noon.*

❿ **Haagensen House.** Behind Hotel 1829, this lovingly restored home was built in the early 1800s by Danish entrepreneur Hans Haagensen and is surrounded by an equally impressive cookhouse, outbuildings, and terraced gardens. A lower-level banquet hall now showcases antique prints and photographs. Guided tours begin at the lookout tower at Blackbeard's Castle and continue to the circa-1860s Villa Notman, Haagensen House, and Hotel 1829. The first tour starts at 9:30 AM. ✉ *Government Hill* ☎ *340/776–1234 or 340/776–1829* 🎟 *Tours $35* ☉ *Oct.–May, daily 9–4; June–Sept., by appointment only.*

㉖ **Hassel Island.** East of Water Island in Charlotte Amalie harbor, Hassel Island is part of the Virgin Islands National Park, as it has the ruins of a British military garrison (built during a brief British occupation of the USVI during the 1800s) and the remains of a marine railway (where ships were hoisted into dry dock for repairs). You can opt for a three-hour guided tour, which departs from the dock at Marriott's Frenchman's Reef Resort. For $49 per person you can see the ruins as well as the island's flora and fauna.

❼ Hotel 1829. As its name implies, the hotel was built in 1829, albeit as the private residence of a prominent merchant named Alaxander Lavalette. The building's coral-color façade is accented with fancy wrought-iron railings, and the interior is paneled in dark wood, which makes it feel delightfully cool. From the terrace there's an exquisite view of the harbor framed by brilliant orange bougainvillea. You can combine a visit to this hotel with a walking tour of Haagensen House, Villa Notman, and the lookout tower at Blackbeard's Castle just behind the hotel. ⌂ *Government Hill* ☏ *340/776–1829 or 340/776–1234* ⊕ *www.hotel1829. com* ☞ *Tour $20* ☉ *Oct.–May, daily 9–4; June–Sept., by appointment only.*

⓱ Legislature Building. Its pastoral-looking lime-green exterior conceals the vociferous political wrangling of the Virgin Islands Senate. Constructed originally by the Danish as a police barracks, the building was later used to billet U.S. Marines, and much later it housed a public school. You're welcome to sit in on sessions in the upstairs chambers. ⌂ *Waterfront Hwy., across from Fort Christian* ☏ *340/774–0880* ☉ *Daily 8–5.*

⓰ Market Square. A cadre of old-timers sells local fruits such as mangoes and papayas, strange-looking root vegetables, and bunches of fresh herbs, while sidewalk vendors offer brightly colored fabrics and tie-dyed clothing at good prices. A new roof over the market stalls, completed in 2007, gives the square an inviting feel. ⌂ *North side of Main St., at Strand Gade.*

⓲ Memorial Moravian Church. Built in 1884, this church was named to commemorate the 150th anniversary of the Moravian Church in the Virgin Islands. ⌂ *17 Norre Gade* ☏ *340/776–0066* ☉ *Weekdays 8–5.*

❾ 99 Steps. This staircase "street," built by the Danes in the 1700s, leads to the residential area above Charlotte Amalie and Blackbeard's Castle. The castle's tower, built in 1679, was once used by the notorious pirate Edward Teach. If you count the stairs as you go up, you'll discover, as have thousands before you, that there are more than 99. ⌂ *Look for steps heading north from Government Hill.*

⓮ **Pissarro Building.** Housing several shops and an art gallery, this was the birthplace and childhood home of Camille Pissarro, who later moved to France and became an acclaimed impressionist painter. The art gallery contains three original pages from Pissarro's sketchbook and two pastels by Pissarro's grandson, Claude. ✉*Main St., between Raadets Gade and Trompeter Gade.*

⓳ **Roosevelt Park.** First called Coconut Park, this park was
☾ renamed in honor of Franklin D. Roosevelt in 1945. It's a great place to put your feet up and people-watch. A renovation, complete in 2007, added five granite pedestals representing the five branches of the military, bronze urns that can be lighted to commemorate special events, and bronze plaques inscribed with the names of veterans who died defending the islands. There's also a new children's playground. ✉*Norre Gade.*

⓴ **Seven Arches Museum.** This restored 18th-century home is
★ a striking example of classic Danish–West Indian architecture. There seem to be arches everywhere—seven to be exact—all supporting a "welcoming arms" staircase that leads to the second floor and the flower-framed front doorway. The Danish kitchen is a highlight: it's housed in a separate building away from the main house, as were all cooking facilities in the early days (for fire prevention). Inside the house you can see mahogany furnishings and gas lamps. ✉*Government Hill, 3 bldgs. east of Government House* ☎*340/774–9295* ⊕*www.sevenarchesmuseum.com* ⌂*$5 donation* ☉*Oct.–July, Mon.–Sat. 10–4; Aug. and Sept., by appointment only.*

⓬ **Synagogue of Beracha Veshalom Vegmiluth Hasidim.** The synagogue's Hebrew name translates as the Congregation of Blessing, Peace, and Loving Deeds. The small building's white pillars contrast with rough stone walls, as does the rich mahogany of the pews and altar. The sand on the floor symbolizes the exodus from Egypt. Since the synagogue first opened its doors in 1833 it has held a weekly service, making it the oldest synagogue building in continuous use under the American flag and the second-oldest (after the one on Curaçao) in the western hemisphere. Guided tours can be arranged. Brochures detailing the key structures and history are also available. Next door, the Weibel Museum showcases Jewish history on St. Thomas. ✉*15 Crystal Gade* ☎*340/774–4312* ⊕*new.onepaper.com/ synagogue* ☉*Weekdays 9–4.*

5 U.S. Post Office. While you buy stamps, contemplate the murals of waterfront scenes by *Saturday Evening Post* artist Stephen Dohanos. His art was commissioned as part of the Works Project Administration (WPA) in the 1930s. ✉*Tolbod Gade and Main St.*

3 Vendors Plaza. Here merchants sell everything from T-
☼ shirts to African attire to leather goods. Look for local art among the ever-changing selections at this busy market. ✉*Waterfront, west of Fort Christian* ☉*Weekdays 8–6, weekends 9–1.*

27 Water Island. This island, the fourth-largest of the U.S. Vir-
☼ gin Islands, floats about ¼ mi (½ km) out in Charlotte Amalie Harbor. A ferry goes between Crown Bay Marina and the island several times daily, at a cost of $9 round-trip. The hike from the ferry dock is less than half a mile to Honeymoon Beach, where Brad Pitt and Cate Blanchett filmed a scene of the movie *The Curious Case of Benjamin Button.* Get picnic supplies at Pirate's Ridge Deli, above the beach; or from Heidi's Honeymoon Grill, a mobile food van that pulls up on the weekends; or from the boat that often delivers hot pizza around noon.

13 Weibel Museum. In this museum next to the synagogue, 300 years of Jewish history on St. Thomas are showcased. The small gift shop sells a commemorative silver coin celebrating the anniversary of the Hebrew congregation's establishment on the island in 1796. There are also tropically inspired items, like menorahs painted to resemble palm trees. ✉*15 Crystal Gade* ☎*340/774–4312* ⊠*Free* ☉*Weekdays 9–4.*

AROUND THE ISLAND

To explore outside Charlotte Amalie, rent a car or hire a taxi. Your rental car should come with a good map; if not, pick up the pocket-size "St. Thomas–St. John Road Map" at a tourist information center. Roads are marked with route numbers, but they're confusing and seem to switch numbers suddenly. Roads are also identified by signs bearing the St. Thomas–St. John Hotel and Tourism Association's mascot, Tommy the Starfish. More than 100 of these color-coded signs line the island's main routes. Orange signs trace the route from the airport to Red Hook, green signs identify the road from town to Magens Bay, Tommy's face on a yellow background points from Mafolie to Crown Bay through the north side, red signs lead from Smith Bay

In Search of Pirates

The line between fact and fiction is often fluid, and it ebbs and flows according to who is telling the tale. So it is with the swashbuckling seafarers of St. Thomas such as Bluebeard, Blackbeard, and Sir Francis Drake. But you'll find the story—we don't promise that it's completely true—if you follow the pirate trail.

Start atop Bluebeard's Hill to the east of Charlotte Amalie. Today, this is the site of Bluebeard's Castle Hotel. According to legend, it was Bluebeard—in reality Eduard de Barbe-Bleue—who picked this prime location to build a stone watchtower from which he could keep an eye on approaching enemies. Bluebeard kept his most prized booty, the lovely Senorita Mercedes, prisoner in the tower. That is, of course, until Mercedes broke free and discovered his gold-filled treasure chests along with gushing love letters to several other young ladies. Just as mean as her mate, Mercedes invited all of Bluebeard's paramours to the tower to pillage his plunder. Today you can walk the hotel grounds, gaze up at the still-standing watchtower, and enjoy an incredible view of the harbor. From this outlook, you can spot yet another pirate-named tower.

High atop Blackbeard's Hill, rising north of Fort Christian and

Government House, is Blackbeard's Castle. No one knows if Blackbeard—better known as Edward Teach—ever visited this site, but historians agree this infamous pirate did indeed sail the Caribbean Sea in the early 18th century. Learn all about Teach and his treacherous band via guided tours that take place between 9 and 3 when a cruise ship is in port. The cost is $35 per person. Life-size, and life-like, statues of pirates dot the route and look ready to issue an "Argh," "Aye," and "Ahoy, Matey!"

Drive over the hill to Drake's Seat. Named for the English privateer, Sir Francis Drake, this popular scenic overlook is supposedly where Drake spied ships approaching from what are now the British Virgin Islands. Don't let anyone tell you the wooden bench is where Drake sat, however. Scholars have a hard enough time trying to prove Drake really stood on this spot.

Finally, head back into downtown Charlotte Amalie and to Royal Dane Mall. This winding trio of brick-and-stone-paved alleyways is home to a couple of bronze plaques inscribed with historical facts about the island. One of them tells about buried pirate treasure. Some doubt it's really here. Others never stop dreaming of the day they'll find it.

to Four Corners via Skyline Drive, and blue signs mark the route from the cruise-ship dock at Havensight to Red Hook. These color-coded routes are not marked on most visitor maps, however. Allow yourself a day to explore, especially if you want to stop to take pictures or to enjoy a light bite or refreshing swim. Most gas stations are on the island's more populated eastern end, so fill up before heading to the north side. And remember to drive on the left!

Although the eastern end has many major resorts and spectacular beaches, don't be surprised if a cow or a herd of goats crosses your path as you drive through the relatively flat, dry terrain. The north side of the island is more lush and hush—fewer houses and less traffic. Here there are roller-coaster routes (made all the more scary because the roads have no shoulders) and incredible vistas. Leave time in the afternoon for a swim. Pick up some sandwiches from delis in the Red Hook area for a picnic lunch, or enjoy a slice of pizza at Magens Bay. A day in the country will reveal the tropical pleasures that have enticed more than one visitor to become a resident.

Numbers in the margin correspond to points of interest on the St. Thomas map.

WHAT TO SEE

30 Compass Point Marina. It's fun to park your car and walk around this marina. The boaters—many of whom have sailed here from points around the globe—are easy to engage in conversation. Turn south off Route 32 at the well-marked entrance road just east of Independent Boat Yard. ⊠*Estate Frydenhoj.*

★ Fodor'sChoice **Coral World Ocean Park.** This interactive aquar-
32 ium and water-sports center lets you experience a variety
☺ of sea life and other animals. The park has several outdoor pools where you can pet baby sharks, feed stingrays, touch starfish, and view endangered sea turtles. There's also a walk-through aviary where colorful rainbow lorikeets might drink nectar from your hands. Other activities include the Sea Trek Helmet Dive that lets you walk along an underwater trail with a high-tech helmet that provides a continuous supply of air. A Shark Encounter program lets you observe juvenile sharks as they swim around you. A sea lion pool, which opened in 2007, is where you can get a big, wet, whiskered kiss. Coral World also has an offshore underwater observatory, an 80,000-gallon coral reef exhibit (one of the largest in the world), and a nature trail

full of lush tropical flowers, ducks, and tortoises. Daily feedings take place at most exhibits. ⊠*Coki Point, north of Rte. 38, Estate Frydendal* ⌂*6450 Estate Smith Bay, St. Thomas 00802* ☎*340/775–1555* ⊕*www.coralworldvi.com* 🖃*$18, Sea Trek $68, Shark Encounter $43* ⊙*Daily 9–5.*

❸❹ Drake's Seat. Sir Francis Drake was supposed to have kept
ॐ watch over his fleet and looked for enemy ships from this vantage point. The panorama is especially breathtaking (and romantic) at dusk, and if you arrive late in the day you can miss the hordes of day-trippers on taxi tours who stop here to take a picture and buy a T-shirt from one of the many vendors. ⊠*Rte. 40, Estate Zufriedenheit.*

❸❺ Estate St. Peter Greathouse & Botanical Gardens. This unusual spot is perched on a mountainside 1,000 feet above sea level, with views of more than 20 islands and islets. You can wander through a gallery displaying local art, sip a complimentary rum punch while looking out at the view, or follow a nature trail that leads you past nearly 70 varieties of tropical plants, including 17 varieties of orchids. ⊠*Rte. 40, Estate St. Peter* ☎*340/774–4999* ⊕*www.greathouse-mountaintop. com* 🖃*$12* ⊙*Mon.–Sat. 9–4:30.*

❷❽ Frenchtown. Popular for its bars and restaurants, Frenchtown is also the home of descendants of immigrants from St. Barthélemy (St. Barths). You can watch them pull up their brightly painted boats and display their equally colorful catch of the day along the waterfront. If you chat with them, you can hear speech patterns slightly different from those of other St. Thomians. Get a feel for the residential district of Frenchtown by walking west to some of the town's winding streets, where tiny wooden houses have been passed down from generation to generation. Next to Joseph Aubain Ballpark, the **French Heritage Museum** (⊠*Intersection of rue de St. Anne and rue de St. Barthélemy* ☎*340/774– 2320*) houses artifacts such as fishing nets, accordions, tambourines, mahogany furniture, and historic photographs that illustrate the lives of the French descendants during the 18th through 20th centuries. The museum is open Monday through Saturday from 9 AM to 6 PM. Admission is free. ⊠*Turn south off Waterfront Hwy. at post office.*

❸❸ Mountain Top. Stop here for a banana daiquiri and spectacu-
ॐ lar views from the observation deck more than 1,500 feet
★ above sea level. There are also shops that sell everything from Caribbean art to nautical antiques, ship models, and T-shirts. Kids will like talking to the parrots—and hearing

them answer back. ✉*Head north off Rte. 33, look for signs* ⊕*www.greathouse-mountaintop.com.*

㉙ **Paradise Point Tramway.** Fly skyward in a gondola to Para-
☾ dise Point, an overlook with breathtaking views of Char-
★ lotte Amalie and the harbor. There are several shops, a bar,
restaurant, and a wedding gazebo; kids enjoy the tropical
bird show held daily at 10:30 AM, 1:30 PM, and 3:30 PM. A
¼-mi (½-km) hiking trail leads to spectacular views of St.
Croix. Wear sturdy shoes, as the trail is steep and rocky.
✉*Rte. 30, across from Havensight Mall, Charlotte Amalie*
☎*340/774–9809* ⊕*www.paradisepointtramway.com* 💲*$18*
☻*Thurs.–Tues. 9–5, Wed. 9–9.*

㉛ **Red Hook.** In this nautical center there are fishing and sailing charter boats, dive shops, and powerboat-rental agencies at the American Yacht Harbor marina. There are also
several bars and restaurants, including Molly Molone's,
Duffy's Love Shack, and Off the Hook. One grocery store
and two delis offer picnic fixings—from sliced meats and
cheeses to rotisserie-roasted chickens, prepared salads, and
freshly baked breads. Ferries depart from Red Hook en
route to St. John and the British Virgin Islands.

WHERE TO EAT

Restaurants are spread all over the island, although fewer
are found on the west and northwest parts of the island.
Most restaurants out of town are easily accessible by taxi
and have ample parking. If you dine in Charlotte Amalie,
take a taxi. Parking close to restaurants can be difficult
to find, and walking around after dark isn't advisable for
safety reasons.

Dining on St. Thomas is informal. Few restaurants require
a jacket and tie. Still, at dinner in the snazzier places shorts
and T-shirts are inappropriate; men would do well to wear
slacks and a shirt with buttons. Dress codes on St. Thomas
rarely require women to wear skirts, but you can never go
wrong with something flowing.

1

CLOSE UP

Prices You Can't Swallow

High food prices in Virgin Islands supermarkets are enough to dull anyone's appetite. According to a report by the U.S. Virgin Islands Department of Labor, food is 36% more expensive than on the mainland.

Although you'll never match the prices back home, you can shop around for the best deals. If you're traveling with a group, it pays to stock up on the basics at warehouse-type stores like Pricesmart and Cost-U-Less. Even the foods not sold in bulk have lower prices than at supermarkets

or convenience stores. Good buys include beverages, meats, produce, and spirits.

After this, head to supermarkets like Plaza Extra, Pueblo, and Food Center. Although the prices aren't as good as at the big-box stores, the selection is better. Finally, if you want to splurge on quality meats, exotic produce, imported cheeses, exotic spices, and imported spirits, then finish off your shopping at high-end shops like Marina Market or Gourmet Gallery.

CHARLOTTE AMALIE

AMERICAN

$–$$$ ✕**Greenhouse Bar & Restaurant.** The eight-page menu at this bustling waterfront restaurant offers burgers, salads, and pizza served all day long, along with more upscale entrées like peel-and-eat shrimp, Maine lobster, Alaskan king crab, and Black Angus prime rib for dinner. This is generally a family-friendly place, though the Two-for-Tuesdays happy hour and Friday-night live reggae music that starts thumping at 10 PM draw a lively young-adult crowd. ⊠*Waterfront Hwy. at Storetvaer Gade* ☎*340/774–7998* ⊟*AE, D, MC, V.*

★ FodorsChoice ✕**Jen's Gourmet Cafe & Deli.** This hole-in-the-
¢–$ wall eatery is the closest thing you'll find to a New York–style Jewish deli. Choose the smoked salmon platter for breakfast or hot pastrami on rye at lunch. Homemade desserts like chocolate layer cake, apple strudel, and peaches-and-cream-cheese strudel are yummy. ⊠*Grand Galleria, 43–46 Norre Gade, Charlotte Amalie* ☎*340/777–4611* ⊟*AE, MC, V* ☺*Closed Sun. No dinner.*

CARIBBEAN

$$ ✕**Cuzzin's Caribbean Restaurant & Bar.** The top picks in this restaurant in a 19th-century livery stage are the Virgin Islands staples. For lunch, order tender slivers of conch stewed in a rich onion butter sauce, savory braised oxtail, or curried chicken. At dinner, the island-style mutton, served in thick gravy and seasoned with locally grown herbs, offers a tasty treat that's deliciously different. Side dishes include peas and rice, boiled green bananas, fried plantains, and potato stuffing. ⊠*7 Wimmelskafts Gade, also called Back St.* ☎*340/777–4711* ▤*AE, MC, V.*

★ Fodor'sChoice ✕**Gladys' Cafe.** Even if the local specialties—
$–$$ conch in butter sauce, salt fish and dumplings, hearty red bean soup—didn't make this a recommended café, it would be worth coming for Gladys's smile. While you're here, pick up a $5 or $10 bottle of her special hot sauce. There are mustard-, oil and vinegar–, and tomato-based versions; the last is the hottest. ⊠*Waterfront, at Royal Dane Mall* ☐*28 Dronningens Gade, Charlotte Amelie, St. Thomas* ☎*340/774–6604* ▤*AE* ☾*No dinner.*

ECLECTIC

★ Fodor'sChoice ✕**Banana Tree Grille.** The eagle's-eye view of the
$$$–$$$$ Charlotte Amalie harbor from this open-air restaurant is as fantastic as the food. Arrive before 6 PM and watch the cruise ships depart from the harbor while you enjoy a drink at the bar. Liz Buckalew, in the restaurant business since the early 1980s, always gives you a warm welcome. For starters, try the combination of lobster, shrimp, scallops, and squid marinated in savory herb vinaigrette. The dark rum, honey, and brown sugar–glazed salmon is an excellent entrée. ⊠*Bluebeard's Castle, Bluebeard's Hill* ☐*Box 302913, Charlotte Amalie, St. Thomas* ☎*340/776–4050* ⚑*Reservations essential* ▤*AE, D, MC, V* ☾*Closed Mon. No lunch.*

FRENCH

$$$–$$$$ ✕**Hervé Restaurant & Wine Bar.** In the glow of candlelight—
★ at tables impeccably dressed with fine linens, silver settings, and sparkling crystal—you can start off with French-trained Hervé Chassin's crispy conch fritters served with a spicy-sweet mango chutney, then choose from such entrées as black-sesame-crusted tuna with a ginger-raspberry sauce or succulent roast duck with a ginger-tamarind sauce. The passion-fruit cheesecake is to die for. For lunch, quiches, salads, and grilled sandwiches are served in the open-air bistro on the first floor. ⊠*Government Hill* ☎*340/777–9703* ⚑*Reservations essential* ▤*AE, MC, V.*

ITALIAN

$$$–$$$$ ×**Virgilio's.** For the island's best northern Italian cuisine,
★ don't miss this intimate, elegant hideaway tucked on a
quiet side street. Eclectic art covers the two-story brick
walls, and the sound of opera sets the stage for a memo-
rable meal. Come here for more than 40 homemade pastas
topped with superb sauces—cappellini with fresh tomatoes
and garlic or peasant-style spaghetti in a rich tomato sauce
with mushrooms and prosciutto. House specialties include
osso buco and tiramisu—expertly crafted by chef Ernesto
Garrigos, who has prepared these two dishes on the Dis-
covery Home Channel's Great Chefs of the World series.
⊠*18 Main St.* ☎*340/776–4920* ⚑*Reservations essential*
☰*AE, MC, V* ☉*Closed Sun.*

$$ ×**Café Amici.** Set within the historic stonework and cascad-
ing tropical blossoms of A. H. Riise Alley, this charming
open-air eatery has an Italian name but boasts a menu with
Caribbean flair. Choose anything from brick-oven pizzas
to fresh salads, open-faced sandwiches, and unique pasta
dishes that are cooked to order. House specialties include
tamarind barbecued shrimp salad and pizza topped with
house-made sausage and apples. ⊠*37 Main St.* ☎*340/776–
0444* ☰*AE, MC, V* ☉*Closed Sun. No dinner.*

SPANISH

$$$–$$$$ ×**Meson Amalia.** Tucked into the alleyway of Palm Passage,
★ this open-air café owned by Antiguan-born Randolph May-
nard and his German wife, Helga, serves authentic Spanish
cuisine. Try tapas such as mussels in brandy sauce, escargots
with mushrooms and herb butter, or Galician-style octopus
and baby eels served in a sizzling garlic sauce. Paella is a
house specialty, as is the caramel flan. ⊠*Palm Passage, 24
Dronnigens Gade* ☎*340/714–7373* ☰*AE, MC, V.*

EAST END

AMERICAN

$$–$$$$ ×**Blue Moon Café.** Watch the serene scene of sailboats float-
☺ ing at anchor while supping; sunsets are especially spec-
tacular here. Enjoy French toast topped with toasted
coconut for breakfast, a grilled mahimahi sandwich with
black olive–caper mayonnaise at lunch, or red snapper
with pecans, bananas, and a coconut rum sauce for dinner. ⊠*Secret Harbour Beach Resort, Rte. 32, Red Hook*
☎*340/779–2080* ☰*AE, D, MC, V.*

ECLECTIC

★ Fodor'sChoice ✕ **Old Stone Farmhouse.** Dine in the splendor of
$$$–$$$$ a beautifully restored plantation house. For a real treat try
executive chef Ric Ade's special tasting menu (a pricey $90
per person). The four-course menu, complete with paired
wines, starts off with appetizer selections such as a differ-
ent sort of surf-and-turf: pan-seared scallops and oxtail
stew. A sauerbraten of North American elk served with
chestnut spaetzle, sweet-and-sour red cabbage, and ginger-
snap gravy shows off Ade's creativity with entrées. Desserts
include the to-die-for hot chocolate cake served with coffee
gelato. Personalized attention makes dining here a delight.
⊠*Rte. 42, 1 mi (1½ km) west of entrance to Mahogany
Run Golf Course, Estate Lovenlund* ☎*340/777–6277*
⌂*Reservations essential* ⊜*AE, MC, V* ⊘*Closed Mon.*

$ ✕ **Duffy's Love Shack.** If the floating bubbles don't attract
you to this zany eatery, the lime-green shutters, loud rock
music, and fun-loving waitstaff just might. It's billed as the
"ultimate tropical drink shack," and the bartenders shake
up such exotic concoctions as the Love Shack Volcano—a
50-ounce flaming extravaganza. The menu has a selec-
tion of burgers, tacos, burritos, and salads. Try the grilled
mahimahi taco salad or jerk Caesar wrap. Wednesday night
is usually a theme party complete with giveaways. ⊠*Rte.
32, Red Hook* ☎*340/779–2080* ⊜*No credit cards.*

IRISH

$$–$$$ ✕ **Molly Molone's.** This open-air eatery has a devout follow-
☾ ing among locals who live and work on the boats docked
nearby. Traditional Irish dishes include bangers and mash
(sausage and mashed potatoes), as well as fresh fish and
rich soups and stews. Beware: the resident iguanas will beg
for table scraps—bring your camera. Upstairs, the same
owners run A Whale of a Tale, a pricier seafood eatery
that also serves freshly made pasta dishes and fine wines.
⊠*Rte. 32, at American Yacht Harbor, Bldg. D, Red Hook*
☎*340/775–1270* ⊜*MC, V.*

ITALIAN

$$$–$$$$ ✕ **Romanos.** Inside this huge old stucco house is a delightful
★ surprise: a spare yet elegant restaurant serving superb north-
ern Italian cuisine. Try the pastas, either with a classic ragout
or a more unique creation such as cream sauce with mush-
rooms, prosciutto, pine nuts, and Parmesan. ⊠*Rte. 388, at
Coki Point, Estate Frydendal* ☎*340/775–0045* ⌂*Reserva-
tions essential* ⊜*MC, V* ⊘*Closed Sun. No lunch.*

SEAFOOD

$$–$$$$ ✕**Agave Terrace.** At this open-air restaurant in the Point Pleasant Resort, the catch of the day—fresh fish served as a steak or a fillet—is listed on the blackboard. More than a dozen sauces, including teriyaki-mango and lime-ginger, liven up your entrée. If you get lucky on a sportfishing day charter, the chef will cook your fish if you bring it in by 3 PM. Come early and have a drink at the Lookout Lounge, which has breathtaking views of the British Virgins. ⊠*Point Pleasant Resort, Rte. 38, Estate Smith Bay* ☎*340/775–4142* ⊟*AE, MC, V* ⊙*No lunch*.

$$–$$$ ✕**Off the Hook.** The fish is so fresh here that you may see it coming in from one of the boats tied up at the dock just steps away. For starters, try the crispy conch fritters with sweet-hot banana-chili chutney. Entrées include a rib-sticking fish stew with scallops, shrimp, mahimahi, mussels, conch, and calamari swimming in a coconut curry broth. Steak, poultry, and pasta lovers will also find something to please at this open-air eatery. There's also a children's menu. ⊠*Rte. 32, Red Hook* ☎*340/775–6350* ⊟*AE, MC, V* ⊙*No lunch*.

SOUTH SHORE

AMERICAN

★ Fodor'sChoice ✕**W!kked.** Gaze at the boats bobbing in the
$–$$$ waves at Yacht Haven Grande while forking into casual fare prepared by executive chef Brian Katz. Hip cheeseburgers are topped with roasted onions, peppers, mushrooms, and smoked Gouda, cheddar, or gorgonzola cheese. Pasta dishes, sizzling steaks, and chicken wings with a choice of five sauces, including ginger-coconut, round out the menu. ⊠*Yacht Haven Grande, 5403 Yacht Haven Grande, Charlotte Amalie* ☎*340/775–8953* ⊟*AE, MC, V*.

ECLECTIC

★ Fodor'sChoice ✕**Havana Blue.** The cuisine here is described
$$–$$$$ as Cuban–Asian, but the dining experience is out of this world. You're met by a glowing wall of water as you enter, then sit at a table laid with linen and silver that's illuminated in a soft blue light radiating from above. Be sure to sample the mango mojito, made with fresh mango, crushed mint, and limes. Entrées include coconut-chipotle ceviche, sugarcane-glazed pork tenderloin medallions, and the signature dish, miso sea bass. Hand-rolled cigars and aged rums finish the night off in true Cuban style. For

something really special, request an exclusive table for two set on Morning Star Beach—you get a seven-course tasting menu, champagne, and your own personal waiter, all for $375 for two. ✉*Morningstar Beach Resort, Rte. 315,* ☎*340/715–2583* ⚓*Reservations essential* ⊗*No lunch.*

$$–$$$ ✕**Randy's Bar & Bistro.** There's no view here—even though ★ you're at the top of a hill—but the somewhat hidden location has helped to keep this one of the island's best dining secrets. This wineshop and deli caters to a local lunch crowd. At night, you forget you're tucked into a nearly windowless building. The table-side bread for starters is a thick, crusty focaccia flavored with nearly 10 different vegetables. Try the Brie-stuffed filet mignon or rack of lamb. After-dinner cigars and wine complete the experience. ✉*Al Cohen's Plaza, atop Raphune Hill, ½ mi (¾ km) east of Charlotte Amalie* ☎*340/777–3199* ▭*AE, D, MC, V.*

WEST END

AMERICAN

$–$$$ ✕**Tickle's Dockside Pub.** Nautical types as well as the local ☾ working crowd come here for casual fare with homey appeal: chicken-fried steak, meat loaf with mashed potatoes, and baby back ribs. Hearty breakfasts feature eggs and pancakes, while lunch is a full array of burgers, salads, sandwiches, and soups. From November through April, the adjacent marina is full of megayachts that make for some great eye candy while you dine. ✉*Crown Bay Marina, Rte. 304, Estate Contant* ☎*340/776–1595* ▭*AE, D, MC, V.*

ECLECTIC

★ Fodor'sChoice ✕**Craig & Sally's.** In the heart of Frenchtown, $$–$$$$ culinary wizard Sally Darash creates menus with a passionate international flavor using fresh ingredients and a novel approach that makes for a delightful dining experience. Sally's constantly changing menu is never the same, which means your favorite dish may not appear again. But there's always something new to tantalize your taste buds, such as yellowtail tuna swimming in a mango, key lime, and habanero sauce. Husband Craig maintains a 300-bottle wine list that's won accolades. ✉*22 Honduras St., Frenchtown* ☎*340/777–9949* ▭*AE, MC, V* ⊗*Closed Mon. and Tues. No lunch weekends.*

SEAFOOD

$$ ×**Hook, Line & Sinker.** Anchored right on the breezy French-
☾ town waterfront, adjacent to the pastel-painted boats of
the local fishing fleet, this harbor-view eatery serves quality
fish dishes. The almond-crust yellowtail snapper is a house
specialty. Spicy jerk-seasoned swordfish and grilled tuna
topped with a yummy mango-rum sauce are also good
bets. This is one of the few independent restaurants serv-
ing Sunday brunch. ⊠ *2 Honduras, in Frenchtown Mall,
Frenchtown* ☎*340/776–9708* ▤*AE, MC, V.*

WHERE TO STAY

The island's first hotels were all based in Charlotte Amalie,
the hub of action at the time. Most people choose lodgings
here to be close to the airport, to experience the charm of
the historic district, or for convenience when on business.
Over the years, tourism has trickled eastward, and today
the major hotel chains have perched their properties on the
beach. Those who want a self-contained resort that feels
like an island unto itself head here. The location of these
resorts makes island-hopping to St. John or the British Vir-
gin Islands a breeze. Private villas dot the island, especially
in the less-populated north.

CHARLOTTE AMALIE

Accommodations in town and near town offer the ben-
efits of being close to the airport, shopping, and a num-
ber of casual and fine-dining restaurants. The downside is
that this is the most crowded and noisy area of the island.
Crime can also be a problem. Don't go for a stroll at night
in the heart of town. Use common sense and take the same
precautions you would in any major city. Properties along
the hillsides are less likely to have crime problems, plus
they command a steady breeze from the cool trade winds.
This is especially important if you're visiting in summer
and early fall.

$$–$$$ ▦**Holiday Inn St. Thomas.** Business travelers, those on their
way to the British Virgin Islands, or laid-back vacation-
ers who want the convenience of being able to walk to
duty-free shopping, sights, and restaurants stay at this har-
borfront hotel. But if your ideal Caribbean beach vacation
means having the beach at your doorstep, this isn't the
place for you, despite the presence of a free beach shuttle.

Contemporary rooms have such amenities as coffeemakers, hair dryers, ironing boards, and irons. An introductory dive lesson with Admiralty Dive Center is complimentary. Pros: walking distance to Charlotte Amalie, nice harbor views. Cons: basic rooms, on busy street, no waters ports. ⊠*Waterfront Hwy., Box 640, 00804* ☎*340/774–5200 or 800/524–7389* ☐*340/774–1231* ⊕*www.holidayinn. st-thomas.com* ⇆*140 rooms, 11 suites* &*In-room: safe, refrigerator, dial-up. In-hotel: restaurant, room service, bar, pool, gym, diving, laundry service, public Internet* ⊟*AE, D, DC, MC, V* ⚏*EP.*

$–$$$ ▨**Hotel 1829.** Antique charm is readily apparent in this rambling 19th-century merchant's house, from the hand-painted Moroccan tiles to a Tiffany window. Rooms on several levels range from stylish and spacious suites with vaulted ceilings to small and cozy rooms. The bar is open nightly and attracts locals as well as hotel guests. The second-floor botanical gardens and open-air champagne bar are romantic spots for sunset viewing. Main Street, with its duty-free shops, is a block away. Pros: close to attractions, old-world charm, breakfast served on the veranda. Cons: small rooms, tour groups during the day, neighborhood dicey at night. ⊠*Government Hill, Box 1567, 00804* ☎*340/776–1829 or 800/524–2002* ☐*340/776– 4313* ⊕*www.hotel1829.com* ⇆*15 rooms* &*In-room: no phone, refrigerator. In-hotel: bar, pool, no kids under 11, no elevator* ⊟*AE, D, MC, V* ⚏*CP.*

$–$$ ▨**The Green Iguana.** Atop Blackbeard's Hill, this B&B offers the perfect mix of gorgeous harbor views, proximity to town and shopping (five minutes away by foot), and secluded privacy provided by the surrounding flamboyant trees and bushy hibiscus. Accommodations range from a roomy, top-floor junior suite with two queen beds to a balcony room with queen bed and full kitchen. All rooms have refrigerators, microwave ovens, and coffeemakers. There's also a picnic area with a gas barbecue grill. The managing couple lives on the property and is very helpful in giving restaurant, sightseeing, or beach suggestions. Pros: personalized service, near town, laundry on premises. Cons: car needed to get around, crime at night. ⊠*37B Blackbeard's Hill, 00802* ☎*340/776–7654 or 800/484–8825* ☐*340/777–4312* ⊕*www.thegreeniguana.com* ⇆*6 rooms* &*In-room: kitchen (some), refrigerator. In-hotel: pool, laundry facilities, no-smoking rooms, no elevator* ⊟*AE, D, MC, V* ⚏*EP.*

★ Fodor'sChoice ⚜**Villa Santana.** Built by exiled General Anto-
$-$$ nio López Santa Anna of Mexico, this 1857 landmark
provides a panoramic view of the harbor and plenty of
West Indian charm, which will make you feel as if you're
living in a charming slice of Virgin Islands history. Each
of the rooms is unique and lovely. Our two favorites are
La Mansion, a former library that is now an elegant villa
with a large living area crowned by cathedral ceilings, full
kitchen, two baths, and four-poster bed; and El Establo,
a three-bedroom house with a full kitchen and laundry
facilities that is rented by the week. Modern amenities
aren't lacking; you can even sit by the pool with your lap-
top and indulge in wireless Internet access. Pros: on-site
property, historic charm, privacy. Cons: no beach, no restaurant, car needed to get around. ⊠*2D Denmark Hill,
00802* ☎*340/776–1311* ᵫ*340/776–1311* ⊕*www.villasan-
tana.com* ⌖*6 rooms* ♨*In-room: no a/c (some), no phone,
kitchen (some), no TV (some), Wi-Fi. In-hotel: pool, no
elevator* ⊟*AE, MC, V* ⦿*EP.*

EAST END

You can find most of the large, luxurious beachfront resorts
on St. Thomas's east end. The downside is that these properties are about a 30-minute drive from town and 45-min-
ute drive from the airport (substantially longer during peak
hours). On the upside, these properties tend to be self-con-
tained, plus there are a number of good restaurants, shops,
and water-sports operators in the area. Once you've settled
in, you don't need a car to get around.

★ Fodor'sChoice ⚜**Ritz-Carlton, St. Thomas.** Everything sparkles at
$$$$ the island's most luxurious resort, especially after a $40 mil-
☺ lion renovation that upgraded everything from in-room furnishings to tiling for the walkways. Spacious guest rooms,
with high-speed Internet access, private balconies, and
marble bathrooms with deep soaking tubs, are in buildings
fanning out from the main building. Six somewhat insti-
tutional-looking buildings, with two- and three-bedroom
condos, sit on their own adjacent beach. The spa, salon,
and fitness center serve adults, both body and soul; the
Ritz Kids program packs in a full day of activities for kids,
including collecting seashells and feeding iguanas. A 54-foot
catamaran is a must-do for a day or sunset sail. Pros: gorgeous view, great water sports, beautiful beach. Cons: service is spotty, food can lack flair, isolated location. ⊠*Rte.
317, Box 6900, Estate Great Bay 00802* ☎*340/775–3333*

or 800/241–3333 🖨340/775–4444 ⊕*www.ritzcarlton.com* 🛏*255 rooms, 20 suites, 2 villas, 81 condos* ♻*In-room: safe, refrigerator, Wi-Fi. In-hotel: 4 restaurants, room service, bars, tennis courts, pools, gym, spa, beachfront, water sports, concierge, children's programs (ages 4–12), laundry service, public Internet, airport shuttle, no-smoking rooms* ⊟*AE, D, DC, MC, V* ⊠*EP.*

★ FodorsChoice ⊡**Wyndham Sugar Bay Resort & Spa.** Though
$$$$ this terra-cotta high-rise is surrounded by palm trees and
♻ lush greenery, rooms and the walkways between them have a bit of a generic feel. However, the sixth and seventh levels of building D have spectacular ocean views. A complete renovation added plantation-style guest room furnishings, plush carpeting, and marble-tile bathrooms. The beach is small, although the nearby pool is replete with waterfalls and colorful cabanas housing hair braiders and henna tattoo artists that make a day of lounging here idyllic. It's a 99-step hike from guest rooms, however. Health buffs enjoy the full-service spa and health club, as well as the outdoor fitness trail. If you're feeling lucky, head to the Ocean Club Gaming Center, where there are 95 video slot machines. Pros: fun pool, full-service spa, casino. Cons: steps to climb, small beach, limited dining options. ⊠*Rte. 38, Box 6500, Estate Smith Bay 00802* ☎340/777–7100 *or* 800/927–7100 🖨340/777–7200 ⊕*www.wyndham.com* 🛏*300 rooms, 9 suites* ♻*In-room: safe, refrigerator, dial-up. In-hotel: 2 restaurants, room service, bar, tennis courts, pool, gym, spa, beachfront, water sports, concierge, children's programs (ages 4–12), laundry service* ⊟*AE, D, DC, MC, V* ⊠*AI.*

$$$–$$$$ ⊡**Point Pleasant Resort.** Hilltop suites give you an eagle's-eye view of the east end and beyond, while those in a building adjacent to the reception area offer incredible sea views. Sea-level junior suites, where the sounds of lapping waves will lull you to sleep, are smaller. There's a resort shuttle, but some walking up steep hills is necessary. The beach is tiny, though some may call it wonderfully private, but three pools give you more swimming and sunning options. The property also has a labyrinth of well-marked nature trails to explore. If you like seafood, don't miss dinner at the Agave Terrace restaurant; Fungi's on the Beach is a casual alternative. Pros: lush setting, kitchens, pleasant pools. Cons: steep climb from beach, car needed to get around, some rooms need refurbishing. ⊠*6600 Rte. 38, Estate Smith Bay 00802* ☎340/775–7200 *or* 800/524–2300 🖨340/776–5694 ⊕*www.pointpleasantresort.com*

🛏128 suites ♿In-room: safe, kitchen, dial-up. In-hotel: 2 restaurants, bar, tennis court, pools, gym, beachfront, concierge, laundry facilities, public Internet, no elevator ═AE, D, DC, MC, V ⦿EP.

$$$–$$$$ 🏨 **Secret Harbour Beach Resort & Villas.** There's not a bad view from these low-rise studio, one-, and two-bedroom condos, which are either beachfront or perched on a hill overlooking an inviting cove. All units, which have white-tile floors and tropical-print wood and wicker furnishings, are spacious; even the studios are more than 600 square feet and certainly big enough for a family with two children. The pool is small, but the beach is the real focal point here. Calm seas make for excellent swimming, and snorkeling is especially good near the small dock to the east of the cove, where coral outcroppings attract a bevy of marine life. Watch spectacular sunsets from your balcony or the beachfront bar. Kids under 13 stay free, making this a good value for families. Pros: beautiful beach, good restaurant, secluded feel. Cons: some small rooms, car needed to get around, condo owners get territorial about beach chairs. ✉Rte. 317, Box 6280, Estate Nazareth 00802-1104 ☎340/775–6550 or 800/524–2250 📠340/775–1501 ⊕www.secretharbourvi.com 🛏49 suites, 15 studios ♿In-room: kitchen. In-hotel: restaurant, bar, tennis courts, pool, gym, beachfront, diving, water sports, no elevator ═AE, MC, V ⦿CP.

$$–$$$ 🏨 **Sapphire Beach Resort & Marina.** A beautiful half-mile-long white-sand beach is the real ace here. After a long succession of owners, Antilles Resorts took control of the property in 2006 and began much-needed refurbishments to the rooms. Changes include new curtains and bedspreads. The property is nicely landscaped on the ocean side, but away from the beach are a long-awaited convention center, marina office, and shopping complex that is still just a big grassy spot occupied by the odd car and piece of construction equipment. Only the pool bar and restaurant are open, but the resort runs a nightly shuttle to the Wyndham Sugar Bay Beach Club & Resort to give guests two more dinner options. Snorkeling equipment, floating mats, one windsurfing lesson and one sail on a Sunfish are complimentary, as is a two-day car rental. Pros: on the beach, water sports available, near ferries. Cons: rooms need refurbishing, restaurant fare limited, unattractive construction area. ✉6720 Estate Smith Bay 00802 ☎800/524–2090, 340/773–9150, or 800/874–7897 📠340/778–4009 ⊕ www.sapphirebeach stthomas.com 🛏171 suites ♿In-room: kitchen (some).

In-hotel: restaurant, bar, tennis courts, pool, gym, beach-front, water sports, concierge, laundry facilities, no elevator ▭*AE, MC, V* ⧈*EP.*

WEST END

A few properties are in the hills overlooking Charlotte Amalie to the west or near French Town, which is otherwise primarily residential.

$$$ ▩**Best Western Emerald Beach Resort.** You get beachfront ambience at this reasonably priced miniresort tucked beneath the palm trees, but the tradeoff is that it's directly across from a noisy airport runway. You'll definitely want to spend time on the white-sand beach, which can be seen from nearly every room in the four three-story, peach-color buildings. Rooms are acceptable, but the tropical-print bedspreads and rattan furnishings look worn. Stay here if you need the beach on a budget or if you have an early-morning flight. Pros: on the beach, close to airport, great Sunday brunch. Cons: airport noise until 10 PM, on a busy road, limited watersports. ⊠*8070 Lindberg Bay, 00802* ☎*340/777–8800 or 800/780—7234* ⊟*340/776–3426* ⊕*www.emeraldbeach. com* ⟐*90 rooms* ⚹*In-room: refrigerator, dial-up. In-hotel: restaurant, bar, tennis courts, pool, gym, beachfront, no elevator* ▭*AE, D, MC, V* ⧈*CP.*

$ ▩**Island View Guesthouse.** Perched 545 feet up the face of Crown Mountain, this small inn has a homey feel; the hands-on owners can book tours or offer tips about the best sightseeing spots. Rooms range from a suite with a kitchenette that's perfect for families to two simply furnished verandah rooms that share a bath. The two verandah rooms and six poolside rooms have no air-conditioning, but at this altitude there's always a breeze. Six of the rooms have kitchenettes, so you wouldn't have to eat out for every meal. There's an honor bar for drinks and snacks and a communal verandah where guests congregate for Continental breakfasts and home-cooked dinners. Pros: spectacular view, friendly atmosphere, good value. Cons: small pool, need a car to get around. ⊠*Rte. 332, Box 1903, Estate Contant 00803* ☎*340/774–4270 or 800/524–2023* ⊟*340/774–6167* ⊕*www.islandviewstthomas.com* ⟐*16 rooms, 14 with private bath* ⚹*In-room: no a/c (some), kitchen (some). In-hotel: pool, laundry facilities, no elevator* ▭*AE, MC, V* ⧈*CP.*

SOUTH SHORE

The south shore of St. Thomas connects town to the east end of the island via a beautiful road that rambles along the hillside with frequent peeks between the hills for a view of the ocean and, on a clear day, of St. Croix some 40 mi (60 km) to the south. The resorts here are on their own beaches. They offer several opportunities for water sports, as well as land-based activities, fine dining, and evening entertainment.

$$$$ **Marriott Frenchman's Reef & Morning Star Beach Resorts.** Set majestically on a promontory overlooking the east side of Charlotte Amalie's harbor, Frenchman's Reef is the high-rise full-service superhotel, while Morning Star is the even more upscale boutique property nestled along the fine white-sand beach. Nice touches include 8-foot-wide mahogany headboards, flat-screen televisions, and Wi-Fi in all the rooms. Meals here include lavish buffets for breakfast and dinner. A rum bar featuring bottles from around the Caribbean and beyond. Live entertainment and dancing, scheduled activities for all ages, and an hourly boat that shuttles guests to town make having fun easy. Pros: on beach, good dining options, plenty of activities. Cons: musty smell on lower levels, long walk between resorts. ⊠*Rte. 315, Box 7100, Estate Bakkeroe 00801* ☎*340/776–8500 or 800/233–6388* 🖷*340/715–6193* ⊕*www.marriott.com/property/propertypage/sttfr* ➪*479 rooms, 27 suites* ⌂*In-room: safe, refrigerator, dial-up, Wi-Fi. In-hotel: 4 restaurants, room service, bar, tennis courts, pools, gym, spa, beachfront, concierge, children's programs (ages 4–12)* ⊟*AE, D, DC, MC, V* ⃝*EP.*

$$$ **Bolongo Bay Beach Club.** All the rooms at this family-run resort tucked along a 1,000-foot-long palm-lined beach have balconies with ocean views; down the beach are 12 studio and two-bedroom condos with full kitchens. This place is more homey than fancy, but the friendliness of the longtime staff keeps visitors coming back. The beach is a bit rocky for swimming, but sails aboard the resort's 53-foot catamaran and excursions arranged by the on-site dive shop are popular. You can opt out of the all-inclusive plan and pay less, but then you'd have to rent a car because the resort is a bit isolated. The creative cuisine at the Beach House, especially the seven-course tasting menu, shouldn't be missed. Pros: family-owned and -operated, on the beach, water sports available. Cons: run-down feel, on busy road, need a car to get around. ⊠*Rte. 30, Box 7150,*

*Estate Bolongo 00802 ☎340/775–1800 or 800/524–4746
🖷340/775–3208 ⊕www.bolongobay.com ⇘65 rooms,
12 studio and 2-bedroom condos ☖In-room: safe, kitchen
(some), refrigerator. In-hotel: 2 restaurants, bar, tennis
courts, pool, beachfront, diving, water sports, no elevator
▤AE, D, DC, MC, V ❗◦EP.*

VILLAS & CONDOMINIUMS

You can arrange private villa rentals through various
agents that represent luxury residences and usually have
both Web sites and brochures that show photos of the
properties they represent. Some are suitable for travelers with disabilities, but be sure to ask specific questions
regarding your own needs. **Calypso Realty** (⊡*Box 12178,
00801* ☎*340/774–1620 or 800/747–4858* ⊕*www.caly-
psorealty.com*) specializes in rental properties around St.
Thomas. **McLaughlin-Anderson Villas** (⊠*100 Blackbeard's
Hill, Suite 3, 00802* ☎*340/776–0635 or 800/537–6246
⊕www.mclaughlinanderson.com*) handles rental villas
throughout the U.S. Virgin Islands, British Virgin Islands,
and Grenada. Many villas and and condominiums are in
complexes on the East End of St. Thomas.

CONDOMINIUM COMPLEXES

$$$–$$$$ 🖾**The Anchorage.** A beachfront setting and homey conve-
♻ niences that include full kitchens and washer-dryer units are
what you can find in these two- and three-bedroom suites
on Cowpet Bay next to the St. Thomas Yacht Club. The
complex has two lighted tennis courts, a freshwater pool,
and an informal restaurant. Pros: on the beach, good ameni-
ties, dining options. Cons: small pool, noisy neighbors, need
car to get around. ⊠*Rte. 317, Estate Nazareth* ⊕*Antilles
Resorts, Box 24786, Christiansted, St. Croix 00824-0786*
☎*800/874–7897* 🖷*340/778–4009* ⊕*www.antillesresorts.
com* ⇘*11 suites* ☖*In-room: kitchen. In-hotel: restaurant,
bar, gym, tennis courts, pool, beachfront, laundry facilities,
no elevator* ▤*AE, D, MC, V* ❗◦*EP.*

$$ 🖾**Sapphire Village.** These high-rise towers feel more like
apartment buildings than luxury resorts, so if you're look-
ing for a home away from home, this might be the place.
There are full kitchens, so you can avoid pricey restaurant meals. The view from your balcony is the marina
and the ocean. The beach, a spectacular half mile of white
sand, is a five-minute walk down the hill. There's a restaurant on property and two more down the hill at the

Sapphire Beach Resort & Marina. Additional restaurants, a shopping complex, and ferries to St. John are a mile away in Red Hook. Pros: walking distance to Red Hook, nice views, secluded feel. Cons: small rooms, limited dining options, noisy neighbors. ⊠ *Rte. 38, Sapphire Bay* ⚲ *Antilles Resorts, Box 24786, Christiansted, St. Croix 00824-0786* ☎ *340/779–1540 or 800/874–7897* 🖷 *340/778–4009* ⊕ *www.antillesresorts.com* ➷ *15 condos* ⚖ *In-room: kitchen. In-hotel: restaurant, bar, tennis courts, pools, beachfront, water sports, laundry facilities, no elevator* ⊟ *AE, D, MC, V* ⭐ *EP.*

$ ▣ **Caribbean Style.** Couples will enjoy the romantic feel of
★ these private, individually decorated condos. Each has a king-size bed, a reading and video library, and a kitchen stocked with breakfast foods and special requests, such as your favorite ice cream or preferred brand of rum. You can literally toss an ice cube into the sea from the hammock or lounge chairs on the private porches of the two smaller condos, while the two larger condos are only about 20 feet away from the rocky waterfront. Vessup Beach and water sports are a 10-minute walk away. Couples who would like to tie the knot will find that wedding arrangements, including professional photography, are the owner's specialty. Pros: on the beach, homey rooms, romantic atmosphere. Cons: no water sports, need car to get around, bugs a problem. ⊠ *Rte. 317, at Cabrita Point, Estate Vessup Bay* ⚲ *6501 Red Hook Plaza, Suite 201, 00802* ☎ *340/715–1117 or 800/593–1390* ⊕ *www.cstylevi.com/cstyle_new/ html* ➷ *4 1-bedroom condos* ⚖ *In-room: kitchen. In-hotel: pool, water sports, no kids under 15, no-smoking rooms, no elevator* ⊟ *AE, MC, V* ⭐ *CP.*

BEACHES

All 44 St. Thomas beaches are open to the public, although you can reach some of them only by walking through a resort. Hotel guests frequently have access to lounge chairs and floats that are off-limits to nonguests; for this reason you may feel more comfortable at one of the beaches not associated with a resort, such as Magens Bay (which charges an entrance fee to cover beach maintenance) or Coki Beach. Whichever one you choose, remember to remove your valuables from the car and keep them out of sight when you go swimming.

Brewer's Beach. Watch jets land at the Cyril E. King Airport as you dip into the usually calm seas. Rocks at either end of the shoreline, patches of grass poking randomly through the sand, and shady tamarind trees 30 feet from the water give this beach a wild, natural feel. Civilization has arrived, as one or two mobile food vans park on the nearby road. Buy a fried-chicken leg and johnnycake or burgers and chips to munch on at the picnic tables. ⊠ *Rte. 30, west of University of the Virgin Islands.*

★ Fodor'sChoice **Coki Beach.** Funky beach huts selling local foods
☾ like meat pates (fried turnovers with a spicy ground-beef filling), picnic tables topped with umbrellas sporting beverage logos, and a brigade of hair braiders and taxi men give this beach overlooking picturesque Thatch Cay a Coney Island feel. But this is the best place on the island to snorkel and scuba dive. Fish, including grunts, snappers, and wrasses, are like an effervescent cloud you can wave your hand through. Ashore you'll find conveniences like rest rooms, changing facilities, mask and fin rentals, and even fish food. ⊠ *Rte. 388, next to Coral World Ocean Park.*

Hull Bay. Watch surfers ride the waves here from December to March, when huge swells roll in from north Atlantic storms. The rest of the year, tranquillity prevails. Homer's Snorkel & Scuba Tours is based here, and Homer himself will happily lead you on a day or night snorkel trip to the nearby reefs and out to the uninhabited island of Hans Lollick. Enjoy hot pizza, barbecue ribs, and a game of darts the Hull Bay Hideaway bar and restaurant. ⊠ *Rte. 37, at end of road on north side.*

★ Fodor'sChoice **Magens Bay.** Deeded to the island as a public
☾ park, this heart-shape stretch of white sand is considered one of the most beautiful in the world. The bottom of the bay is flat and sandy, so this is a place for sunning and swimming rather than snorkeling. On weekends and holidays the sounds of music from groups partying under the sheds fill the air. There's a bar, snack shack, and beachwear boutique; bathhouses with rest rooms, changing rooms, and saltwater showers are close by. Sunfish and paddleboats are the most popular rentals at the water-sports kiosk. East of the beach is Udder Delight, a one-room shop at St. Thomas Dairies that serves a Virgin Islands tradition—a milk shake with a splash of Cruzan rum. Kids can enjoy virgin versions, which have a touch of soursop, mango, or banana flavoring. If you arrive between 8 AM and 5 PM, you pay

an entrance fee of $3 per person, $1 per vehicle, and 25¢ per child under age 12. ⊠*Rte. 35, at end of road on north side of island.*

★ **Morningstar Beach.** Nature and nurture combine at this ¼-mi-long (½-km-long) beach between Marriott Frenchman's Reef and Morning Star Beach Resorts, where amenities range from water-sports rentals to beachside bar service. A concession rents floating mats, snorkeling equipment, sailboards, and Jet Skis. Swimming is excellent; there are good-size rolling waves year-round, but do watch the undertow. If you're feeling lazy, rent a lounge chair with umbrella and order a libation from one of two full-service beach bars. At 7 AM and again at 5 PM, watch the cruise ships glide majestically out to sea from the Charlotte Amalie harbor. ⊠*Rte. 315, 2 mi (3 km) southeast of Charlotte Amalie, past Havensight Mall and cruise-ship dock.*

★ **Sapphire Beach.** A steady breeze makes this beach a boardsailor's paradise. The swimming is great, as is the snorkeling, especially at the reef near Pettyklip Point. Beach volleyball is big on the weekends. There's also a restaurant, bar, and water-sports rentals at Sapphire Beach Resort & Marina. ⊠*Rte. 38, Sapphire Bay.*

Secret Harbour. Placid waters make it an easy job to stroke your way out to a swim platform offshore from the Secret Harbour Beach Resort & Villas. Nearby reefs give snorkelers a natural show. There's a bar and restaurant, as well as a dive shop. ⊠*Rte. 32, Red Hook.*

Vessup Beach. This wild, undeveloped beach is lined with sea-grape trees and century plants. It's close to Red Hook harbor, so you can watch the ferries depart. Calm waters are excellent for swimming. West Indies Windsurfing is here, so you can rent Windsurfers, kayaks, and other water toys. There are no rest rooms or changing facilities. It's popular with locals on weekends. ⊠*Off Rte. 322, Vessup Bay.*

DID YOU KNOW? While driving on the left side is the rule on St. Thomas, steering wheels are not on the right. That's because most cars are imported from the U.S.

SPORTS & THE OUTDOORS

AIR TOURS

On the Charlotte Amalie waterfront next to Tortola Wharf, **Air Center Helicopters** (⊠ *Waterfront, Charlotte Amalie, St. Thomas* ☎ *340/775–7335 or 800/619–0013* ⊕ *www.air-centerhelicopters.com*) offers two tours, both pretty pricey: a 17-minute tour of St. Thomas and St. John for $385, and a 25-minute tour that includes St. Thomas, St. John, and Jost Van Dyke priced at $565. Prices are for the entire helicopter, which can accommodate five passengers and a pilot. If you can afford the splurge, it's a nice ride, but in truth, you can see most of the aerial sights from Mountain Top or Paradise Point, and there's no place you can't reach easily by car or boat.

BOATING & SAILING

Calm seas, crystal waters, and nearby islands (perfect for picnicking, snorkeling, and exploring) make St. Thomas a favorite jumping-off spot for day- or weeklong sails or powerboat adventures. With more than 100 vessels from which to choose, St. Thomas is the charter-boat center of the U.S. Virgin Islands. You can go through a broker to book a sailing vessel with a crew or contact a charter company directly. Crewed charters start at $2,000 per person per week, while bareboat charters can start at $1,500 per person for a 50- to 55-foot sailboat (not including provisioning), which can comfortably accommodate up to six people. If you want to rent your own boat, hire a captain. Most local captains are excellent tour guides.

Single-day charters are also a possibility. You can hire smaller power boats for the day, including the services of a captain if you wish to have someone take you on a guided snorkel trip around the islands.

Island Yachts (⊠ *6100 Red Hook Quarter, 18B, Red Hook* ☎ *340/775–6666 or 800/524–2019* ⊕ *www.iyc.vi*) offers sail- or powerboats with or without crews. Luxury is the word at **Magic Moments** (⊠ *American Yacht Harbor, Red Hook* ☎ *340/775–5066* ⊕ *www.yachtmagicmoments.com*), where the crew of a 45-foot Sea Ray offers a pampered island-hopping snorkeling cruise. Nice touches include icy-cold eucalyptus-infused washcloths to freshen up and a gourmet wine and lobster lunch. **Stewart Yacht Charters** (⊠ *6501 Red Hook Plaza, Suite 20, Red Hook* ☎ *340/775–1358 or 800/432–6118* ⊕ *www.stewartyachtcharters.com*) is run by longtime sailor Ellen Stewart, who is an expert at matching clients with yachts for weeklong crewed charter holidays. Bareboat sail and powerboats, including a selection of stable trawlers, are available at **VIP Yacht Charters** (⊠*South off Rte. 32, Estate Frydenhoj* ☎*340/774–9224 or 866/847–9224* ⊕*www.vipyachts.com*), at Compass Point Marina.

Awesome Powerboat Rentals (⊠*6100 Red Hook Quarter, Red Hook* ☎*340/775–0860* ⊕*www.powerboatrentalsvi.com*), at "P" dock next to the Off the Hook restaurant, offers 22- to 26-foot twin-engine catamarans for day charters. Rates range from $345 to $385 for half- or full-day. A captain can be hired for $115 for a day. If you want to explore the east end of St. Thomas, **Mangrove Adventures** (⊠*Rte. 32, Estate Nadir* ☎*340/779–2155* ⊕*www.viecotours.com*) offers inflatable boat rentals for $100 per day. **Nauti Nymph** (⊠*6501 Red Hook Plaza, Suite 201, Red Hook* ☎☎*340/775–5066* ☎*800/734–7345* ⊕*www.st-thomas.com/nautinymph*) has a large selection of 25- to 29-foot powerboats. Rates vary from $345 to $540 a day, including snorkel gear, water skis, and outriggers, but not including fuel. You can hire a captain for $115 more.

CYCLING

Water Island Adventures (⊠*Water Island* ☎*340/714–2186 or 340/775–5770* ⊕*www.waterislandadventures.com*) offers a cycling adventure to the USVI's "newest" Virgin. You take a ferry ride from the West Indian Company dock near Havensight Mall to Water Island before jumping on a Cannondale mountain bike for a 90-minute tour over rolling hills on dirt and paved roads. Explore the remains of the Sea Cliff Hotel, the inspiration for Herman Wouk's book *Don't Stop the Carnival,* then take a cooling swim at beautiful Honeymoon Beach. Helmets, water, a guide, juices, and ferry fare are included in the $75 cost.

DIVING & SNORKELING

Popular dive sites include such wrecks as the *Cartanser Sr.,* a beautifully encrusted World War II cargo ship sitting in 35 feet of water, and the *General Rogers,* a Coast Guard cutter resting at 65 feet. Here you can find a gigantic resident barracuda. Reef dives offer hidden caves and archways at **Cow and Calf Rocks,** coral-covered pinnacles at **Frenchcap,** and tunnels where you can explore undersea from the Caribbean to the Atlantic at **Thatch Cay, Grass Cay,** and **Congo Cay.** Many resorts and charter yachts offer dive packages. A one-tank dive starts at $80; two-tank dives are $99 and up. Call the USVI Department of Tourism to obtain a free eight-page guide to Virgin Islands dive sites. There are plenty of snorkeling possibilities, too.

🕃 **Admiralty Dive Center** (✉*Holiday Inn St. Thomas, Waterfront Hwy., Charlotte Amalie* ☎*340/777–9802 or 888/900–3483* ⊕*www.admiraltydive.com*) provides boat dives, rental equipment, and a retail store. Four-tank to 12-tank packages are available if you want to dive over several days. **BOB Underwater Adventure** (✉*Crown Bay Marina, Rte. 304, Charlotte Amalie* ☎*340/715–0348* ⊕*www.bobusvi.com*) offers an alternative to traditional diving in the form of an underwater motor scooter called BOB, or Breathing Observation Bubble. A half-day tour, including snorkel equipment, rum punch, and towels, is $99 per person. **Blue Island Divers** (✉*Crown Bay Marina, Rte. 304, Estate Contant* ☎*340/774–2001* ⊕*www.blueislanddivers.com*) is a full-service dive shop that offers both day and night dives to wrecks and reefs. **Chris Sawyer Diving Center** (☎*340/775–7320 or 877/929–3483* ⊕*www.sawyerdive.vi*) is a PADI five-star outfit that specializes in dives to the 310-foot-long *Rhone,* in the British Virgin Islands. Hotel-dive packages are offered through the Wyndham Sugar Bay Beach Club & Resort.

🕃 **Coki Beach Dive Club** (✉*Rte. 388, at Coki Point, Estate Frydendal* ☎*340/775–4220* ⊕*www.cokidive.com*) is a PADI Gold Palm outfit run by avid diver Peter Jackson. Snorkel and dive tours in the fish-filled reefs off Coki Beach are available, as are classes from beginner to underwater photography. **Snuba of St. Thomas** (✉*Rte. 388, at Coki Point, Estate Smith Bay* ☎*340/693–8063* ⊕*www.visnuba.com*) offers something for nondivers, a cross between snorkeling and scuba diving: a 20-foot air hose connects you to the surface. The cost is $68. Children must be eight or older to participate. **Underwater Safaris** (✉*Havensight Mall, Bldg. VI, Rte. 30, Charlotte Amalie* ☎*340/774–1350* ⊕*www.scubadivevi.com*) is another PADI five-star center that offers boat dives to the reefs around Buck Island and nearby offshore wrecks.

FISHING

★ Fishing here is synonymous with blue marlin angling—especially from June through October. Four 1,000-pound-plus blues, including three world records, have been caught on the famous North Drop, about 20 mi (32 km) north of St. Thomas. A day charter for marlin with up to six anglers costs $1,500 for the day. If you're not into marlin fishing, try hooking sailfish in winter, dolphin (the fish, not the mammal) in spring, and wahoo in fall. Inshore trips for two to four hours range from $275 to $550, respectively. To find the trip that will best suit you, walk down the docks at either American Yacht Harbor or Sapphire Beach Marina in the late afternoon and chat with the captains and crews.

For marlin, Captain Red Bailey's **Abigail III** (⊠*Rte. 38, Sapphire Bay* ☎*340/775–6024* ⊕*www.sportfishvi.com*) operates out of the Sapphire Beach Resort & Marina. The **Charter Boat Center** (⊠*6300 Red Hook Plaza, Red Hook* ☎*340/775–7990* ⊕*www.charterboat.vi*) is a major source for sportfishing charters, both marlin and inshore. Captain Eddie Morrison, aboard the 45-foot Viking **Marlin Prince** (⊠*American Yacht Harbor, Red Hook* ☎*340/693–5929* ⊕*www.marlinprince.com*), is one of the most experienced charter operators in St. Thomas and specializes in fly-fishing for blue marlin. For inshore trips, **Peanut Gallery Charters** (⊠*Crown Bay Marina, Rte. 304, Estate Contant* ☎*340/775–5274* ⊕*www.fishingstthomas.com*) offers trips on its 18-foot *Dauntless* or 28-foot custom sportfishing catamaran.

GOLF

★ The **Mahogany Run Golf Course** (⊠*Rte. 42, Estate Lovenlund* ☎*340/777–6006 or 800/253–7103* ⊕*www.mahoganyrungolf.com*) attracts golfers for its spectacular view of the British Virgin Islands and the challenging 3-hole Devil's Triangle. At this Tom and George Fazio–designed par-70, 18-hole course, there's a fully stocked pro shop, snack bar, and open-air club house. Greens and half-cart fees for 18 holes are $150. The course is open daily, and there are frequently informal weekend tournaments. It's the only course on St. Thomas.

PARASAILING

The waters are so clear around St. Thomas that the outlines of coral reefs are visible from the air. Parasailers sit in a harness attached to a parachute that lifts them off a boat deck until they're sailing through the sky. Parasailing trips average a 10-minute ride in the sky that costs $75 per person. Friends who want to ride along pay $15 for the boat trip. **Caribbean Watersports & Tours** (⊠*6501 Red Hook Plaza, Red Hook* ☎*340/775–9360* ⊕*www.viwatersports.com*) makes parasailing pickups from 10 locations around the island, including many major beachfront resorts. It also rents Jet Skis, kayaks, and floating battery-power chairs.

SEA EXCURSIONS

Landlubbers and seafarers alike will enjoy the wind in their hair and salt spray in the air while exploring the waters surrounding St. Thomas. Several businesses can book you on a snorkel-and-sail to a deserted cay for a half day that starts at $65 per person or a full day that begins at $110 per person. An excursion over to the British Virgin Islands starts at $115 per person, not including customs fees. A luxury daylong motor-yacht cruise complete with gourmet lunch is $375 or more per person.

For a soup-to-nuts choice of sea tours, contact the **Adventure Center** (⊠*Marriott's Frenchman's Reef Hotel, Rte. 315, Estate Bakkeroe* ☎*340/774–2992 or 866/868–7784* ⊕*www.adventurecenters.net*). The **Charter Boat Center** (⊠*6300 Red Hook Plaza, Red Hook* ☎*340/775–7990* ⊕*www.charterboat.vi*) specializes in day trips to the British Virgin Islands and day- or weeklong sailing charters. **Limnos Charters** (⊠*Compass Point Marina, Rte. 32, Estate Frydenhoj* ☎*340/775–3203* ⊕*www.limnoscharters.com*) offers one of the most popular British Virgin Islands day trips, complete with lunch, open bar, and snorkel gear. Destinations include the Baths in Virgin Gorda and the sparsely inhabited island of Jost Van Dyke. Enjoy sailboat racing with **OnDeck Ocean Racing** (⊠*9100 Havensight, Suite 10, Port of Sale Mall* ☎*340/777–4944* ⊕*www.ondeckoceanracing.com*). During two-hour excursions you are one of the crew. Work the winches, take a turn at the wheel, and maneuver straight to the finish line. Jimmy Loveland at **Treasure Isle Cruises** (⊠*Rte. 32, Box 6616, Estate Nadir* ☎*340/775–9500* ⊕*www.treasureislecruises.com*) can set you up with everything from a half-day sail to a seven-day U.S. and British Virgin Islands trip that combines sailing with accommodations and sightseeing trips onshore.

SEA KAYAKING

Fish dart, birds sing, and iguanas lounge on the limbs of dense mangrove trees deep within a marine sanctuary on St. Thomas's southeast shore. Learn about the natural history here in a guided kayak-snorkel tour to Patricia Cay or via an inflatable boat tour to Cas Cay for snorkeling and hiking. Both are 2½ hours long. The cost is $65 per person. **Mangrove Adventures** (⊠*Rte. 32, Estate Nadir* ☎*340/779–2155* ⊕*www.viecotours.com*) rents its two-person sit-atop

ocean kayaks and inflatable boats for self-guided exploring. In addition, many resorts on St. Thomas's eastern end
also rent kayaks.

SUBMARINE TRIPS

Dive 90 feet under the sea to one of St. Thomas's most beautiful reefs without getting wet. **Atlantis Adventures** (⊠ *Havensight Mall, Bldg. VI, Charlotte Amalie* ☎ *340/776–5650
⊕www.atlantisadventures.com*) has a 46-passenger sub-
marine that takes you to a watery world teeming with
brightly colored fish, vibrant sea fans, and the occasional
shark. A guide narrates the one-hour underwater journey,
while a diver makes a mid-tour appearance for a fish-feed-
ing show. The cost is $89. No children shorter than 36
inches are allowed.

WINDSURFING

Ⓒ Expect some spills, anticipate the thrills, and try your luck
clipping through the seas. Most beachfront resorts rent
Windsurfers and offer one-hour lessons for about $80. If
you want to learn, try Pual Stoken's **Island Sol** (☎ *340/775–
6530 ⊕www.islandsol.com*). The two-time Olympic athlete
charges $125 per hour for private lessons, $75 per hour for
group lessons. One of the island's best-known independent
windsurfing companies is **West Indies Windsurfing** (⊠ *Vessup
Beach, No. 9, Estate Nazareth* ☎ *340/775–6530*). Owner
John Phillips is the board buff who introduced the sport
of kite boarding to the USVI; it entails using a kite to lift
a boardsailor off the water for an airborne ride. A private
kite-boarding lesson costs $125 per hour, while a semipri-
vate lesson starts at $85 per hour.

SHOPPING

★ **Fodor's Choice** St. Thomas lives up to its billing as a duty-free
shopping destination. Even if shopping isn't your idea of
how to spend a vacation, you still may want to slip in on a
quiet day (check the cruise-ship listings—Monday and Sunday are usually the least crowded) to browse. Among the
best buys are liquor, linens, china, crystal (most stores will
ship), and jewelry. The amount of jewelry available makes
this one of the few items for which comparison shopping is
worth the effort. Local crafts include shell jewelry, carved
calabash bowls, straw brooms, woven baskets, and dolls.
Creations by local doll maker Gwendolyn Harley—like her
costumed West Indian market woman—have been little

goodwill ambassadors, bought by visitors from as far away as Asia. Spice mixes, hot sauces, and tropical jams and jellies are other native products.

On St. Thomas, stores on Main Street in Charlotte Amalie are open weekdays and Saturday 9 to 5. The hours of the shops in the Havensight Mall (next to the cruise-ship dock) and the Crown Bay Commercial Center (next to the Crown Bay cruise-ship dock) are the same, though occasionally some stay open until 9 on Friday, depending on how many cruise ships are anchored nearby. You may also find some shops open on Sunday if cruise ships are in port. Hotel shops are usually open evenings, as well.

There's no sales tax in the USVI, and you can take advantage of the $1,200 duty-free allowance per family member (remember to save your receipts). Although you can find the occasional salesclerk who will make a deal, bartering isn't the norm.

AREAS & MALLS

The prime shopping area in **Charlotte Amalie** is between Post Office and Market squares; it consists of two parallel streets that run east–west (Waterfront Highway and Main Street) and the alleyways that connect them. Particularly attractive are the historic **A.H. Riise Alley, Royal Dane Mall, Palm Passage,** and pastel-painted **International Plaza.**

Vendors Plaza, on the waterfront side of Emancipation Gardens in Charlotte Amalie, is a central location for vendors selling handmade earrings, necklaces, and bracelets; straw baskets and handbags; T-shirts; fabrics; African artifacts; and local fruits. Look for the many brightly colored umbrellas.

West of Charlotte Amalie, the pink-stucco **Nisky Center,** on Harwood Highway about ½ mi (¾ km) east of the airport, is more of a hometown shopping center than a tourist area, but there's a bank, clothing store, record shop, and Radio Shack.

At the Crown Bay cruise-ship pier, the **Crown Bay Center,** off the Harwood Highway in Sub Base about ½ mi (¾ km) has quite a few shops.

Havensight Mall, next to the cruise-ship dock, may not be as charming as downtown Charlotte Amalie, but it does have more than 60 shops. It also has an excellent book-

CLOSE UP

Made in St. Thomas

1

Justin Todman, aka the Broom Man, keeps the dying art of broom-making alive. It's a skill he learned at the age of six from his father. From the fronds of the date palm, Todman delicately cuts, strips, and dries the leaves, a process that can take up to a week. Then he creatively weaves the leaves into distinctively shaped brooms with birch-berry wood for handles. There are feather brooms, cane brooms, multicolor yarn brooms, tiny brooms to fit into a child's hand, and tall long-handled brooms to reach cobwebs on the ceiling. Some customers buy Todman's brooms—sold at the Native Arts & Crafts Cooperative—not for cleaning but rather for celebrating their nuptials. It's an old African custom for the bride and groom to jump over a horizontally laid broom to start their new life.

Gail Garrison puts the essence of local flowers, fruits, and leaves into perfumes, powders, and body splashes. Her Island Fragrances line includes frangipani-, white ginger-, and jasmine-scented perfumes; aromatic mango, lime, and coconut body splashes; and bay rum aftershave for men. Garrison compounds, mixes, and bottles the products herself in second-floor offices on Charlotte Amalie's Main Street. You can buy the products in the Tropicana Perfume Shop.

Gwendolyn Harley preserves Virgin Islands culture in the personalities of her hand-sewn, softly sculptured historic dolls for sale at the Native Arts & Crafts Cooperative. There are quadrille dancers clad in long, colorful skirts; French women with their neat peaked bonnets; and farmers sporting handwoven straw hats. Each one-of-kind design is named using the last three letters of Harley's first name; the dolls have names like Joycelyn, Vitalyn, and Iselyn.

Cheryl Miller cooks up ingredients like sun-sweetened papayas, fiery Scotch bonnet peppers, and aromatic basil leaves into the jams, jellies, and hot sauces she sells under her Cheryl's Taste of Paradise line. Five of Miller's products—Caribbean Mustango Sauce, Caribbean Sunburn, Mango Momma Jam, Mango Chutney, and Hot Green Pepper Jelly—have won awards at the National Fiery Foods Show in Albuquerque, New Mexico.

Jason Budsan traps the enticing aromas of the islands into sumptuous candles he sells at his Tillett Gardens workshop. Among the scents are Ripe Mango, Night Jasmine, Lime in de Coconut, Frenchie Connection (with vanilla and lavender), and Ripe Pineapple.

store, a bank, a pharmacy, a gourmet grocery, and smaller branches of many downtown stores. The shops at **Port of $ale,** adjoining Havensight Mall (its buildings are pink instead of brown), sell discount goods. Next door to Port of $ale is the **Yacht Haven Grande** complex, with many upscale shops.

East of Charlotte Amalie on Route 38, **Tillett Gardens** is an oasis of artistic endeavor across from the Tutu Park Shopping Mall. The late Jim and Rhoda Tillett converted this old Danish farm into an artists' retreat in 1959. Today you can watch artisans produce silk-screen fabrics, candles, watercolors, jewelry, and other handicrafts. Something special is often happening in the gardens as well: the Classics in the Gardens program is a classical music series presented under the stars, Arts Alive is an annual arts-and-crafts fair held in November, and the Pistarckle Theater holds its performances here. **Tutu Park Shopping Mall,** across from Tillett Gardens, is the island's one and only enclosed mall. More than 50 stores and a food court are anchored by Kmart and Plaza Extra grocery store. Archaeologists have discovered evidence that Arawak Indians once lived near the grounds.

Red Hook has **American Yacht Harbor,** a waterfront shopping area with a dive shop, a tackle store, clothing and jewelry boutiques, a bar, and a few restaurants.

SPECIALTY ITEMS

ART

Camille Pissarro Art Gallery. This second-floor gallery, in the birthplace of St. Thomas's famous artist, offers a fine collection of original paintings and prints by local and regional artists. ⊠ *14 Main St., Charlotte Amalie* ☎ *340/774–4621.*

The Color of Joy. Find locally made arts and crafts here, including pottery, batik, hand-painted linen and cotton clothing, glass plates and ornaments, and watercolors by owner Corinne Van Rensselaer. There are also original prints by many local artists. ⊠ *Rte. 317, about 100 yards west of Ritz-Carlton, Red Hook* ☎ *340/775–4020.*

Gallery St. Thomas. Fine art and collectibles are found in this charming gallery, including paintings, wood sculpture, glass, and jewelry that are from or inspired by the Virgin Islands. ⊠ *1 Main St., 2nd fl., Charlotte Amalie* ☎ *340/777–6363.*

1

Kilnworks Pottery & Caribbean Art Gallery. A 12-foot statue of a green iguana marks the entrance to this pottery paradise. Owner Peggy Seiwert is best known for her lizard-theme ceramic cups, bowls, and platters. There are also pottery pieces by other local artists, as well as paintings and gift items. ⊠*Rte. 38, across from Toad & Tart English Pub, Estate Smith Bay* ☎*340/775–3979.*

Mango Tango. Works by popular local artists—originals, prints, and note cards—are displayed (there's a one-person show at least one weekend a month) and sold here. There's also the island's largest humidor and a brand-name cigar gallery. ⊠*Al Cohen's Plaza, ½ mi (¾ km) east of Charlotte Amalie* ☎*340/777–3060.*

BOOKS

🕭 **Dockside Bookshop.** This place is packed with books for children, travelers, cooks, and historians, as well as a good selection of paperback mysteries, best sellers, art books, calendars, and prints. It also carries a selection of books written in and about the Caribbean and the Virgin Islands. ⊠*Havensight Mall, Bldg. VI, Rte. 30, Charlotte Amalie* ☎*340/774–4937.*

CAMERAS & ELECTRONICS

Boolchand's. Brand-name cameras, audio and video equipment, and binoculars are sold here. ⊠*31 Main St., Charlotte Amalie* ☎*340/776–0794* ⊠*Havensight Mall, Bldg. II, Rte. 30, Charlotte Amalie* ☎*340/776–0302.*

Royal Caribbean. Shop here for cameras, camcorders, stereos, watches, and clocks. ⊠*23 Main St., Charlotte Amalie* ☎*340/776–5449* ⊠*33 Main St., Charlotte Amalie* ☎*340/776–4110* ⊠*Havensight Mall, Bldg. I, Rte. 30, Charlotte Amalie* ☎*340/776–8890.*

CHINA & CRYSTAL

The Crystal Shoppe at A. H. Riise. All that glitters is here, from the Swarovski and Waterford crystal to the figurines by Hummel, Daum, and Royal Copenhagen, and china by Belleek, Kosta Boda, and several Limoges factories. There's also a large selection of Lladró figurines. ⊠*37 Main St., at Riise's Alley, Charlotte Amalie* ☎*340/776–2303.*

Little Switzerland. All of this establishment's shops carry crystal from Baccarat, Waterford, and Orrefors; and china from Kosta Boda, Rosenthal, and Wedgwood, among others. There's also an assortment of Swarovski cut-crystal animals, gemstone globes, and many other affordable collectibles. It also does a booming mail-order business; ask for a catalog. ⌧*5 Dronningens Gade, across from Emancipation Garden, Charlotte Amalie* ☎*340/776–2010* ⌧*3B Main St., Charlotte Amalie* ☎*340/776–2010* ⌧*Havensight Mall, Bldg. II, Rte. 30, Charlotte Amalie* ☎*340/776–2198.*

Scandinavian Center. The best of Scandinavia is here, including Royal Copenhagen, Georg Jensen, Kosta Boda, and Orrefors. Owners Soøren and Grace Blak make regular buying trips to northern Europe and are a great source of information on crystal. Online ordering is available if you want to add to your collection once home. ⌧*Havensight Mall, Bldg. III, Rte. 30, Charlotte Amalie* ☎*340/776–5030 or 800/524–2063.*

CLOTHING

🕒 **Fresh Produce.** You won't find lime-green mangoes, peachy-pink guavas, or sunny-yellow bananas in this store. But you will find these fun, casual colors in the Fresh Produce clothing line. This is one of only 16 stores to stock 100% of this California-created, tropical-feel line of apparel for women. Find dresses, shirts, slacks, and skirts in small to plus sizes as well as accessories such as bags and hats. ⌧*Riise's Alley, Charlotte Amalie* ☎*340/774–0807.*

🕒 **Keep Left.** This friendly shop features something for everyone in the family, including Patagonia dresses, Quiksilver swim wear, Jams World shirts, Watership Trading hats, and NAOT sandals. ⌧*American Yacht Harbor, Bldg. C, Rte. 32, Red Hook* ☎*340/775–9964.*

🕒 **Local Color.** Men, women, and children will find something to choose from among brand-name wear like Jams World, Fresh Produce, and Urban Safari. There's also St. John artist Sloop Jones's colorful, hand-painted island designs on cool dresses, T-shirts, and sweaters. Find tropically oriented accessories like big-brim straw hats, bold-color bags, and casual jewelry. ⌧*Royal Dane Mall, at Waterfront, Charlotte Amalie* ☎*340/774–2280.*

Nicole Miller. The New York designer has created an exclusive motif for the USVI: a map of the islands, a cruise ship, and a tropical sunset. Find this print, and Miller's full line of other designs, on ties, scarves, boxer shorts, sarongs, and dresses. ⌧*24 Main St., at Palm Passage, Charlotte Amalie* ☎*340/774–8286.*

Tommy Hilfiger Boutique. Stop by this shop for classic American jeans and sportswear, as well as trendy bags, belts, ties, socks, caps, and wallets. ⊠ *Waterfront Hwy. at Trompeter Gade, Charlotte Amalie* ☎340/777–1189.

FOODSTUFFS

☺ **The Belgian Chocolate Company.** Everything at this confectionery shop tastes as good as it smells. Watch chocolates made before your eyes. Specialties include triple-chocolate rum truffles. You can also find imported chocolates here as well. Both the homemade and imported come in decorative boxes, so they make great gifts. ⊠*Royal Dane Alley, Charlotte Amalie* ☎340/774–6675.

Cost-U-Less. The Caribbean equivalent of Costco and Sam's Club sells everything from soup to nuts, but in giant sizes and case lots. The meat-and-seafood department, however, has family-size portions. A well-stocked fresh produce section and a case filled with rotisserie chicken were added in 2006. ⊠*Rte. 38, ¼ mi (½ km) west of Rte. 39 intersection, Estate Donoe* ☎340/777–3588.

Food Center. Fresh produce, meats, and seafood, plus an on-site bakery and deli with hot-and-cold prepared foods, are the draw here, especially for those renting villas, condos, or charter boats in the East End area. ⊠*Rte. 32, Estate Frydenhoj* ☎340/777–8806.

Fruit Bowl. For fresh fruits and vegetables, this is the best place on the island to go. ⊠ *Wheatley Center, Rtes. 38 and 313 intersection, Charlotte Amalie* ☎340/774–8565.

Gourmet Gallery. Visiting millionaires buy their caviar here. There's also an excellent and reasonably priced wine selection, as well as specialty ingredients for everything from tacos to curries to chow mein. A full-service deli offers imported meats, cheeses, and in-store prepared foods that are perfect for a gourmet picnic. ⊠*Crown Bay Marina, Rte. 304, Estate Contant* ☎340/776–8555 ⊠*Havensight Mall, Bldg. VI, Rte. 30, Charlotte Amalie* ☎340/774–4948.

Marina Market. You won't find better fresh meat or seafood anywhere on the island. ⊠*Rte. 32, across from Red Hook ferry, Red Hook* ☎340/779–2411.

Plaza Extra. This large U.S.-style supermarket has everything you need from produce to meat, including fresh seafood, an excellent deli, and a bakery. There's a liquor department, too. ⊠*Tutu Park Shopping Mall, Rte. 38, Estate Tutu* ☎*340/775–5646.*

PriceSmart. Everything from electronics to housewares is found in this warehouse-size store. The meat, poultry, and seafood departments are especially popular. A small café in front sells pizzas, hot dogs, and the cheapest bottled water on the island—just 75¢ a pop. ⊠*Rte. 38, west of Fort Mylner, Estate Tutu* ☎*340/777–3430.*

Pueblo Supermarket. This Caribbean chain carries stateside brands of most products—but at higher prices because of shipping costs to the islands. ⊠*Sub Base, ½ mi (¾ km) east of Crown Bay Marina, Estate Contant* ☎*340/774–4200* ⊠*Rte. 30, 1 mi (1½ km) north of Havensight Mall, Estate Thomas* ☎*340/774–2695.*

HANDICRAFTS

☼ **Caribbean Marketplace.** This is a great place to buy handicrafts from the Caribbean and elsewhere. Also look for Sunny Caribee spices, teas from Tortola, and coffee from Trinidad. ⊠*Havensight Mall, Rte. 30, Charlotte Amalie* ☎*340/776–5400.*

☼ **Dolphin Dreams.** Look for gaily painted Caribbean-theme Christmas ornaments, art glass from the Mitchell-Larsen studio, and jewelry made from recycled coral. Signature clothing lines include Bimini Bay and Rum Reggae. This boutique is the exclusive Red Hook source for the famous Caribbean Hook Bracelet, originated by the Caribbean Bracelet Company on St. Croix. ⊠*American Yacht Harbor, Bldg. C, Rte. 32, Red Hook* ☎*340/775–0549.*

Down Island Traders. These traders deal in hand-painted calabash bowls; finely printed Caribbean note cards; jams, jellies, spices, hot sauces, and herbs; teas made of lemongrass, passion fruit, and mango; coffee from Jamaica; and handicrafts from throughout the Caribbean. ⊠*Waterfront Hwy. at Post Office Alley, Charlotte Amalie* ☎*340/776–4641.*

Native Arts & Crafts Cooperative. More than 40 local artists—including schoolchildren, senior citizens, and people with disabilities—create the handcrafted items for sale here: African-style jewelry, quilts, calabash bowls, dolls, carved-wood figures, woven baskets, straw brooms, note cards, and cookbooks. ⊠*Tolbod Gade, across from Emancipation Garden, Charlotte Amalie* ☎*340/777–1153.*

JEWELRY

Amsterdam Sauer. Many fine one-of-a-kind designs are displayed at this jeweler's three locations. The Imperial Topaz Collection at the Main Street store is a stunner. ✉ *1 Main St., Charlotte Amalie* ☎ *340/774–2222* ✉ *Havensight Mall, Rte. 30, Charlotte Amalie* ☎ *340/776–3828* ✉ *Ritz-Carlton, Rte. 317, Estate Great Bay* ☎ *340/779–2308.*

Cardow Jewelry. A chain bar—with gold in several lengths, widths, sizes, and styles—awaits you here, along with diamonds, emeralds, and other precious gems. You're guaranteed 40% to 60% savings off U.S. retail prices or your money will be refunded within 30 days of purchase. ✉ *33 Main St., Charlotte Amalie* ☎ *340/776–1140* ✉ *Havensight Mall, Bldg. I, Rte. 30, Charlotte Amalie* ☎ *340/774–0530 or 340/774–5905* ✉ *Marriott Frenchman's Reef Resort, Rte. 315, Estate Bakkeroe* ☎ *340/774–0434.*

Colombian Emeralds. Well known in the Caribbean, this store offers set and unset emeralds as well as gems of every description. The watch boutique carries upscale brands like Ebel, Tissot, and Jaeger LeCoultre. ✉ *30 Main St., Charlotte Amalie* ☎ *340/777–5400* ✉ *Waterfront at A. H. Riise Mall, Charlotte Amalie* ☎ *340/774–1033* ✉ *Havensight Mall, Bldg. V, Rte. 30, Charlotte Amalie* ☎ *340/774–2442.*

Diamonds International. Choose a diamond, emerald, or tanzanite gem and a mounting, and you can have your dream ring set in an hour. Famous for having the largest inventory of diamonds on the island, this shop welcomes trade-ins, has a U.S. service center, and offers free diamond earrings with every purchase. ✉ *31 Main St., Charlotte Amalie* ☎ *340/774–3707* ✉ *3 Drakes Passage, Charlotte Amalie* ☎ *340/775–2010* ✉ *7AB Drakes Passage, Charlotte Amalie* ☎ *340/774–1516* ✉ *Havensight Mall, Bldg. II, Rte. 30, Charlotte Amalie* ☎ *340/776–0040* ✉ *Wyndham Sugar Bay Beach Club & Resort, Rte. 38, Estate Smith Bay* ☎ *340/714–3248.*

H. Stern Jewelers. The World Collection of jewels set in modern, fashionable designs and an exclusive sapphire watch have earned this Brazilian jeweler a stellar name. ✉ *8 Main St., Charlotte Amalie* ☎ *340/776–1939* ✉ *Havensight Mall, Bldg. II, Rte. 30, Charlotte Amalie* ☎ *340/776–1223* ✉ *Marriott Frenchman's Reef Resort, Rte. 315, Estate Bakkeroe* ☎ *340/776–3550.*

Jewels. Name-brand jewelry and watches are in abundance here. Designer jewelry lines include David Yurman, Bulgari, Chopard, and Penny Preville. The selection of watches is extensive, with brand names including Jaeger le Coultre, Tag Heuer, Breitling, Movado, and Gucci. ✉*Main St., at Riise's Alley, Charlotte Amalie* ☎*340/777–4222* ✉*Waterfront at Hibiscus Alley, Charlotte Amalie* ☎*340/777–4222* ✉*Havensight Mall, Bldg. II, Rte. 30, Charlotte Amalie* ☎*340/776–8590.*

Rolex Watches at A.H. Riise. As the Virgin Islands' official Rolex retailer, this shop offers one of the largest selections of these fine timepieces in the Caribbean. An After Sales Service Center assures that your Rolex keeps on ticking for a lifetime. ✉*37 Main St., at Riise's Alley, Charlotte Amalie* ☎*340/776–2303* ✉*Havensight Mall, Bldg. II, Rte. 30, Charlotte Amalie* ☎*340/776–4002.*

LEATHER GOODS

Coach Boutique at Little Switzerland. Find a full line of fine leather handbags, belts, gloves, and more for women, plus briefcases and wallets for men. Accessories for both sexes include organizers, travel bags, and cell-phone cases. ✉*5 Main St., Charlotte Amalie* ☎*340/776–2010.*

☾ **Zora's.** Fine made-to-order leather sandals are the specialty here. There's also a selection of locally made backpacks, purses, and briefcases in durable, brightly colored canvas. ✉*Norre Gade, across from Roosevelt Park, Charlotte Amalie* ☎*340/774–2559.*

LINENS

Fabric in Motion. Fine Italian linens share space with Liberty's of London silky cottons, colorful batiks, cotton prints, ribbons, and accessories at this small shop. ✉*Storetvaer Gade, Charlotte Amalie* ☎*340/774–2006.*

Mr. Tablecloth. The friendly staff here will help you choose from the floor-to-ceiling selection of linens, from Tuscany lace tablecloths to Irish linen pillowcases. The prices will please. ✉*6–7 Main St., Charlotte Amalie* ☎*340/774–4343.*

LIQUOR & TOBACCO

A.H. Riise Liquors & Tobacco. This Riise venture offers a large selection of tobacco (including imported cigars), as well as cordials, wines, and rare vintage Armagnacs, cognacs, ports, and Madeiras. It also stocks fruits in brandy and barware from England. Enjoy rum samples at the tasting bar. ⊠*37 Main St., at Riise's Alley, Charlotte Amalie* ☎*340/776–2303* ⊠*Havensight Mall, Bldg. I, Rte. 30, Charlotte Amalie* ☎*340/776–7713.*

Al Cohen's Discount Liquor. The wine selection at this warehouse-style store is extremely large. ⊠*Rte. 30 across from Havensight Mall, Charlotte Amalie* ☎*340/774–3690.*

Tobacco Discounters. Find here a full line of discounted brand-name cigarettes, cigars, and tobacco accessories. ⊠*Port of $ale Mall, Rte. 30, next to Havensight Mall, Charlotte Amalie* ☎*340/774–2256.*

MUSIC

☾ **Modern Music.** Shop for the latest stateside and Caribbean CD releases, plus oldies, classical, and New Age music. ⊠*Rte. 30, across from Havensight Mall, Charlotte Amalie* ☎*340/774–3100* ⊠*Nisky Center, Rte. 30, Charlotte Amalie* ☎*340/777–8787.*

☾ **Parrot Fish Music.** A stock of standard stateside CDs, plus a good selection of Caribbean artists, including local groups, can be found here. You can browse through the collection of calypso, soca, steel band, and reggae music online at *www.parrotfishmusic.com.* ⊠*Back St., Charlotte Amalie* ☎*340/776–4514.*

PERFUME

Tropicana Perfume Shoppe. Displayed in an 18th-century Danish building is a large selection of fragrances for men and women, including those locally made by Gail Garrison from the essential oils of tropical fruits and flowers like mango and jasmine. ⊠*2 Main St., Charlotte Amalie* ☎*340/774–0010.*

SUNGLASSES

Fashion Eyewear. Take your pick from name-brand eyewear. A real plus here is prescription sunglasses, copied from your present eyewear, ready in a half hour for $99. ⊠*International Plaza, Charlotte Amalie* ☎*340/776–9075.*

TOYS

☾ **Quick Pics.** Birds sing, dogs bark, and fish swim in this animated toy land, which is part of a larger electronics and souvenir store. Adults have as much fun trying out the wares as do kids. ⊠*Havensight Mall, Bldg. IV, Rte. 30, Charlotte Amalie* ☎*340/774–3500.*

NIGHTLIFE & THE ARTS

On any given night, especially in season, you can find steel-pan orchestras, rock and roll, piano music, jazz, broken-bottle dancing (actual dancing atop broken glass), disco, and karaoke. Pick up a free copy of the bright yellow *St. Thomas–St. John This Week* magazine when you arrive (it can be found at the airport, in stores, and in hotel lobbies). The back pages list who's playing where. The Friday edition of the *Daily News* carries complete listings for the upcoming weekend.

NIGHTLIFE

BARS

Agave Terrace. Island-style steel-pan bands are a treat that should not be missed. Steel-pan music resonates after dinner here on Tuesday and Thursday. ✉*Point Pleasant Resort, Rte. 38, Estate Smith Bay* ☎*340/775–4142.*

Duffy's Love Shack. A live band and dancing under the stars are the big draws for locals and visitors alike. ✉*Red Hook Plaza, Red Hook* ☎*340/779–2080.*

Epernay Bistro. This intimate nightspot has small tables for easy chatting, wine and champagne by the glass, and a spacious dance floor. Mix and mingle with island celebrities. The action runs from 4 PM until the wee hours Monday through Saturday. ✉*Frenchtown Mall, 24-A Honduras, Frenchtown* ☎*340/774–5348.*

Greenhouse Bar & Restaurant. Once this favorite eatery puts away the salt and pepper shakers at 10 PM, it becomes a rock-and-roll club with a DJ or live reggae bands raising the weary to their feet six nights a week. ✉*Waterfront Hwy. at Storetvaer Gade, Charlotte Amalie* ☎*340/774–7998.*

Iggies Beach Bar. Sing along karaoke-style to the sounds of the surf or the latest hits at this beachside lounge. There are live bands on the weekends, and you can dance inside or kick up your heels under the stars. At the adjacent Beach House restaurant, there's Carnival Night, complete with steel-pan music on Wednesday. ✉*Bolongo Bay Beach Club & Villas, Rte. 30, Estate Bolongo* ☎*340/775–1800.*

Ritz-Carlton, St. Thomas. On Monday nights, catch steel-pan music at this resort's bar. ✉*Rte. 317, Estate Great Bay* ☎*340/775–3333.*

CLOSE UP

Mocko Jumbie Magic

Mocko Jumbies, the island's otherworldly stilt walkers, trace their roots back to West Africa. The steps of the stilt walkers held religious significance in West Africa, but today's West Indian version is more secular—bending backward to gravity-defying lengths and high kicking to the pulsating beat of drums, bells, and whistles.

Today, satins and sequins have replaced costumes made of grasses, shells, and feathers. Festive headpieces—braids of feathers, glittering crowns, tall hats, and even spiky horns—attract plenty of atten-tion from onlookers. A mask completes the outfit, assuring that the dancer's identity is concealed from spectators, thus maintaining the magic of the Mocko Jumbie.

Beyond Carnival celebrations, the Mocko Jumbie is so popular that it's a mainstay at many hotels. Mocko Jumbie dancers also perform at store openings, when cruise ships dock, or even at weekend beach jams. Old-fashioned or newfangled, Mocko Jumbies will always be loved best for driving away "jumbie spirits," as they say in the islands.

THE ARTS

THEATER

Pistarkle Theater. In the Tillett Gardens complex, this air-conditioned theater with more than 100 seats is host to a dozen or more productions annually, plus a children's summer drama camp. ⊠*Tillett Gardens, Rte. 38, across from Tutu Park Shopping Mall, Estate Tutu* ☎*340/775-7877.*

Reichhold Center for the Arts. This amphitheater has its more expensive seats covered by a roof. Schedules vary, so check the paper to see what's on when you're in town. Throughout the year there's an entertaining mix of local plays, dance exhibitions, and music of all types. ⊠*Rte. 30, across from Brewers Beach, Estate Lindberg Bay* ☎*340/693-1559.*

ST. THOMAS ESSENTIALS

To research prices, get advice from other travelers, and book travel arrangements, visit www.fodors.com.

TRANSPORTATION

BY AIR

Of all the Virgin Islands, St. Thomas is the most accessible by air, with an abundance of nonstop and connecting flights that can have you at the beach in three to four hours from most East Coast airports. Moving on is also easy because there are small island-hopper planes (as well as seaplane service) from St. Thomas to St. Croix (and ferries to St. John). American, Continental, Delta, Spirit, United, and US Airways fly to St. Thomas; some flights connect through San Juan, Puerto Rico. Cape Air flies from San Juan; Cape Air has code-share arrangements with all major airlines, so your luggage can transfer seamlessly.

BY BOAT & FERRY

Ferries are a great way to travel around the islands. There's frequent service between St. Thomas and St. John and their neighbors, the BVI. At this writing, proof of citizenship (passport or birth certificate plus government-issued photo ID) is required to travel between the USVI and BVI by ferry, but sometime in 2008 it is expected that a passport will be required. The actual schedules change, so you should check with the ferry companies to determine the current schedules. The Virgin Islands Vacation Guide & Community (⊕ *www.vinow.com*) publishes current ferry schedules on its Web site. For contact information for all the ferry companies, see ⇨ Virgin Islands Essentials.

Ferries to St. John leave daily from both Charlotte Amalie and Red Hook. From Charlotte Amalie the trip takes 45 minutes and costs $10. The first ferry to St. John leaves at 9, the last at 5:30; from St. John to Charlotte Amalie, the first ferry leaves at 7:15 AM, the last at 3:45.

More frequent ferries to St. John leave from Red Hook, take 15 to 20 minutes, and costs $5; there's an additional charge of $2 for each piece of luggage. The first ferry from Red Hook to St. John leaves at 6:30 AM, the last at midnight; from St. John back to Red Hook, the first ferry leaves at 6 AM, the last at 11 PM. About every hour, there is a car ferry, which costs $52 round-trip; you should arrive at least 25 minutes before departure.

Reefer is the name given to both of the brightly colored 26-passenger skiffs that run between the Charlotte Amalie waterfront and Marriott Frenchman's Reef hotel every day on the half hour from 8 to 5. It's a good way to beat the traffic (and is about the same price as a taxi) to Morning Star Beach. The one-way fare is $6 per person, and the trip takes about 15 minutes.

There's daily service between both Charlotte Amalie or Red Hook, on St. Thomas, and West End or Road Town, Tortola, BVI, by either Smith's Ferry or Native Son, and to Virgin Gorda, BVI, by Smith's Ferry. The fare is $22 one-way or $40 round-trip, and the trip from Charlotte Amalie takes 45 minutes to an hour to West End, up to 90 minutes to Road Town; from Red Hook the trip is only a half hour.

The 2¼-hour trip from Charlotte Amalie to Virgin Gorda costs $35 one-way and $60 round-trip. From Red Hook and Cruz Bay, Inter-Island offers service on Thursday and Sunday; Speedy's offers service on Tuesday, Thursday, and Saturday.

On Friday, Saturday, and Sunday a ferry operates among Red Hook, Cruz Bay, and Jost Van Dyke; the trip takes 45 minutes and costs $50 per person round-trip.

BY BUS

On St. Thomas, the island's large buses make public transportation a very comfortable—though slow—way to get from east and west to Charlotte Amalie and back (service to the north is limited). Buses run about every 30 minutes from stops that are clearly marked with VITRAN signs. Fares are $1 between outlying areas and town and 75¢ in town.

BY CAR

On St. Thomas traffic can get pretty bad, especially in Charlotte Amalie at rush hour (7 to 9 and 4:30 to 6). Cars often line up bumper to bumper along the waterfront. If you need to get from an East End resort to the airport during these times, find the alternate route (starting from the East End, Route 38 to 42 to 40 to 33) that goes up the mountain and then drops you back onto Veterans Highway. If you plan to explore by car, be sure to pick up the latest edition of "Road Map St. Thomas–St. John," which includes the route numbers *and* the names of the roads that are used by locals. It's available anywhere you find maps and guidebooks.

CAR RENTALS

Avis, Budget, and Hertz all have counters at Cyril E. King Airport. Dependable Car Rental offers pickups and drop-offs at the airport and to and from major hotels. Cowpet Rent-a-Car is on the east end of the island. Discount has a location at Bluebeard's Castle hotel. Avis is at the Marriott Frenchman's Reef, Havensight Mall (adjacent to the cruise-ship dock), and Seaborn Airlines terminal on the Charlotte Amalie waterfront; Budget has branches at the Sapphire Beach Resort & Marina and at the Havensight Mall, adjacent to the main cruise-ship dock.

Information **Avis** (☎340/774–1468). **Budget** (☎340/776–5774). **Cowpet Rent-a-Car** (☎340/775–7376). **Dependable Car Rental** (☎340/774–2253 or 800/522–3076). **Discount** (☎340/776–4858). **Hertz** (☎340/774–1879).

BY TAXI

USVI taxis don't have meters because fare rates are standard. Fares are per person, not per destination, and drivers usually take multiple fares, especially from the airport, ferry docks, and the cruise-ship terminal. Many taxis are open safari vans, but some are air-conditioned vans. Taxis of all shapes and sizes are available at various ferry, shopping, resort, and airport areas, and they also respond to phone calls. There are taxi stands in Charlotte Amalie across from Emancipation Garden (in front of Little Switzerland, behind the post office) and along the waterfront. But you probably won't have to look for a stand, as taxis are plentiful and routinely cruise the streets.

Information **East End Taxi** (☎340/775–6974). **Islander Taxi** (☎340/774–4077). **VI Taxi Association** (☎340/774–4550).

CONTACTS & RESOURCES

BANKS

First Bank has locations in Market Square, Waterfront, Estate Thomas, Port of $ale, Red Hook, and Tutu. There are waterfront locations for Banco Popular, as well as branches in Hibiscus Alley, Sugar Estate, Fort Mylner, Red Hook, and Altona, a mile east of the airport. Scotia Bank has branches at Havensight Mall, Nisky Center, Tutu Park Mall, and the Waterfront.

EMERGENCIES

Coast Guard **Marine Safety Detachment** (☎340/776–3497). **Rescue Coordination Center** (☎787/289–2041 in San Juan, PR).

Emergency Services **Air Ambulance Network** (☎800/327–1966). **Ambulance and fire emergencies** (☎911). **Medical Air Services** (☎340/777–8580 or 800/643–9023). **Police emergencies** (☎911).

Hospitals **Roy L. Schneider Hospital & Community Health Center** (✉Sugar Estate ✛1 mi [1½ km] east of Charlotte Amalie ☎340/776–8311).

Pharmacies **Doctor's Choice Pharmacy** (✉Wheatley Shopping Center, across from Roy L. Schneider Hospital, Sugar Estate ☎340/777–1400 ✉Medical Arts Complex, off Rte. 30, 1½ mi [2½ km] east of Cyril E. King Airport ☎340/774–8988). **Havensight Pharmacy** (✉Havensight Mall, Charlotte Amalie ☎340/776–1235). **Kmart Pharmacy** (✉Tutu Park Mall, Tutu ☎340/777–3854).

Scuba-Diving Emergencies **Roy L. Schneider Hospital & Community Health Center** (✉Sugar Estate ✛1 mi [1½ km] east of Charlotte Amalie ☎340/776–2686).

INTERNET, MAIL & SHIPPING

The main U.S. Post Office on St. Thomas is near the hospital, with branches in Charlotte Amalie, Frenchtown, Havensight, and Tutu Mall. Postal rates are the same as if you were in the mainland United States, but Express Mail and Priority Mail aren't as quick.

FedEx offers overnight service if you get your package to the office before 5 PM. Shipping services on St. Thomas are also available at Fast Shipping & Communications Nisky Mail Center and at Red Hook Mail Services.

On St. Thomas, Beans, Bytes & Websites is an Internet café in Charlotte Amalie. East End Secretarial Services offers long-distance dialing, copying, and fax services. At Little Switzerland, there's free Internet access along with an ATM, big-screen TV, telephones, and a bar with cold drinks. Near Havensight Mall, go to Soapy's Station or the Cyber Zone at Port of $ale, where there are 16 computers. Rates for Internet access range from $4 to $6 for 30 minutes to $8 to $12 per hour.

Internet Cafés **Beans, Bytes & Websites** (✉Royal Dane Mall, behind Tavern on Waterfront, Charlotte Amalie, St. Thomas ☎340/775–5262 ⊕www.usvi.net/cybercafe). **Cyber Zone** (✉Port of $ale, Charlotte Amalie, St. Thomas ☎340/714–7743). **East End**

Secretarial Services (✉ *Upstairs at Red Hook Plaza, Red Hook, St. Thomas* ☎ *340/775–5262*). **Little Switzerland** (✉ *5 Dronnigens Gade, across from Emancipation Garden, Charlotte Amalie, St. Thomas* ☎ *340/776–2010*). **The Crew Hub** (✉ *Havensight Mall, above Budget, Charlotte Amalie, St. Thomas* ☎ *340/715–2233*).

Shipping **Fast Shipping & Communications** (✉ *Rte. 30, across from Havensight Mall, Charlotte Amalie, St. Thomas* ☎ *340/714–7634*). **FedEx** (✉ *Cyril E. King Airport, St. Thomas* ☎ *340/777–4140* ⊕ *www. fedex.com*). **Red Hook Mail Services** (✉ *Red Hook Plaza, Rte. 32, 2nd fl., Red Hook, St. Thomas* ☎ *340/779–1890*).

SAFETY

To be safe, keep your hotel or vacation villa door locked at all times, stick to well-lighted streets at night, and use the same kind of street sense that you would in any unfamiliar territory. Don't wander the streets of Charlotte Amalie alone at night. If you plan to carry things around, rent a car—not an open-air vehicle—and lock possessions in the trunk. Keep your rental car locked wherever you park. Don't leave cameras, purses, and other valuables lying on the beach while you snorkel for an hour (or even for a minute), no matter how many people are nearby.

TOUR OPTIONS

Accessible Adventuresprovides a 2- to 2½-hour island tour aboard a special trolley that's especially suitable for those in wheelchairs. Tours go to major sights like Magens Bay and Mountain Top and include a stop for shopping and refreshments. The cost is $34 per person. The V.I. Taxi Association gives a two-hour tour for two people in an open-air safari bus or enclosed van; aimed at cruise-ship passengers, this $29 tour includes stops at Drake's Seat and Mountain Top. Other tours include a three-hour trip to Coki Beach with a shopping stop in downtown Charlotte Amalie for $35 per person, a three-hour tour that includes a trip up the St. Thomas Skyride for $38 per person, a three-hour trip to the Coral World Ocean Park for $45 per person, and a five-hour beach tour to St. John for $75 per person. For $35 to $40 for two, you can hire a taxi for a customized three-hour drive around the island. Make sure to see Mountain Top, as the view is wonderful.

Information **Accessible Adventures** (☎ *340/775–2346* ⊕ *www.accessvi.com*) **V. I. Taxi Association St. Thomas City-Island Tour** (☎ *340/774–4550* ⊕ *www.vitaxi.com*)

WALKING TOURS

The *St. Thomas–St. John Vacation Handbook,* available free at hotels and tourist centers, has an excellent self-guided walking tour of Charlotte Amalie on St. Thomas. Blackbeard's Castle conducts a 45-minute to one-hour historic walking tour that starts at Blackbeard's Castle, then heads downhill to Villa Notman, Haagensen House, and the 99 steps. The cost is $35 per person and includes a tour of Haagensen House and a rum punch. The St. Thomas Historical Trust has published a self-guided tour of the historic district; it's available in book and souvenir shops for $2. Trust members also conduct a two-hour guided historic walking tour by reservation only. Call for more information and to make a reservation.

Information **Blackbeard's Castle** (☎*340/776–1234 or 340/776–1829 ⊕www.blackbeardscastle.com*)

The **St. Thomas Historical Trust** (☎*340/774–5541 ⊕www. stthomashistoricaltrust.org*)

WEDDINGS

Superior Court Offices **St. Thomas Superior Court** (✆*Box 70, St. Thomas 00804 ☎340/774-6680*).

Wedding Planners **Weddings the Island Way** (✆*Box 11694, St. Thomas 00801 ☎340/777-6505 or 800/582-4784 ⊕www.weddings theislandway.com*).

St. John

WORD OF MOUTH

"Much has been written here of the beauty of St. John. All I can say is; its all true! The island is absolutely gorgeous and definitely a place I plan to get back to for a longer visit."

—cmerrell

By Lynda
Lohr

The sun slipped up over the horizon like a great orange ball, streaking the sky with wisps of gold. Watching from my porch overlooking Coral Bay, I thanked Mother Nature, as I do almost every day, for providing glorious sunrises, colorful rainbows and green hillsides, and the opportunity to enjoy them all. It was a magnificent start to another gorgeous St. John day, an island where nature is the engine that fuels the island's economy and brings more than 800,000 visitors a year.

St. John's heart is Virgin Islands National Park, a treasure that takes up a full two-thirds of St. John's 20 square mi (53 square km). The park helps keep the island's interior in its pristine and undisturbed state, but if you go at midday, you'll probably have to share your stretch of beach with others, particularly at Trunk Bay.

The island is booming, and it can get a tad crowded at the ever-popular Trunk Bay Beach during the busy winter season; parking woes plague the island's main town of Cruz Bay, but you won't find traffic jams or pollution. It's easy to escape from the fray, however: just head off on a hike or go early or late to the beach. The sun won't be as strong, and you may have that perfect crescent of white sand all to yourself.

St. John doesn't have a grand agrarian past like her sister island, St. Croix, but if you're hiking in the dry season, you can probably stumble upon the stone ruins of old plantations. The less adventuresome can visit the repaired ruins at the park's Annaberg Plantation and Caneel Bay resort.

In 1675 Jorgen Iverson claimed the unsettled island for Denmark. By 1733 there were more than 1,000 slaves working more than 100 plantations. In that year the island was hit by a drought, hurricanes, and a plague of insects that destroyed the summer crops. With famine a real threat and the planters keeping them under tight reign, the slaves revolted on November 23, 1733. They captured the fort at Coral Bay, took control of the island, and held on to it for six months. During this period, about 20% of the island's total population was killed, the tragedy affecting both black and white residents in equal percentages. The rebellion was eventually put down with the help of French troops from Martinique. Slavery continued until 1848, when slaves in St. Croix marched on Frederiksted to demand their freedom from the Danish government. This time it was granted. After emancipation, St. John fell into decline, with its inhabitants eking out a living on small farms. Life continued in much the same way until the national park opened in 1956 and tourism became an industry.

Of the three U.S. Virgin Islands, St. John, which has 5,000 residents, has the strongest sense of community, which is primarily rooted in a desire to protect the island's natural beauty. Despite the growth, there are still many pockets of tranquillity. Here you can truly escape the pressures of modern life for a day, a week—perhaps, forever.

EXPLORING ST. JOHN

St. John is an easy place to explore. One road runs along the northern shore, another across the center of the mountains. There are a few roads that branch off here and there, but it's hard to get lost. Pick up a map at the visitor center before you start out and you'll have no problems. Few residents remember the route numbers, so have your map in hand if you stop to ask for directions. Bring along a swimsuit for stops at some of the most beautiful beaches in the world. You can spend all day or just a couple of hours exploring, but be advised that the roads are narrow and wind up and down steep hills, so don't expect to get anywhere in a hurry. There are lunch spots at Cinnamon Bay and in Coral Bay, or you can do what the locals do—find a secluded spot for a picnic. The grocery stores in Cruz Bay sell Styrofoam coolers just for this purpose.

If you plan to do a lot of touring, renting a car will be cheaper and will give you much more freedom than relying on taxis; on St. John, taxis are shared safari vans, and drivers are reluctant to go anywhere until they have a full load of passengers. Although you may be tempted by an open-air Suzuki or Jeep, a conventional car can get you just about everywhere on the paved roads, and you'll be able to lock up your valuables. You may be able to share a van or open-air vehicle (called a safari bus) with other passengers on a tour of scenic mountain trails, secret coves, and eerie bush-covered ruins.

ABOUT THE RESTAURANTS

The cuisine on St. John seems to get better every year, with culinary-school-trained chefs vying to see who can come up with the most imaginative dishes. There are restaurants to suit every taste and budget—from the elegant establish-

St. John

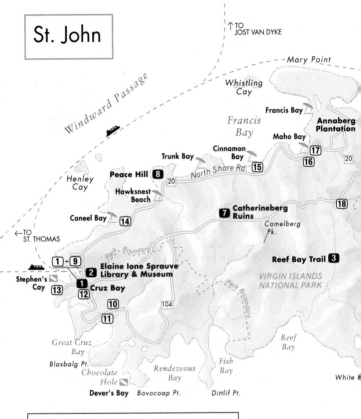

↑ TO
JOST VAN DYKE

Mary Point

Windward Passage

Whistling
Cay

Francis
Bay

Francis Bay

Annaberg
Plantation

Maho Bay

Cinnamon
Bay

Trunk Bay

North Shore Rd.

Peace Hill

Hawksnest
Beach

Henley
Cay

Caneel Bay

Catherineberg
Ruins

Camelberg
Pk.

Reef Bay Trail

VIRGIN ISLANDS
NATIONAL PARK

←TO
ST. THOMAS

Elaine Ione Sprauve
Library & Museum

Stephen's
Cay

Cruz Bay

Park Boundary

Great Cruz
Bay

Blasbalg Pt.

Chocolate
Hole

Rendezvous
Bay

Reef
Bay

Fish
Bay

Dever's Bay   Bovocoap Pt.   Dittlif Pt.

White

Hotels

Caneel Bay Resort, **14**

Cinnamon Bay
Campground, **15**

Coconut Coast Villas, **13**

Estate Lindholm, **3**

Estate Zootenvaal, **21**

Gallows Point Resort, **2**

Garden by the Sea
Bed & Breakfast, **12**

Harmony Studios, **17**

Maho Bay Camps, **16**

Serendip, **10**

Westin St. John Resort, **11**

Restaurants

Asolare, **8**

Café Roma, **1**

Chateau Bordeaux, **18**

Chilly Billy's, **9**

Chloe & Bernard's, **11**

Donkey Diner, **20**

Fish Trap, **4**

Lime Inn, **5**

Miss Lucy's Restaurant, **22**

Skinny Legs Bar
& Restaurant, **19**

Stone Terrace Restaurant, **7**

Tage, **6**

Vie's Snack Shack, **23**

Zozo's Ristorante, **2**

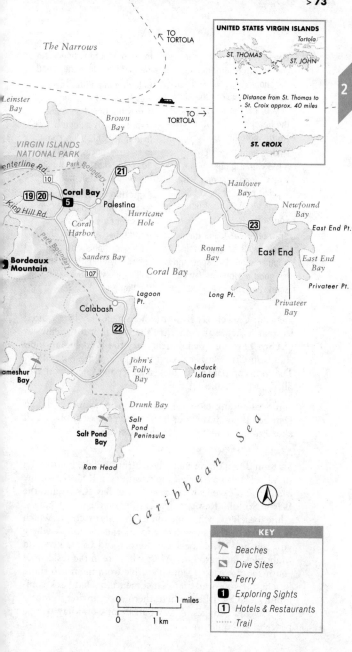

The Narrows

TO TORTOLA

UNITED STATES VIRGIN ISLANDS

Tortola

ST. THOMAS   ST. JOHN

Distance from St. Thomas to St. Croix approx. 40 miles

ST. CROIX

2

Leinster Bay

Brown Bay

TO → TORTOLA

VIRGIN ISLANDS NATIONAL PARK

Park Boundary

Haulover Bay

enterline Rd.

10

21

19 **20** **Coral Bay**

5 Palestina

King Hill Rd.

Coral Harbor

Newfound Bay

23

East End Pt.

Hurricane Hole

Park Boundary

Round Bay

East End

East End Bay

Bordeaux Mountain

Sanders Bay

Coral Bay

107

Privateer Pt.

Long Pt.

Privateer Bay

Calabash

Lagoon Pt.

22

ameshur Bay

John's Folly Bay

Leduck Island

Drunk Bay

Salt Pond Peninsula

Salt Pond Bay

Ram Head

C a r i b b e a n   S e a

	1 miles
0	
0	1 km

KEY

Beaches

Dive Sites

Ferry

1 Exploring Sights

1 Hotels & Restaurants

······· Trail

ST. JOHN TOP 5

Beach Hopping: Fill your cooler with cold drinks, grab the snorkeling gear, and stash your beach chair in the back of your car for a day spent at the beaches along St. John's North Shore Road.

Hiking Reef Bay: Opt for a trip with a ranger with Virgin Islands National Park. A safari bus takes you to the trailhead, and a boat brings you back.

Snorkeling at Trunk Bay: Trunk Bay is St. John's most popular snorkeling spot, and for good reason. The famed snorkeling trail is a good way

to learn about the undersea life that surrounds the island.

Relaxing in a Villa: There are about 500 vacation villas across the island, so it's no surprise this is a popular way to visit St. John. Villas come in all sizes, prices, and locations, and most give you all the comforts of home.

Exploring Cruz Bay: Spend a half day poking around Cruz Bay's varied stores, shopping for that perfect gift for the folks back home. You can spend anything from a few dollars to—well, the sky's the limit.

ments at Caneel Bay Resort (where men may be required to wear a jacket at dinner) to the casual in-town eateries of Cruz Bay. For quick lunches, try the West Indian food stands in Cruz Bay Park and across from the post office. The cooks prepare fried chicken legs, pates (meat- and fish-filled pastries), and callaloo.

Some restaurants close for vacation in September and even October. If you have your heart set on a special place, call ahead to make sure it's open during these months.

ABOUT THE HOTELS

St. John doesn't have many beachfront hotels, but that's a small price to pay for all the pristine sand. However, the island's two excellent resorts—Caneel Bay Resort and the Westin St. John Resort & Villas—*are* on the beach. Sandy, white beaches string out along the north coast, which is popular with sunbathers and snorkelers and is where you can find the Caneel Bay Resort and Cinnamon and Maho Bay campgrounds. Most villas are in the residential south-shore area, a 15-minute drive from the north-shore beaches. If you head east you come to the laid-back community of Coral Bay, where there are growing numbers of villas and cottages. A stay outside of Coral Bay will be peaceful and quiet.

If you're looking for West Indian village charm, there are a few inns in Cruz Bay. Just know that when bands play at any of the town's bars (some of which stay open until the wee hours), the noise can be a problem. Your choice of accommodations also includes condominiums and cottages near town; two campgrounds, both at the edges of beautiful beaches (bring bug repellent); ecoresorts; and luxurious villas, often with a pool or a hot tub (sometimes both) and a stunning view.

If your lodging comes with a fully equipped kitchen, you'll be happy to know that St. John's handful of grocery stores sell everything from the basics to sun-dried tomatoes and green chilies—though the prices will take your breath away. If you're on a budget, consider bringing some staples (pasta, canned goods, paper products) from home. Hotel rates throughout the island, though considered expensive by some, do include endless privacy and access to most water sports.

WHAT IT COSTS IN DOLLARS				
$$$$	$$$	$$	$	¢
RESTAURANTS				
OVER $30	$20–$30	$12–$20	$8–$12	UNDER $8
HOTELS				
* OVER $350	$250–$350	$150–$250	$80–$150	UNDER $80
** OVER $450	$350–$450	$250–$350	$125–$250	UNDER $125

*EP, BP, CP **AI, FAP, MAP Restaurant prices are for a main course at dinner. Hotel prices are for two people in a double room during high season.

TIMING

St. John is a year-round destination, but those from cooler climates head here in winter. Summer is also popular, especially with honeymooners and families. That's also when the weather is the hottest, and when some restaurants and shops close for a month or so.

WHAT TO SEE

Numbers in the margin correspond to points of interest on the St. John map.

❻ Annaberg Plantation. In the 18th century, sugar plantations
★ dotted the steep hills of this island. Slaves and free Danes
and Dutchmen toiled to harvest the cane that was used
to create sugar, molasses, and rum for export. Built in the
1780s, the partially restored plantation at Leinster Bay was
once an important sugar mill. Although there are no official visiting hours, the National Park Service has regular
tours, and some well-informed taxi drivers will show you
around. Occasionally you may see a living-history demon-
stration—someone making johnnycake or weaving baskets.
For information on tours and cultural events, contact the
St. John National Park Service Visitors Center. ⊠*Leinster
Bay Rd., Annaberg* ☎*340/776–6201* ⊕*www.nps.gov/viis*
⊠*Free* ☉*Daily dawn–dusk.*

❹ Bordeaux Mountain. St. John's highest peak rises to 1,277
★ feet. Route 10 passes near enough to the top to offer breathtaking vistas. Don't stray into the road here—cars whiz by
at a good clip along this section. Instead, drive nearly to the
end of the dirt road that heads off next to the restaurant
and gift shop for spectacular views at Picture Point and the
trailhead of the hike downhill to Lameshur. Get a trail map
from the park service before you start. ⊠*Rte. 10.*

❼ Catherineberg Ruins. At this fine example of an 18th-century
sugar and rum factory, there's a storage vault beneath the
windmill. Across the road, look for the round mill, which
was later used to hold water. In the 1733 slave revolt,
Catherineberg served as headquarters for the Amina war-
riors, a tribe of Africans captured into slavery. ⊠*Rte. 10,
Catherineberg.*

❺ Coral Bay. This laid-back community at the island's dry,
eastern end is named for its shape rather than for its underwater life—the word *coral* comes from *krawl,* Dutch for
"corral." It's a small, quiet, neighborhoody settlement—a
place to get away from it all. You'll probably need a four-
wheel-drive vehicle if you plan to stay at this end of the
island, as some of the rental houses are up unpaved roads
that wind around the mountain. If you come just for lunch,
a regular car will be fine.

❶ Cruz Bay. St. John's main town may be compact (it consists of only several blocks), but it's definitely a hub: the ferries from St. Thomas and the British Virgin Islands pull in here, and it's where you can get a taxi or rent a car to travel around the island. There are plenty of shops in which to browse, a number of watering holes where you can stop for a breather, many restaurants, and a grassy square with benches where you can sit back and take everything in. Look for the current edition of the handy, amusing "St. John Map" featuring Max the Mongoose. To pick up a useful guide to St. John's hiking trails, see various large maps of the island, and find out about current park service programs, including guided walks and cultural demonstrations, stop by the **V.I. National Park Visitors Center** (✉*Near baseball field, Cruz Bay* ☎*340/776–6201* ⊕*www.nps.gov/ viis*). It's open daily from 8 to 4:30.

❷ Elaine Ione Sprauve Library. On the hill just above Cruz Bay is the Enighed Estate greathouse, built in 1757. *Enighed* is the Danish word for "concord" (unity or peace). The greathouse and its outbuildings (a sugar factory and horse-driven mill) were destroyed by fire and hurricanes, and the house sat in ruins until 1982. The library offers Internet access for $2 an hour. ✉*Rte. 104, make a right past Texaco station, Cruz Bay* ☎*340/776–6359* ☐*Free* ⊙*Weekdays 9–5.*

❸ Peace Hill. It's worth stopping at this spot just past the Hawksnest Bay overlook for great views of St. John, St. Thomas, and the BVI. On the flat promontory is an old sugar mill. ✉*Off Rte. 20, Denis Bay.*

❸ Reef Bay Trail. Although this is one of the most interest-
★ ing hikes on St. John, unless you're a rugged individualist who wants a physical challenge (and that describes a lot of people who stay on St. John), you can probably get the most out of the trip if you join a hike led by a park ser- vice ranger who can identify the trees and plants on the hike down, fill you in on the history of the Reef Bay Plan- tation, and tell you about the petroglyphs on the rocks at the bottom of the trail. A side trail takes you to the plantation's greathouse, a gutted but mostly intact struc- ture that maintains vestiges of its former beauty. Take the safari bus from the park's visitor center. A boat takes you from the beach at Reef Bay back to the visitor center, sav- ing you the uphill climb. ✉*Rte. 10, Reef Bay* ☎*340/776– 6201 Ext. 238 reservations* ⊕*www.nps.gov/viis* ☐*Free, safari bus $6, return boat trip to Cruz Bay $15* ⊙*Tours at 9:30* AM, *days change seasonally.*

St. John Archaeology

Archaeologists continue to unravel St. John's past through excavations at Trunk Bay and Cinnamon Bay, both prime tourist destinations within Virgin Islands National Park.

Work began back in the early 1990s, when the park wanted to build new bathhouses at the popular Trunk Bay. In preparation for that project, the archaeologists began to dig, turning up artifacts and the remains of structures that date to AD 900. The site was once a village occupied by the Taino, a peaceful group that lived in the area for many centuries. A similar but not quite as ancient village was discovered at Cinnamon Bay.

By the time the Tainos got to Cinnamon Bay—they lived in the area from about AD 1000 to 1500—their society had developed to include chiefs, commoners, workers, and slaves. The location of the national park's busy Cinnamon Bay campground was once a Taino temple that belonged to a king or chief. When archaeologists began digging in 1998, they uncovered several dozen *zemis*, which are small clay gods used in ceremonial activities, as well as beads, pots, and many other artifacts.

Near the end of the Cinnamon Bay dig, archaeologists turned up another less ancient but still surprising discovery. A burned layer indicated that a plantation slave village had also stood near Cinnamon Bay campground; it was torched during the 1733 revolt because its slave inhabitants had been loyal to the planters. Since the 1970s, bones from slaves buried in the area have been uncovered at the water's edge by beach erosion.

WHERE TO EAT

With the exception of the grown-on-the-island greens, which you can find in salads at a wide variety of local restaurants, and an occasional catch of local fish, almost all of the food served at here is imported from the mainland. This means that you may find prices on restaurant menus and supermarket shelves on the high side, since the shipping costs are passed along to the consumer.

For approximate costs, see the dining and lodging price chart at the beginning of this chapter.

BORDEAUX

CONTINENTAL

$$$$ × **Chateau Bordeaux.** This rustic restaurant with a to-die-for
★ view of Coral Bay is a bit out of the way, but worth the
trip. Its interior is made elegant with lace tablecloths, glow-
ing candles, and stylish dinner presentations. Start with the
flaky yellowfin tuna served with an Asian-inspired sauce,
then segue into pan-roasted lobster tail in a red curry sauce
served wasabi mashed potatoes, or the rack of lamb topped
with a blackstrap rum glaze. Save room for dessert—the
warm flourless chocolate cake is served with a sweet goat
cheese mousse and pineapple relish. ⊠*Rte. 10, Bordeaux*
☎*340/776–6611* ⊟*AE, MC, V* ⊗*No lunch.*

CORAL BAY & ENVIRONS

AMERICAN

¢–$ × **Skinny Legs Bar & Restaurant.** Sailors who live aboard boats
★ anchored just offshore and an eclectic coterie of residents
gather for lunch and dinner at this funky spot in the middle of a boatyard-cum-shopping complex. If owner Moe
Chabuz is around, take a gander at his gams; you'll see
where the restaurant got its name. It's a great place for
burgers, fish sandwiches, and whatever sports event is on
the satellite TV. ⊠*Rte. 10, Coral Bay* ☎*340/779–4982*
⊟*AE, D, MC, V.*

CARIBBEAN

$$–$$$ × **Miss Lucy's Restaurant.** Sitting seaside at remote Friis Bay,
★ Miss Lucy's dishes up Caribbean food with a contempo-
rary flair. Dishes like tender conch fritters, a spicy West
Indian stew called callaloo, and fried fish make up most
of the menu, but you also find a generous paella filled
with seafood, sausage, and chicken on the menu. Sunday
brunches are legendary, and if you're around when the
moon is full, stop by for the monthly full-moon party. The
handful of small tables near the water are the nicest, but if
they're taken or the mosquitoes are bad, the indoor tables
do nicely. ⊠*Rte. 107, Friis Bay* ☎*340/693–5244* ⊟*AE, D,
MC, V* ⊗*Closed Mon. No dinner Sun.*

¢–$ × **Vie's Snack Shack.** Stop by Vie's when you're out explor-
★ ing the island. Although it's just a shack by the side of
the road, Vie's serves up some great cooking. The garlic
chicken legs are crisp and tasty, and the conch fritters are
really something to write home about. Plump and filled
with fresh herbs, a plateful will keep you going for the rest

of the afternoon. Save room for a wedge of coconut pie—called a tart in this neck of the woods. When you're done eating, a spectacular white-sand beach across the road beckons. ⊠*Rte. 10, Hansen Bay* ☎*340/693–5033* ▭*No credit cards* ⊙*Closed Sun. and Mon. No dinner.*

ECLECTIC

$$–$$$ ✕**Donkey Diner.** In an odd combination that works well for Coral Bay visitors and residents, this tiny spot along the main road through Coral Bay sells yummy breakfasts and pizza. Breakfasts can be as ordinary or as innovative as you like, with the menu running from fried eggs with bacon to blueberry pancakes to scrambled tofu served with home fries. Pizzas are equally eclectic, with toppings that include everything from the usual pepperoni and mushrooms to more exotic corn, raisins, and kalamata olives. ⊠*Rte. 10, Coral Bay* ☎*340/693–5240* ▭*No credit cards* ⊙*Closed Mon. and Tues.*

CRUZ BAY & ENVIRONS

CONTINENTAL

$$$$ ✕**Tage.** This place gets rave reviews from locals and visi-
★ tors alike for its imaginative cuisine. The menu isn't large, but changes seasonally; look for dishes like Thai-style bouillabaisse with shellfish and salmon in a coconut milk, ginger, and lemongrass broth. Save room for desserts such as the Veracruz flan, a tasty dish of custard served with chocolate cake and lavender ice cream. Although you may be tempted to eat outside, resist the urge—it's much quieter indoors. ⊠*Rte. 104, across from Julius E. Sprauve School* ☎*340/715–4270* ▭*AE, MC, V* ⊙*Closed Mon. No lunch.*

$$$–$$$$ ✕**Chloe & Bernard's.** With a cuisine that draws from all corners of the globe, Chloe & Bernard's is always delightful. The menu changes regularly, but you might start with sliced sirloin on a bed of caramelized onions and roasted cherry tomatoes, or a salad of wild field greens, plump grapes, and candied walnuts drizzled with a roasted apple vinaigrette. Dinner might be scallops over egg noodles tossed with asparagus tips and strips of fried prosciutto. ⊠*Westin St. John Resort & Villas, Rte. 104* ☎*340/693–8000* ▭*AE, MC, V* ⊙*No lunch.*

$$$–$$$$ ✕**Stone Terrace Restaurant.** A delightful harbor view, soft
★ lantern light, and white-linen tablecloths provide the backdrop for this restaurant's imaginative cuisine. To standards like rack of lamb, the chef adds a crisp Dijon mustard–onion crust, a few savory carrot gnocchi, and a Stilton cheese cream

sauce and rosemary glaze. The salad is jazzed up with a confit of duck perched on arugula, figs, and plantain chips drizzled with a tamarind-balsamic dressing. The desserts change daily, but are always as intriguing as the other courses. ⊠*Bay St.* ☎*340/693–9370* ☐*MC, V* ⊘*Closed Mon. No lunch.*

$$–$$$ ✕**Lime Inn.** Vacationers and mainland transplants who call St. John home flock to this alfresco spot for the congenial hospitality and good food, including all-you-can-eat shrimp on Wednesday nights. Fresh lobster is the specialty, and the menu also includes shrimp-and-steak dishes and such specials as coconut-encrusted chicken breast with plantains and a Thai curry–cream sauce. ⊠*Lemon Tree Mall, King St.* ☎*340/776–6425* ☐*AE, MC, V* ⊘*Closed Sun. No lunch Sat.*

ECLECTIC

$$–$$$$ ✕**Fish Trap.** The rooms here all open to the breezes and buzz
ↂ with a mix of locals and visitors. Start with a tasty appetizer like conch fritters or fish chowder (a creamy combination of snapper, white wine, paprika, and secret spices). You can always find steak and chicken dishes, as well as the interesting pasta of the day. ⊠*Bay and Strand sts., next to Our Lady of Mount Carmel Church* ☎*340/693–9994* ☐*MC, V* ⊘*Closed Mon. No lunch.*

$ ✕**Chilly Billy's.** Although you might stop by this restaurant at lunchtime for a heartburn-inducing St. John Reuben (with turkey, cheese, sauerkraut, and mustard on rye), this restaurant's claim to fame is breakfast. The stuffed French toast is one step this side of heaven: before it's fried, the bread is soaked in a mixture of eggs and Bailey's. If you're not one for morning sweets, try a savory breakfast burrito filled with eggs and jalepeño jack cheese. ⊠*Lumberyard Shopping Center, Boulon Center Rd.* ☎*340/693–8708* ☐*MC, V* ⊘*No dinner.*

ITALIAN

★ Fodor'sChoice ✕**Zozo's Ristorante.** Creative takes on old stan-
$$$$ dards coupled with lovely presentations draw the crowds to this restaurant at Gallows Point Resort. Start with crispy fried calamari served with a pesto mayonnaise. The chef dresses up roasted mahimahi with a pistachio crust and serves it with a warm goat cheese and arugula salad. The slow-simmered osso buco comes with prosciutto-wrapped asparagus and saffron risotto. The sunset views will take your breath away. ⊠*Gallows Point Resort, Bay St.* ☎*340/693–9200* ☐*AE, MC, V* ⊘*No lunch.*

$$–$$$ ✕ **Café Roma.** This second-floor restaurant in the heart of
⏱ Cruz Bay is *the* place for traditional Italian cuisine: lasagna, spaghetti and meatballs, and seafood puttanesca. Small pizzas are available at the table, but larger ones are for takeout only. Rum-caramel bread pudding is a dessert specialty. This casual eatery can get crowded in winter, so show up early. ✉ *Vesta Gade* ☎ *340/776–6524* ▭ *MC, V* ⊘ *No lunch*.

PAN-ASIAN

$$$–$$$$ ✕ **Asolare.** Contemporary Asian cuisine dominates the menu
★ at this elegant open-air eatery in an old St. John house. Come early and relax over drinks while you enjoy the sunset lighting up the harbor. Start with an appetizer such as pork dumplings served with a glass noodle salad, then move on to entrées such as beef fillet served with roasted haystack potatoes and napa cabbage, or seared tuna served with an apple-and-greens salad. If you still have room for dessert, try the spring roll drizzled with a mango puree and chocolate sauce. ✉ *Estate Lindholm, Rte. 20 on Caneel Hill* ☎ *340/779–4747* ▭ *AE, MC, V* ⊘ *No lunch*.

WHERE TO STAY

St. John attracts so many different kinds of travelers because accommodations come in all price ranges. Folks on a budget can sleep at Cinnamon Bay Campground. Cruz Bay has a few moderately priced guesthouses and no-frills vacation villas. Those with fatter wallets will have no trouble finding a room at the island's resorts or luxury vacation villas.

For approximate costs, see the dining and lodging price chart at the beginning of this chapter.

HOTELS & INNS

★ **Fodor's**Choice 🏨 **Caneel Bay Resort.** Well-heeled honeymooners,
$$$$ couples celebrating anniversaries, and extended families all enjoy Caneel Bay Resort's laid-back luxury. If you want to spend your days sunning on any one of its seven gorgeous beaches, taking a kayak out for a paddle, or enjoy lingering dinners at its fine restaurants, you can find no finer resort on St. John. Your room, which has air-conditioning or can be opened to catch the breezes, won't come with a TV or even a telephone (though management will loan you a cellular)—all the better to get away from it all. Rooms look

as if they're right out of a magazine; if you opt for one of the beachfront rooms, you can get out of bed and stumble a few steps across the sand to the Caribbean. Otherwise, you can look out on the gardens or the tennis courts. Nightlife runs to steel-pan music or an easy-listening combo; if you want lots of action, go elsewhere. Pros: lovely beaches, gorgeous rooms, lots of amenities. Cons: staff can be chilly, isolated location, high prices. ⊠*Rte. 20, Caneel Bay ⏣Box 720, Cruz Bay 00830 ☎340/776–6111 or 888/767–3966 🖶340/693–8280 ⊕www.caneelbay.com ➷166 rooms ⚇In-room: no phone, no TV. In-hotel: 4 restaurants, tennis courts, pool, spa, beachfront, diving, water sports, no elevator, children's programs (ages 4–12), public Internet, public Wi-Fi, no-smoking rooms* ⊟*AE, DC, MC, V* ⏅*CP.*

$$$$ 🖾**Westin St. John Resort & Villas.** Other than Caneel Bay, this is the island's only big resort. Although it doesn't provide the same casual luxury, it does have a nice beachfront location and enough activities to keep you busy. That said, most guests rent a car for at least a couple of days to explore the area's many lovely beaches. The hotel is spread over 47 beachfront acres adjacent to Great Cruz Bay, with lushly planted gardens, a white sandy beach that beckons sunbathers, and nice—but not luxurious—rooms with tropical touches. Those strung out behind the beach put you closest to the water, but even the hillside villas are only a seven-minute stroll to the sand. Pros: good children's programs, nice pool, many activities. Cons: mediocre beach, long walk to some facilities, need car to get around ⊠*Rte. 104, Great Cruz Bay ⏣Box 8310, Cruz Bay 00831 ☎340/693–8000 or 800/808–5020 🖶340/779–4985 ⊕www.westinresortstjohn.com ➷174 rooms, 146 villas ⚇In-room: safe, refrigerator, Ethernet. In-hotel: 4 restaurants, tennis courts, pool, gym, beachfront, diving, water sports, no elevator, children's programs (ages 3–12), public Wi-Fi, no-smoking rooms* ⊟*AE, D, DC, MC, V* ⏅*EP.*

$$$–$$$$ 🖾**Estate Lindholm Bed & Breakfast.** Built among old stone ruins on a lushly planted hill overlooking Cruz Bay, Estate Lindholm has a charming setting. The location puts you close to Cruz Bay's restaurants, shopping, and nightlife. You'll feel as if you're out of the fray, but still near enough to run into town when you want. Rooms are sophisticated, with crisp white spreads accented by teak furniture. The sunset views from Asolare restaurant, on the property, provide a stunning end to your day. **Pros:** lovely landscaping, gracious host, pleasant decor. Cons: can be noisy, some uphill walks, on busy road. ⏣*Box 1360, Cruz Bay 00831*

☎*340/776–6121* 🖷*800/322–6335* ⊕*www.estatelindholm. com* 🛏*10 rooms* ☆*In-room: refrigerator. In-hotel: restaurant, pool, gym, no elevator, no kids under 18, no-smoking rooms* ▭*AE, D, MC, V* ⊚*CP.*

$$$ ☷**Garden by the Sea Bed & Breakfast.** A stay here will allow you to live like a local in a middle-class residential neighborhood near a bird-filled salt pond. This cozy B&B is also an easy walk from Cruz Bay. White spreads and curtains provide pristine counterpoints to the blue and green hues in your room. Your hosts serve a delightful breakfast—piña colada French toast is a specialty—on the front deck. It's perfect for folks who enjoy peace and quiet: there are no phones or TVs in the rooms. Pros: homey atmosphere, great breakfasts, nice view from deck. Cons: nearby utility, some uphill walks, basic amenities. ✉*Enighed* ☍*5004A Enighed 87, Cruz Bay 00830* ☎🖷*340/779–4731* ⊕*www. gardenbythesea.com* 🛏*3 rooms* ☆*In-room: no phone, no TV. In-hotel: no elevator, no-smoking rooms* ▭*No credit cards* ⊚*BP.*

CAMPING

St. John has a handful of camping spots ranging from the basic Cinnamon Bay Campground to the relatively comfortable Concordia Studios & Eco-tents. They appeal to those who don't mind bringing their own beach towels from home or busing their own tables at dinner. If you want your piña colada delivered beachside by a smiling waiter, you'd be better off elsewhere.

☾ ⚠**Cinnamon Bay Campground.** Cinnamon Bay Campground sits in the heart of Virgin Islands National Park, a stellar location right at the beach. Tents and rustic cottages are nestled in the trees that stretch behind the shore, and you have easy access to hiking, water sports, and ranger-led evening programs. The amenities are basic, but include propane stoves, cooking equipment, and bed linens; reserve early if you'd like a cottage right behind the beach. Only the screened cottages have electric lights; tenters depend on propane lanterns. Showers and flush toilets, as well as a restaurant and a small store, are a short walk away from the camping area. Pros: lovely beach, hiking nearby, lots of activities. Cons: cold showers, can be buggy, traffic noise. ☆*Flush toilets, drinking water, showers (cold), picnic tables, food service, electricity (some), public telephone, general store, swimming (ocean)* 🛏*55 tents, 40 cottages, 31 tent sites* ✉*Rte. 20, Cinnamon Bay* ☍*Box 720,*

2

Cruz Bay 00830-0720 ☎*340/776–6330 or 800/539–9998* 🖷*340/776–6458* ⊕*www.cinnamonbay.com* ⚷*Reservations essential* ⊟*AE, MC, V* ⊙*Oct.–Aug.*

★ FodorsChoice ⚠**Maho Bay Camps.** Tucked into the greenery
☾ along the island's north shore, ecoconscious Maho Bay Camps attracts a sociable crowd that likes to explore the undersea world off the campground's beach or attend on-site seminars. The "tents" (wooden platforms protected from the elements by canvas and screening) are linked by wooden stairs, ramps, and walkways—all of them elevated—so that you can trek around camp, down to the beach, and to the coolish public showers without disturbing the terrain. Although the tents have amenities like real beds and electricity, there are no refrigerators; ice-filled coolers keep your food from spoiling. Pros: friendly atmosphere, good restaurant, ecofriendly facility. Cons: many stairs, can be buggy, need car to get around. ⚷*Flush toilets, drinking water, showers (cold), picnic tables, food service, electricity, public telephone, general store, swimming (beach).* ⚐*114 tent cottages* ✉*Maho Bay* ⊡*Box 310, Cruz Bay 00830* ☎*340/776–6240 or 800/392–9004* 🖷*340/776–6504* ⊕*www.maho.org* ⚷*Reservations essential* ⊟*AE, MC, V.*

CONDOMINIUM RESORTS & COTTAGES

Many of the island's condos are just minutes from the hustle and bustle of Cruz Bay, but you'll find more scattered around the island.

$$$$ ⊡**Gallows Point Resort.** Gallows Point Resort has an excellent waterfront location just outside Cruz Bay's center. You're a short walk to restaurants and shops, but once you step into your condo, the hustle and bustle are left behind. The upper-level apartments have loft bedrooms and the best views. The harborside villas get better trade winds, but they're a tad noisier. Tropical rooms have wicker furniture, tile floors, and brightly colored spreads in colors that reflect the sea and sky. Zozo's Ristorante, a popular spot for sunset watching, serves northern Italian cuisine above the lobby. Pros: walk to shopping, excellent restaurant, comfortable rooms. Cons: some noisy rooms, mediocre beach, little parking. ✉*Gallows Point, Bay St., Box 58, Cruz Bay 00831* ☎*340/776–6434 or 800/323–7229* 🖷*340/776–6520* ⊕*www.gallowspointresort.com* ⚐*60 units* ⚷*In-room: kitchen, in-room Wi-Fi. In-hotel: restaurant, pool, beach-*

front, water sports, no elevator, public Internet, public Wi-Fi ⊟*AE, MC, V* ⍟*EP.*

$$$–$$$$ ⊡**Coconut Coast Villas.** This small condominium complex with studio, two-, and three-bedroom apartments is a 10-minute walk from Cruz Bay, but is insulated from the town's noise in a sleepy suburban neighborhood. You can swim and snorkel at the small beach or relax poolside and catch some rays. Rooms have a fresh feel; each is a little bit different in decor, with whites, blues, and greens predominating in the color scheme. Colorful artwork by St. John artist Elaine Estern graces the walls. Pros: good snorkeling, full kitchens, walk to Cruz Bay. Cons: small beach, some uphill walks, nearby utility plant can be noisy. ⊠*Turner Bay* ⍐*Box 618, Cruz Bay 00831* ☎*340/693–9100 or 800/858–7989* ⎙*340/779–4157* ⊕*www.coconutcoast.com* ⌁*9 units* ⌂*In-room: kitchen. In-hotel: pool, beachfront, no elevator, public Internet.* ⊟*MC, V* ⍟*EP.*

$$$–$$$$ ⊡**Estate Zootenvaal.** Comfortable and casual, this small cottage colony gives you the perfect place to relax. It's certainly out of the way, along the island's East End Road. Although you'll feel that you're getting away from it all, a five-minute drive will bring you to Coral Bay's restaurants, a handful of shops, and tiny grocery store. The small but very private beach across the road is a major plus. Pros: lovely beach, very private, near restaurants. Cons: some traffic noise, no air-conditioning. ⊠*Rte. 10, Hurricane Hole, Zootenvaal 00830* ☎*340/776–6321* ⊕*www.estatezootenvaal.com* ⌁*4 units* ⌂*In-room: no a/c, no phone (some), kitchen, no TV. In-hotel: beachfront, no elevator* ⊟*No credit cards* ⍟*EP.*

$$ ⊡**Harmony Studios.** These condominium-style units sit hillside at Maho Bay, giving you more of the comforts of home than the tents at the nearby Maho Bay Camp. An ecologically correct environment is one of the draws here. Entryway mats are made of recycled tires, the pristine walls of recycled newspapers, and the electricity comes from the wind and the sun. Best of all, you share access to interesting evening programs and a nice beach at Maho. Be prepared to hike up and down long flights of steep, wooden stairs. Pros: friendly guests, near beach, comfortable units. Cons: lots of stairs, no air-conditioning, need car to get around. ⊠*Maho Bay* ⍐*Box 310, Cruz Bay 00830* ☎*340/776–6240 or 800/392–9004* ⎙*340/776–6504* ⊕*www.maho.org* ⌁*12 units* ⌂*In-room: no a/c, no phone, kitchen, no TV. In-hotel: restaurant, beachfront, water sports, no elevator, children's programs (ages 8–16), public Internet, no-smoking rooms* ⊟*AE, MC, V* ⍟*EP.*

$$ ⛫ **Serendip.** We'd pick Serendip for a budget vacation in a residential locale. This complex offers modern apartments on lush grounds with lovely views. Although this is a property from the 1960s, the units don't feel dated. There are colorful spreads, fully equipped kitchens, and bookshelves filled with good vacation reads. You definitely need a car if you stay here, though; it's about 1 mi (1½ km) up a steep hill from Cruz Bay. Pros: comfortable accommodations, good views, nice neighborhood. Cons: no beach, need car to get around, nearby construction. ✉ *Enighed* ⬚ *Box 273, Cruz Bay 00831* ☎ *340/776–6646 or 888/800–6445* ⊕ *www. serendipstjohn.com* ⤙*10 apartments* ⚴*In-room: kitchen, Wi-Fi. In-hotel: pool, no elevator* ☰*MC, V* ⍟*EP.*

PRIVATE CONDOS & VILLAS

Tucked here and there between Cruz Bay and Coral Bay are about 350 private villas and condos (prices range from $ to $$$$). With pools or hot tubs, full kitchens, and living areas, these lodgings provide a fully functional home away from home. They're perfect for couples and extended groups of family or friends. You need a car, since most lodgings are in the hills and very few are at the beach. Villa managers usually pick you up at the dock, arrange for your rental car, and answer questions upon arrival as well as during your stay. Prices drop in the summer season, which is generally after April 15. Some companies begin off-season pricing a week or two later, so be sure to ask.

If you want to be close to Cruz Bay's restaurants and boutiques, a villa in the Chocolate Hole and Great Cruz Bay areas will put you a few minutes away. The Coral Bay area has a growing number of villas, but you'll be about 20 minutes from Cruz Bay. Beaches string out along the North Shore, so you won't be more than 15 minutes from the water no matter where you stay.

RENTAL AGENTS

Book-It VI (⬚*5000 Estate Enighed, PMB 15, Cruz Bay 00830* ☎*340/693–8555 or 800/416–1205* 🖷*340/693–8480* ⊕*www. bookitvi.com*) handles villas all across St. John. **Carefree Get-Aways** (⬚*Box 1626, Cruz Bay 00831* ☎*340/779–4070 or 888/643–6002* 🖷*340/774–6000* ⊕*www.carefreegetaways.com*) manages vacation villas on the island's southern and western edges. **Caribbean Villas & Resorts** (⬚*Box 458, Cruz Bay 00831* ☎*340/776–6152 or 800/338–0987* 🖷*340/779–4044* ⊕*www.caribbeanvilla.com www.caribbe-*

anvilla) handles condo rentals for Cruz Views and Gallow's Point Resort, as well as for many private villas. **Caribe Havens** (✉*Box 455, Cruz Bay 00831* ☎*340/776–6518* 🖷*340/776– 6518* ⊕*www.caribehavens.com*) has mainly budget properties scattered around the island.

Catered to Vacation Homes (✉*Marketplace Suite 206, 5206 Enighed, Cruz Bay 00830* ☎*340/776–6641 or 800/424– 6641* 🖷*340/693–8191* ⊕*www.cateredto.com*) has luxury homes, mainly in the middle of the island and on the western edge. **Cloud 9 Villas** (✉*Box 102, Cruz Bay 00831* ☎*340/693–8495 or 866/693–8496* 🖷*340/693–8191* ⊕*www. cloud9villas.com*) has several homes, with most in the Gifft Hill and Chocolate Hole area **Destination St. John** (✎*Box 8306, Cruz Bay 00831* ☎*340/779–4647 or 800/562–1901* 🖷*340/715–0073* ⊕*www.destinationstjohn.com*) manages villas across the island. **Great Caribbean Getaways** (✎*Box 8317, Cruz Bay 00831* ☎*340/693–8692 or 800/341– 2532* 🖷*340/693–9112* ⊕*www.greatcaribbeangetaways. com*) handles private villas from Cruz Bay to Coral Bay.

Island Getaways (✎*Box 1504, Cruz Bay 00831* ☎*340/693– 7676 or 888/693–7676* 🖷*340/693–8923* ⊕*www.island-get- aways.net*) has villas in the Great Cruz Bay–Chocolate Hole area, with a few others scattered around the island. **On-Line Vacations** (✎*Box 9901, Emmaus 00830* ☎*340/776–6036 or 888/842–6632* 🖷*340/693–5357* ⊕*www.onlinevacations. com*) books vacation villas around St. John. **Private Homes for Private Vacations** (✉*7605 Mamey Peak, Coral Bay 00830* ☎🖷*340/776–6876* ⊕*www.privatehomesvi.com*) has homes across the island. **Seaview Vacation Homes** (✎*Box 644, Cruz Bay 00831* ☎*340/776–6805 or 888/625–2963* 🖷*340/779– 4349* ⊕*www.seaviewhomes.com*) handles homes with views of the ocean in the Chocolate Hole, Great Cruz Bay, and Fish Bay areas.

Star Villas (✎*1202 Gallows Point, Cruz Bay 00830* ☎*340/776–6704 or 888/897–9759* 🖷*340/776–6183* ⊕*www. starvillas.com*) has cozy villas just outside Cruz Bay. **Vacation Vistas** (✎*Box 476, Cruz Bay 00831* ☎*340/776–6462* ⊕*www.vacationvistas.com*) manages villas mainly in the Chocolate Hole, Great Cruz Bay, and Rendezvous areas. **Windspree** (✉*7924 Emmaus, Cruz Bay 00830* ☎*340/693– 5423 or 888/742–0357* 🖷*340/693–5623* ⊕*www.wind spree.com*) handles villas mainly in the Coral Bay area.

BEACHES

St. John is blessed with many beaches, and all of them fall into the good, great, and don't-tell-anyone-else-about-this-place categories. Those along the north shore are all within the national park. Some are more developed than others—and many are crowded on weekends, holidays, and in high season—but by and large they're still pristine. Beaches along the south and eastern shores are quiet and isolated.

Cinnamon Bay Beach. This long, sandy beach faces beautiful cays and abuts the national park campground. The facilities are open to the public and include cool showers, toilets, a commissary, and a restaurant. You can rent water-sports equipment here—a good thing, because there's excellent snorkeling off the point to the right; look for the big angelfish and large schools of purple triggerfish. Afternoons on Cinnamon Bay can be windy—a boon for windsurfers but an annoyance for sunbathers—so arrive early to beat the gusts. The Cinnamon Bay hiking trail begins across the road from the beach parking lot; ruins mark the trailhead. There are actually two paths here: a level nature trail (signs along it identify the flora) that loops through the woods and passes an old Danish cemetery, and a steep trail that starts where the road bends past the ruins and heads straight up to Route 10. Rest rooms are on the main path from the commissary to the beach and scattered around the campground. ⊠*North Shore Rd., Rte. 20, about 4 mi (6 km) east of Cruz Bay.*

Francis Bay Beach. Because there's little shade, this beach gets toasty warm in the afternoon when the sun comes around to the west, but the rest of the day, it's a delightful stretch of white sand. The only facilities are a few picnic tables tucked among the trees and a portable rest room, but folks come here to watch the birds that live in the swampy area behind the beach. The park offers bird-watching hikes here on Sunday morning; sign up at the visitor center in Cruz Bay. To get here, turn left at the Annaberg intersection. ⊠*North Shore Rd., Rte. 20, ¼ mi (½ km) from Annaberg intersection.*

Hawksnest Beach. Sea grape and waving palm trees line this narrow beach, and there are rest rooms, cooking grills, and a covered shed for picnicking. A patchy reef just offshore means snorkeling is an easy swim away, but the best underwater views are reserved for ambitious snorkelers who head farther to the east along the bay's fringes. Watch out for boat traffic—a channel guides dinghies to the beach, but the occasional boater strays into the swim area. It's the closest drivable beach to Cruz Bay, so it's often crowded with locals and visitors. ⊠*North Shore Rd., Rte. 20, about 2 mi (3 km) east of Cruz Bay.*

Lameshur Bay Beach. This sea grape–fringed beach is toward the end of a partially paved road on the southeast coast. The reward for your long drive is solitude, good snorkeling, and a chance to spy on some pelicans. The beach has a couple of picnic tables, rusting barbecue grills, and a portable rest room. The ruins of the old plantation are a five-minute walk down the road past the beach. The area has good hiking trails, including a trek (more than a mile) up Bordeaux Mountain before an easy walk to Yawzi Point. ⊠*Off Rte. 107, about 1½ mi (2½ km) from Salt Pond.*

Maho Bay Beach. This popular beach is below Maho Bay Camps, a wonderful hillside enclave of tent cabins. The campground offers breakfast and dinner at its Pavillion Restaurant, water-sports equipment rentals at the beach, and rest rooms. After a five-minute hike down a long flight of stairs to the beach, snorkelers head off along rocky outcroppings for a look at all manner of colorful fish. Watch for a sea turtle or two to cross your path. Another lovely strip of sand with the same name sits right along the North Shore Road. Turn left at the Annaberg intersection and follow the signs about 1 mi (1½ km) for Maho Bay Camps. ⊠*Off North Shore Rd., Rte. 20, Maho Bay.*

Salt Pond Bay Beach. If you're adventurous, this rocky beach on the scenic southeastern coast—next to Coral Bay and rugged Drunk Bay—is worth exploring. It's a short hike down a hill from the parking lot, and the only facilities are an outhouse and a few picnic tables scattered about. Tide pools are filled with all sorts of marine creatures, and the snorkeling is good, particularly along the bay's edges. A short walk takes you to a pond where salt crystals collect around the edges. Hike farther uphill past cactus gardens to Ram Head for see-forever views. Leave nothing valuable in your car, as reports of thefts are common. ⊠*Rte. 107, about 3 mi (5 km) south of Coral Bay.*

★ Fodor'sChoice **Trunk Bay Beach.** St. John's most-photographed beach is also the preferred spot for beginning snorkelers because of its underwater trail. (Cruise-ship passengers interested in snorkeling for a day flock here, so if you're looking for seclusion, arrive early or later in the day.) Crowded or not, this stunning beach is one of the island's most beautiful. There are changing rooms with showers, bathrooms, a snack bar, picnic tables, a gift shop, phones, lockers, and snorkeling-equipment rentals. The parking lot often overflows, but you can park along the road. ⊠*North Shore Rd., Rte. 20, about 2½ mi (4 km) east of Cruz Bay.*

SPORTS & THE OUTDOORS

BOATING & SAILING

If you're staying at a hotel or campground, your activities desk will usually be able to help you arrange a sailing excursion aboard a nearby boat. Most day sails leaving Cruz Bay head out along St. John's north coast. Those that depart Coral Bay might drop anchor at some remote cay off the island's east end or even in the nearby British Virgin Islands. Your trip usually includes lunch, beverages, and at least one snorkeling stop. Keep in mind that inclement weather could interfere with your plans, though most boats will still go out if rain isn't too heavy. If you're staying in a villa, or if your hotel or campground doesn't have an ★ affiliated charter sailboat, contact **St. John Concierge Services** (⊠*Across from post office, Cruz Bay* ☎*340/777–2665 or 800/808–6025* ⊕*www.adventuresstjohn.com*). The capable staff can find a boat that fits your style and pocketbook. The company also books fishing and scuba trips.

For a speedier trip to the cays and remote beaches off St. John, you can rent a power boat from **Ocean Runner** (⊠*On waterfront, Cruz Bay* ☎*340/693–8809.* The company rents one- and two-engine boats for $295 to $395 per day. Gas and oil will run you $100 to $300 a day extra, depending on how far you're going. It's a good idea to have some skill with power boats for this self-drive adventure, but if you don't, you can hire a captain for $110 a day.

Even novice sailors can take off in a small sailboat from Cruz Bay Beach with **Sail Safaris** (☎*340/626–8181 or 866/820–6906* ⊕*www.sailsafaris.net*) to one of the small islands off St. John. Guided half-day tours, rentals, and lessons each run $70 per person.

DIVING & SNORKELING

Although just about every beach has nice snorkeling—Trunk Bay, Cinnamon Bay, and Waterlemon Cay at Leinster Bay get the most praise—you need a boat to head out to the more remote snorkeling locations and the best scuba spots. Sign on with any of the island's water-sports operators to get to spots farther from St. John. If you use the one at your hotel, just stroll down to the dock to hop aboard. Their boats will take you to hot spots between St. John and St. Thomas, including the tunnels at **Thatch Cay,** the ledges at **Congo Cay,** and the wreck of the *General Rogers.* Dive off St. John at **Stephens Cay,** a short boat ride out of Cruz Bay, where fish swim around the reefs as you float downward. At **Devers Bay,** on St. John's south shore, fish dart about in colorful schools. **Carval Rock,** shaped like an old-time ship, has gorgeous rock formations, coral gardens, and lots of fish. It can be too rough here in winter, though. Count on paying $75 for a one-tank dive and $90 for a two-tank dive. Rates include equipment and a tour. If you've never dived before, try an introductory course, called a resort course. Or if certification is in your vacation plans, the island's dive shops can help you get your card.

Cruz Bay Watersports (☎340/776–6234 ⊕*www.divestjohn. com*) has two locations: in Cruz Bay at the Lumberyard Shopping Complex and at the Westin St. John Resort. Owners Marcus and Patty Johnston offer regular reef, wreck, and night dives and USVI and BVI snorkel tours. The company holds both PADI five-star facility and NAUI Dream Resort status. **Low Key Watersports** (☎340/693–8999 *or 800/835–7718* ⊕*www.divelowkey.com*), at Wharfside Village, offers one- and two-tank dives and specialty courses. It's certified as a PADI five-star training facility.

FISHING

Well-kept charter boats—approved by the U.S. Coast Guard—head out to the north and south drops or troll along the inshore reefs, depending on the season and what's biting. The captains usually provide bait, drinks, and lunch, but you need to bring your own hat and sunscreen. Fishing charters run between $550 and $700 per half day for the boat. **Capt. Byron Oliver** (☎340/693–8339) takes you out to the north and south drops or closer in to St. John. **Gone Ketchin'** (☎340/714–1175 ⊕*www.goneketchin.com*), in St. John, arranges trips with old salt Captain Grizz.

HIKING

Although it's fun to go hiking with a Virgin Islands National Park guide, don't be afraid to head out on your own. To find a hike that suits your ability, stop by the park's visitor center in Cruz Bay and pick up the free trail guide; it details points of interest, trail lengths, and estimated hiking times, as well as any dangers you might encounter. Although the park staff recommends long pants to protect against thorns and insects, most people hike in shorts because it can get very hot. Wear sturdy shoes or hiking boots even if you're hiking to the beach. Don't forget to bring water and insect repellent.

★ Fodor'sChoice The **Virgin Islands National Park** (⊠ *1300 Cruz Bay Creek, St. John* ☎ *340/776–6201* ⊕ *www.nps.gov/ viis*) maintains more than 20 trails on the north and south shores and offers guided hikes along popular routes. A full-day trip to Reef Bay is a must; it's an easy hike through lush and dry forest, past the ruins of an old plantation, and to a sugar factory adjacent to the beach. It can be a bit arduous for young kids, however. Take the $6 safari bus from the park's visitor center to the trailhead, where you can meet a ranger who'll serve as your guide. The park provides a boat ride back to Cruz Bay for $15 to save you the walk back up the mountain. The schedule changes from season to season; call for times and reservations, which are essential.

HORSEBACK RIDING

Clip-clop along the island's byways for a slower-pace tour of St. John. **Carolina Corral** (☎ *340/693–5778*) offers horseback trips and wagon rides down scenic roads with owner Dana Barlett. She has a way with horses and calms even the most novice riders. Rates start at $75 for a 1½-hour horseback ride and $20 for a 45-minute wagon ride.

SEA KAYAKING

Poke around crystal bays and explore undersea life from a sea kayak. Rates run about $90 for a full day in a double kayak. Tours start at $50 for a half day. On the Cruz Bay side of the island, **Arawak Expeditions** (☎ *340/693–8312 or 800/238–8687* ⊕ *www.arawakexp.com*), which operates out of Low Key Watersports in Cruz Bay's Wharfside Village, has professional guides who use traditional and sit-on-top kayaks to ply coastal waters. The company also rents single and double kayaks, so you can head independently to nearby islands like Stephen's Cay. Explore Coral Bay Harbor and Hurricane Hole on the eastern end of the island in a sea kayak from **Crabby's Watersports** (⊠*Rte. 107, outside Coral Bay* ☎*340/714–2415* ⊕*www.crabbys watersports.com*). If you don't want to paddle into the wind to get out of Coral Bay Harbor, the staff will drop you off in Hurricane Hole so you can paddle downwind back to Coral Bay. Crabby's also rents snorkel gear, dinghies, and fishing tackle.

WINDSURFING

Steady breezes and expert instruction make learning to windsurf a snap. Try **Cinnamon Bay Campground** (⊠*Rte. 20, Cinnamon Bay* ☎*340/693–5902*), where rentals are $40 to $80 per hour. Lessons are available right at the waterfront; just look for the Windsurfers stacked up on the beach. The cost for a one-hour lesson starts at $60, plus the cost of the board rental. You can also rent kayaks, boogie boards, and surfboards.

FREE PARKING **Cruz Bay's parking problem is maddening. Your best bet is to rent a car from a company that allows you to park in their lot. Make sure you ask before you sign on the dotted line if you plan to spend time in Cruz Bay.**

SHOPPING

AREAS & MALLS

Luxury goods and handicrafts can be found on St. John. Most shops carry a little of this and a bit of that, so it pays to poke around. The Cruz Bay shopping district runs from **Wharfside Village,** just around the corner from the ferry dock, to **Mongoose Junction,** an inviting shopping center on North Shore Road. (The name of this upscale shopping mall, by the way, is a holdover from a time when those furry island creatures gathered at a nearby garbage bin.) Out on Route 104, stop in at the **Marketplace** to explore its gift and crafts shops. At the island's other end, there are a few stores—selling clothes, jewelry, and artwork—here and there from the village of **Coral Bay** to the small complex at **Shipwreck Landing.**

On St. John, store hours run from 9 or 10 to 5 or 6. Wharf-side Village and Mongoose Junction shops in Cruz Bay are often open into the evening.

SPECIALTY ITEMS

ART

Bajo el Sol. This gallery sells works by owner Livy Hitchcock, plus those from a roster of the island's best artists. Shop for oil and acrylics, sculptures, and ceramics. ✉*Mongoose Junction, North Shore Rd., Cruz Bay* ☎*340/693–7070.*

Coconut Coast Studios. This waterside shop, a five-minute walk from Cruz Bay, showcases the work of Elaine Estern. She specializes in undersea scenes. ✉*Frank Bay, Cruz Bay* ☎*340/776–6944.*

BOOKS

National Park Headquarters. The shop sells several good histories of St. John, including *St. John Back Time,* by Ruth Hull Low and Rafael Lito Valls, and, for linguists, Valls's *What a Pistarckle!*—an explanation of the colloquialisms that make up the local version of English (*pistarckle* is a Dutch Creole word that means "noise" or "din," which pretty much sums up the language here). ✉*Cruz Bay* ☎*340/776–6201.*

CLOTHING

Big Planet Adventure Outfitters. You knew when you arrived that some place on St. John would cater to the outdoor enthusiasts who hike up and down the island's trails. Well, this outdoor-clothing store is where you can find the popular Naot sandals and Reef footware, along with colorful and durable cotton clothing and accessories by Billabong. The store also sells children's clothes. ✉*Mongoose Junction, North Shore Rd., Cruz Bay* ☎*340/776–6638.*

Bougainvillea Boutique. If you want to look as if you stepped out of the pages of the resort-wear spread in an upscale travel magazine, try this store. Owner Susan Stair carries *very* chic men's and women's resort wear, straw hats, leather handbags, and fine gifts. ✉*Mongoose Junction, North Shore Rd., Cruz Bay* ☎*340/693–7190* ✉*Westin Resort and Villas, Rte. 104, Great Cruz Bay* ☎*340/693–8000 Ext. 1784.*

Jolly Dog. Stock up on the stuff you forgot to pack at this store. Sarongs in cotton and rayon, beach towels with tropical motifs, and hats and T-shirts sporting the Jolly Dog logo fill the shelves. ✉*Shipwreck Landing, Rte. 107, Sanders Bay* ☎*340/693–5333* ✉*Skinny Legs Shopping Complex, Rte. 10, Coral Bay* ☎*340/693–5900.*

Sloop Jones. It's worth the trip all the way out to the island's east end to shop for made-on-the-premises clothing, pillows, and fabrics by the yard splashed with tropical colors. Fabrics are in cotton, linen, and rayon and are supremely comfortable. ✉*Off Rte. 10, East End* ☎*340/779–4001.*

St. John Editions. Shop here for nifty cotton dresses that go from beach to dinner with a change of shoes and accessories. Owner Molly Soper also carries attractive straw hats and inexpensive jewelry. ✉*North Shore Rd., Cruz Bay* ☎*340/693–8444.*

FOOD

If you're renting a villa, condo, or cottage and doing your own cooking, there are several good places to shop for food; just be aware that prices are much higher than those at home.

Dolphin Market. Shop for fresh produce, deli items, and all the basics at this small store in Cruz Bay. ✉*Boulon Center, Rte. 10, Cruz Bay* ☎*340/776–5322.*

Lily's Gourmet Market. This small store in Coral Bay carries the basics plus meat, fish, and produce. ✉*Cocoloba Shopping Center, Rte. 107, Coral Bay* ☎*340/777–3335.*

Love City Mini Mart. This market doesn't look like much, but it's just about the only place to shop in Coral Bay and has a surprising selection of items. ✉*Off Rte. 107, Coral Bay* ☎*340/693–5790.*

Starfish Market. The island's largest store usually has the best selection of meat, fish, and produce. ✉*The Marketplace, Rte. 104, Cruz Bay* ☎*340/779–4949.*

GIFTS

Awl Made Here. Shop here for locally made leather goods. Owner Tracey O'Brien creates lovely journal covers, wallets, and belts, but she also does special orders. The store carries other locally made items like imaginative jewelry and hand-painted wine glasses. ✉*Skinny Legs Shopping Complex, Rte. 10, Coral Bay* ☎*340/777–5757.*

Bamboula. Owner Jo Sterling travels the world to find unusual housewares, rugs, bedspreads, accessories, and men's and women's clothes and shoes for this multicultural boutique. ⊠*Mongoose Junction, North Shore Rd., Cruz Bay* ☎*340/693–8699.*

Best of Both Worlds. Pricy metal sculptures and attractive artworks hang from this shop's walls; the nicest are small glass decorations shaped like shells and seahorses. ⊠*Mongoose Junction, North Shore Rd., Cruz Bay* ☎*340/693–7005.*

The Canvas Factory. If you're a true shopper who needs an extra bag to carry home all your treasures, this store offers every kind of tote and carrier imaginable, from simple bags to suitcases with numerous zippered compartments. All are made of canvas, naturally. It also sells great canvas hats. ⊠*Mongoose Junction, North Shore Rd., Cruz Bay* ☎*340/776–6196.*

Donald Schnell Studio. In addition to pottery, this place sells unusual hand-blown glass, wind chimes, kaleidoscopes, fanciful fountains, and more. Your purchases can be shipped worldwide. ⊠*Amore Center, Rte. 108, Cruz Bay* ☎*340/776–6420.*

Every Ting. As its name implies, this store has a bit of this and a bit of that. Shop for Caribbean books and CDs, picture frames decorated with shells, and T-shirts with tropical motifs. Residents and visitors also drop by to have a cup of espresso. ⊠*Gallows Point Resort, Bay St., Cruz Bay* ☎*340/693–5820.*

Fabric Mill. Shop here for women's clothing in tropical brights, as well as place mats, napkins, and batik wraps. Or take home a brilliant-hued bolt from the upholstery-fabric selection. ⊠*Mongoose Junction, North Shore Rd., Cruz Bay* ☎*340/776–6194.*

Mumbo Jumbo. With what may be the best prices in St. John, this cozy shop carries everything from tropical clothing to stuffed sea creatures. ⊠*Skinny Legs Shopping Complex, Rte. 10, Coral Bay* ☎*340/779–4277.*

Nest and Company. In colors that reflect the sea, this cozy store carries perfect take-home gifts. Shop here for soaps in tropical scents, dinnerware, and much more. ⊠*Marketplace Shopping Center, Rte. 108, Cruz Bay* ☎*340/715–2522.*

★ **Pink Papaya.** This store is where you can find the well-known work of longtime Virgin Islands resident M.L. Etre, plus a huge collection of one-of-a-kind gifts, including bright tablecloths, unusual trays, and unique tropical jewelry. ⊠*Lemon Tree Mall, King St., Cruz Bay* ☎*340/693–8535.*

JEWELRY

Caravan Gallery. Owner Radha Speer travels the world to find much of the unusual jewelry she sells here. And the more you look, the more you see—folk art, tribal art, and masks for sale cover the walls and tables, making this a great place to browse. ⊠*Mongoose Junction, North Shore Rd., Cruz Bay* ☎*340/779–4566.*

Free Bird Creations. Head here for special handcrafted jewelry—earrings, bracelets, pendants, chains—as well as the good selection of water-resistant watches for your beach excursions. ⊠*Wharfside Village, Strand St., Cruz Bay* ☎*340/693–8625.*

Jewels. This branch of a St. Thomas store carries emeralds, diamonds, and other jewels in attractive yellow- and white-gold settings, as well as strings of creamy pearls, watches, and other designer jewelry. ⊠*Mongoose Junction, North Shore Rd., Cruz Bay* ☎*340/776–6007.*

R&I Patton Goldsmiths. Rudy and Irene Patton design most of the lovely silver and gold jewelry displayed in this shop. The rest comes from various designer friends. Sea fans (those large, lacy plants that sway with the ocean's currents) in filigreed silver, starfish and hibiscus pendants in silver or gold, and gold sand-dollar-shape charms and earrings are choice selections. ⊠*Mongoose Junction, North Shore Rd., Cruz Bay* ☎*340/776–6548.*

Verace. Jewelry from such well-known designers as Toby Pomeroy and Patrick Murphy fill the shelves. Murphy's stunning gold sailboats with gems for hulls will catch your attention. ⊠*Wharfside Village, Strand St., Cruz Bay* ☎*340/693–7599.*

PHOTO DEVELOPING

Cruz Bay Photo. Pick up disposable cameras, film, and other photo needs, or when your memory card fills up, download your digital photos to a disk or print them out. Shop here also for good-quality sunglasses, a must for your tropical vacation. ⊠*Wharfside Village, Strand St., Cruz Bay* ☎*340/779–4313.*

NIGHTLIFE

St. John isn't the place to go for glitter and all-night party-ing. Still, after-hours Cruz Bay can be a lively little town in which to dine, drink, dance, chat, or flirt. Notices posted on the bulletin board outside the Connections telephone center—up the street from the ferry dock in Cruz Bay—or listings in the island's two small newspapers (the *St. John Sun Times* and *Tradewinds*) will keep you apprised of special events, comedy nights, movies, and the like.

There's calypso and reggae on Friday night at **Fred's** (⊠*King St., Cruz Bay* ☎*340/776–6363*). Young folks like to gather at **Woody's** (⊠*Near ferry dock, across from Subway restaurant, Cruz Bay* ☎*340/779–4625*), where sidewalk tables provide a close-up view of Cruz Bay's action. After a sunset drink at **Zozo's Ristorante** (⊠*Gallows Point Resort, Bay St., Cruz Bay* ☎*340/693–9200*), up the hill from Cruz Bay, you can stroll around town (much is clustered around the small waterfront park). Many of the young people from the U.S. mainland who live and work on St. John will be out sipping and socializing, too.

As its name implies, **Island Blues** (⊠*Rte. 107, Coral Bay* ☎*340/776–6800*) is the hot place to go for music at the eastern end of the island. On the far side of the island, landlubbers and old salts listen to music and swap stories at **Skinny Legs Bar & Restaurant** (⊠*Rte. 10, Coral Bay* ☎*340/779–4982*).

ST. JOHN ESSENTIALS

To research prices, get advice from other travelers, and book travel arrangements, visit www.fodors.com.

TRANSPORTATION

BY AIR
St. John does not have an airport, so you will need to fly into St. Thomas. *See* ⇨*By Air in St. Thomas Essentials for more information.*

BY BOAT & FERRY
There's frequent daily service from both Red Hook and Charlotte Amalie, St. Thomas, to Cruz Bay. There's also frequen service from Cruz Bay to Tortola, aboard an Inter-Island Boat Service ferry. You can take the St. Thomas–

Party with the Locals

Although the U.S. Virgin Islands mark all of the same federal holidays as the mainland, they have a few of their own. Transfer Day, on March 31, commemorates Denmark's sale of the territory to the U.S in 1917. Emancipation Day, on July 3, marks the date slavery was abolished in the Danish West Indies in 1848. Liberty Day, on November 1, honors David Hamilton Jackson, who secured freedom of the press and assembly from King Christian X of Denmark.

While you're on St. John, don't hesitate to attend local events like the annual Memorial Day and Veterans Day celebrations sponsored by the American Legion. These small parades give a poignant glimpse into island life. The St. Patrick's Day Parade is another blink-and-you'll-miss-it event. It's fun to join the islanders who come out decked in green. The annual Friends of Virgin Islands National Park meeting in January is another place to mix and mingle with the locals.

bound *Native Son* from West End because it stops to clear customs in St. John. The half-hour trip costs $45 roundtrip. You need to present proof of citizenship upon entering the BVI; a passport is best, but a birth certificate with a raised seal in addition to a government-issue photo ID will suffice. *For information on ferry companies, see ⇨ By Boat & Ferry in Virgin Islands Essentials.*

BY BUS

Modern Vitran buses on St. John run from the Cruz Bay ferry dock through Coral Bay to the far eastern end of the island at Salt Pond, making numerous stops in between. The fare is $1 to any point.

BY CAR

The terrain in St. John is very hilly, the roads winding, and the blind curves numerous. You may suddenly come upon a huge safari bus careening around a corner or a couple of hikers strolling along the side of the road. Major roads are well paved, but once you get off a specific route, dirt roads filled with potholes are common. For such driving, a four-wheel-drive vehicle is your best bet. Be aware that you can't bring all rental cars over to St. John from St. Thomas. Even more important, the barge service is very busy, so you can't always get a space.

CAR RENTALS

Best is just outside Cruz Bay near the public library, off Route 10. Cool Breeze is in Cruz Bay across from the Creek. Courtesy is in Cruz Bay next to the police station. Delbert Hill Taxi & Jeep Rental Service is in Cruz Bay across from Lemon Tree Mall, just around the corner from the ferry dock. Denzil Clyne is across from the Creek. O'Connor Jeep is in Cruz Bay across from the Islandia building. St. John Car Rental is across from Wharfside Village shopping center on Bay Street in Cruz Bay. Spencer's Jeep is across from the Creek in Cruz Bay.

Information **Best** (☎340/693–8177). **Cool Breeze** (☎340/776–6588 ⊕www.coolbreezecarrental.com). **Courtesy** (☎340/776–6650 ⊕www.courtesycarrental.com). **Delbert Hill Taxi & Jeep Rental Service** (☎340/776–6637). **Denzil Clyne** (☎340/776–6715). **O'Connor Car Rental** (☎340/776–6343 ⊕www.oconnorcarrental. com). **St. John Car Rental** (☎340/776–6103 ⊕www.stjohncarrental. com). **Spencer's Jeep** (☎340/693–8784 or 888/776–6628 ⊕www. spencersjeeprental.com).

BY TAXI

Taxis meet ferries arriving in Cruz Bay. Most drivers use vans or open-air safari buses. You can find them congregated at the dock and at hotel parking lots. You can also hail them anywhere on the road. Amost all trips will be shared, and prices are per person. Paradise Taxi will pick you up if you call, but most of the drivers don't provide that service. If you need one to pick you up at your rental villa, ask the villa manager for suggestions on whom to call or arrange a ride in advance. Some small cruise ships stop at St. John to let passengers disembark for a day. The main town of Cruz Bay is near the area where the ships drop off passengers. If you want to swim, the famous Trunk Bay is a $6 taxi ride per person from town.

Information **Paradise Taxi** (☎340/714–7913).

CONTACTS & RESOURCES

BANKS

St. John has two banks. First Bank is one block up from the ferry dock, and Scotia Bank is at the Marketplace on Route 104.

EMERGENCIES

Coast Guard **Marine Safety Detachment** (☎340/776–3497). **Rescue Coordination Center** (☎787/289–2041 *in San Juan, Puerto Rico*).

Emergency Services **Air Ambulance Network** (☎800/327–1966). **Ambulance and fire emergencies** (☎911). **Medical Air Services** (☎340/777–8580 or 800/643–9023). **Police emergencies** (☎911).

Hospital **Myrah Keating Smith Community Health Center** (✉*Rte. 10, east of Cruz Bay, Susannaberg* ☎340/693–8900).

Pharmacy **Chelsea Drug Store** (✉*The Marketplace, Rte. 104, Cruz Bay* ☎340/776–4888).

Scuba-Diving Emergencies **Roy L. Schneider Hospital & Community Health Center** (✉*Sugar Estate, St. Thomas* ☎340/776–8311).

INTERNET, MAIL & SHIPPING

There is a post office in Cruz Bay, but the lines are often long. The place to go to check your e-mail is Surf da Web in Cruz Bay and Keep Me Posted in Coral Bay. You'll pay $6 a half hour for Internet service.

Internet Cafés **Surf da Web** (✉*St. John Marketplace, 2nd fl., Cruz Bay* ☎340/693–9152 ⊕*www.surfdaweb.com*).

Keep Me Posted (✉*Cocoloba Shopping Center, Coral Bay* ☎340/775–1727 ⊕*www.keepmepostedstjohn.com*).

Shipping **FedEx** (✉*St. John* ☎800/463–3339).

SAFETY

Although crime is not as prevalent in St. John as it is on St. Thomas and St. Croix, it does exist. Keep your hotel or vacation villa door locked at all times, stick to well-lighted streets at night, and use the same kind of street sense that you would in any unfamiliar territory. There are occasional burglaries at villas, even during daylight hours. Lock doors even when you're lounging by the pool. It's not a good idea to walk around Cruz Bay late at night. If you don't have a car, plan on taking a taxi. Since it can be hard to find a taxi in the wee hours of the morning, arrange in advance for a driver to pick you up. If you have valuables, rent a car—not an open-air vehicle—and lock possessions in the trunk. Keep your rental car locked wherever you park. Don't leave cameras, purses, and other valuables lying on the beach while you snorkel for an hour (or even for a minute).

TOUR OPTIONS

In St. John, taxi drivers provide tours of the island, making stops at various sites, including Trunk Bay and Annaberg Plantation. Prices run around $15 a person. The taxi drivers congregate near the ferry in Cruz Bay. The dispatcher will find you a driver for your tour. Along with providing trail maps and brochures about Virgin Islands National Park, the park service also gives several guided tours on- and off-shore. Some are only offered during particular times of the year, and some require reservations. For more information, contact the Virgin Islands National Park Visitors Center.

Information V.I. National Park Visitors Center (⌂ *Cruz Bay* ☎ *340/776–6201* ⊕ *www.nps.gov/viis*).

WEDDINGS

Superior Court Offices In St. Thomas (⌂ *Box 70, St. Thomas 00804* ☎ *340/774–6680*).

Wedding Planners Anne Marie Weddings (⌂ *5000 Enighed PMB 7, St. John 00830* ☎ *340/693–5153 or 888/676–5701* ⊕ *www. stjohnweddings.com*).

St. Croix

WORD OF MOUTH

"Lovely place, lovely people—not a great place for partiers, but for beaches, snorkeling, and quiet fun amid some cool Danish colonial architecture, it was darn near perfect."

—repete

By Lynda
Lohr

As my seaplane skimmed St. Croix's north coast on the flight from St. Thomas, the island's agrarian past played out below. Stone windmills left over from the days when sugar ruled stood like sentinels in the fields. As we closed in on Christiansted, the big yellow Fort Christianvaern loomed on the waterfront, and the city's red roofs created a colorful counterpoint to the turquoise harbor. A visit to St. Croix, once a Danish colony, always puts me in touch with my Danish roots (my grandmother was a Poulsen). Indeed, history is so popular in St. Croix that planes are filled with Danish visitors who, like other vacationers, come to sun at the island's powdery beaches, enjoy pampering at the hotels, and dine at interesting restaurants, but mainly wish to explore the island's colonial history.

Until 1917 Denmark owned St. Croix and her sister Virgin Islands, an aspect of the island's past that is reflected in street names in the main towns of Christiansted and Frederiksted as well as surnames of many island residents. Those early Danish settlers, as well as those from other European nations, left behind slews of 18th- and 19th-century ruins, all of them worked by slaves brought over on ships from Africa, their descendants, and white indentured servants lured to St. Croix to pay off their debt to society. Some—such as the Christiansted National Historic site, Whim Plantation, the ruins at St. George Village Botanical Garden, the Nature Conservancy's property at Estate Princess, and the ruins at Estate Mount Washington and Judith's Fancy—are open for easy exploration. Others are on private land, but a drive around the island reveals the ruins of 100 plantations here and there on St. Croix's 84 square mi. Their windmills, greathouses, and factories are all that's left of the 224 plantations that once grew sugarcane, tobacco, and other agricultural products at the height of the island's plantation glory.

The downturn began in 1801 when the British occupied the island. The demise of the slave trade in 1803, another British occupation from 1807 to 1815, droughts, the development of the sugar beet industry in Europe, political upheaval, and a depression sent the island on a downward spiral.

St. Croix never recovered from these blows. The end of slavery in 1848, followed by labor riots, fires, hurricanes, and an earthquake during the last half of the 19th century, brought what was left of the island's economy to its knees. The start of prohibition in 1922 called a halt to the island's rum industry, further crippling the economy. The situation remained dire—so bad that President Herbert Hoover called the territory an "effective poorhouse" during a 1931 visit—until the rise of tourism in the late 1950s and 1960s. With tourism came economic improvements coupled with an influx of residents from other Caribbean islands and the mainland, but St. Croix depends partly on industries like the huge oil refinery outside Frederiksted to provide employment.

Today, suburban subdivisions fill the fields where sugarcane once waved in the tropical breeze. Condominium complexes line the beaches along the north coast outside Christiansted. Homes that are more elaborate dot the rolling hillsides. Modern strip malls and shopping centers sit along major roads, and it's easy to find a McDonald's as it is Caribbean fare.

Although St. Croix sits definitely in the 21st century, with only a little effort you can easily step back into the island's past.

EXPLORING ST. CROIX

Although there are things to see and do in St. Croix's two towns, Christiansted and Frederiksted (both named after Danish kings), there are lots of interesting spots in between them and to the east of Christiansted. Just be sure you have a map in hand (pick one up at rental-car agencies, or stop by the tourist office for an excellent one that's free). Many secondary roads remain unmarked; if you get confused, ask for help.

ABOUT THE RESTAURANTS

Seven flags have flown over St. Croix, and each has left its legacy in the island's cuisine. You can feast on Italian, French, and American dishes; there are even Chinese and Mexican restaurants in Christiansted. Fresh local seafood is plentiful and always good; wahoo, mahimahi, and conch are most popular. Island chefs often add Caribbean twists to familiar dishes. For a true island experience, stop at a local restaurant for goat stew, curried chicken, or fried pork chops. Regardless of where you eat, your meal will be an informal affair. As is the case everywhere in the Caribbean, prices are higher than you'd pay on the mainland. Some restaurants may close for a week or two in September or

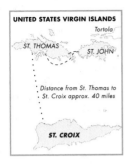

UNITED STATES VIRGIN ISLANDS

Tortola

ST. THOMAS

ST. JOHN

Distance from St. Thomas to St. Croix approx. 40 miles

ST. CROIX

↑ TO
ST. THOMAS

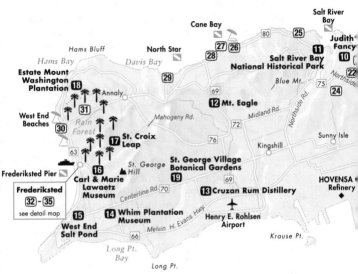

Salt River Bay

Cane Bay

North Star

80   25

Judith Fancy

10

Hams Bluff

Hams Bay   *Davis Bay*

27 26
28

Salt River Bay National Historical Park

22

Estate Mount Washington Plantation

18

Annaly

29

Blue Mt.

75

24

Northside

Northside Rd.

West End Beaches

31

Rain Forest

St. Croix Leap

17

69

12 Mt. Eagle

Mahogany Rd.

72   *Midland Rd.*

76

Kingshill

Sunny Isle

30

63

16

St. George Hill

St. George Village Botanical Gardens

19

HOVENSA Refinery

Frederiksted Pier

Frederiksted

32 – 35

see detail map

13 Cruzan Rum Distillery

Centerline Rd. 70   69

15

14 Whim Plantation Museum

Henry E. Rohlsen Airport

Melvin H. Evans Hwy.

West End Salt Pond

66

Krause Pt.

Long Pt. Bay

Long Pt.

C a r i b b e a n   S e a

KEY

🝔 Beaches

◪ Dive Sites

⛴ Cruise Ship Terminal

■ Exploring Sights

① Hotels & Restaurants

🌴 Rain Forest

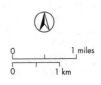

0   1 miles

0   1 km

St. Croix

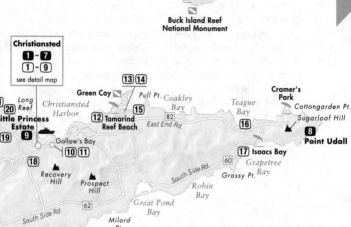

Buck Island

**Buck Island Reef
National Monument**

Christiansted
1 - **7**
(1) - (9)
see detail map

Long **21**
20 Reef
**Little Princess
Estate**
19
*Christiansted
Harbor*
9

13 **14**
Green Cay *Pull Pt.* *Coakley*
Bay
12 **Tamarind
Reef Beach**
15
82
East End Rd.
16

*Teague
Bay*

**Cramer's
Park**
Cottongarden Pt.
Sugarloaf Hill
8
Point Udall

Gallow's Bay
10 **11**
18
*Recovery
Hill*
*Prospect
Hill*

60
17 **Isaacs Bay**
Grapetree
Grassy Pt. Bay

South Side Rd.
*Robin
Bay*

*Great Pond
Bay*
62
South Side Rd.
*Milord
Pt.*

Manchenil
Canegarden Bay
Bay

Hotels		Restaurants
The Buccaneer, **12**	Mount Victory Camp, **31**	Anna's Café, **10**
Cane Bay Reef Club, **26**	Palms at Pelican Cove, **24**	Breezez, **20**
Carringtons Inn, **18**	Renaissance Carambola, **29**	The Deep End, **13**
Chenay Bay Beach Resort, **15**	Sugar Beach, **21**	Elizabeth's, **19**
Club St. Croix, **20**	Tamarind Reef Hotel, **13**	The Galleon, **14**
Colony Cove, **22**	Villa Greenleaf, **24**	Off the Wall, **28**
Divi Carina Bay Resort, **17**	Villa Madeleine, **16**	Sunset Grill, **33**
Hibiscus Beach Hotel, **23**	Villa Margarita, **25**	Tutto Bene, **11**
	Waves at Cane Bay, **27**	

ST. CROIX TOP 5

Sailing to Buck Island: Take a boat to Buck Island Reef National Monument, a national treasure. The beach at the western end of the island is a great spot to relax after a snorkeling adventure or a hike up the hill to take in the stunning view.

Diving the Wall: Every dive boat in St. Croix makes a trip to the Wall, one of the Caribbean's best diving experiences, but it's also accessible from the shore. Diving off Cane Bay Beach is especially popular.

Exploring Fort Christiansvaern: History bluffs flock to Christiansted National Historic Site. Head to the upper ramparts of Fort Christiansvaern to ponder how life was for early settlers.

Experiencing plantation life: Whim Plantation showcases St. Croix's agrarian past. The planter and his family lived a comfortable life in the greathouse, but the slaves, and later, the poorly paid workers, had a much less posh existence.

Strolling around Christiansted: You can easily while away the better part of a day in Christiansted, St. Croix's main town. The shops carry everything from one-of-a-kind artworks to hand-crafted jewelry to simple souvenirs.

October, so if you're traveling during these months it's best to call ahead.

ABOUT THE HOTELS

You can find everything from plush resorts to simple beachfront digs in St. Croix. If you sleep in either the Christiansted or Frederiksted area, you'll be closest to shopping, restaurants, and nightlife. Most of the island's other hotels will put you just steps from the beach. St. Croix has several small but special properties that offer personalized service. If you like all the comforts of home, you may prefer to stay in a condominium or villa. Room rates on St. Croix are competitive with those on other islands, and if you travel off-season, you can find substantially reduced prices. Many properties offer money-saving honeymoon and dive packages. Whether you stay in a hotel, a condominium, or a villa, you'll enjoy up-to-date amenities. Most properties have room TVs, but at some bed-and-breakfasts there might be only one in the common room.

WHAT IT COSTS IN DOLLARS				
$$$$	$$$	$$	$	¢
RESTAURANTS				
OVER $30	$20–$30	$12–$20	$8–$12	UNDER $8
HOTELS				
* OVER $350	$250–$350	$150–$250	$80–$150	UNDER $80
** OVER $450	$350–$450	$250–$350	$125–$250	UNDER $125

*EP, BP, CP; **AI, FAP, MAP; Restaurant prices are for a main course at dinner, excluding tip. Hotel prices are for two people in a double room during high season, excluding 8% tax, service charge and energy surcharges (which can vary significantly), and meal plans (except for all-inclusives).

TIMING

St. Croix celebrates Carnival in late December with the St. Croix Christmas Festival. If you don't book far ahead, it can be hard to find a room because of the influx of visitors from around the region and around the world.

WHAT TO SEE

Numbers in the margin correspond to points of interest on the St. Croix, Christiansted, and Frederiksted maps.

CHRISTIANSTED

Christiansted is a historic Danish-style town that always served as St. Croix's commercial center. Your best bet is to see the historic sights in the morning, when it's still cool. Break for lunch at an open-air restaurant before spending as much time as you like shopping.

In the 1700s and 1800s Christiansted was a trading center for sugar, rum, and molasses. Today there are law offices, tourist shops, and restaurants, but many of the buildings, which start at the harbor and go up the gently sloped hillsides, still date from the 18th century. You can't get lost. All streets lead back downhill to the water.

If you want some friendly advice, stop by the **Visitor Center** (⊠*53A Company St.* ☎*340/773–0495* ⊕*www.usvitourism. vi*) weekdays between 8 and 5 for maps and brochures.

Christiansted

KEY

- **1** *Exploring Sights*
- **1** *Hotel & Restaurants*

Dining
Avocado Pit, **3**
Café Christine, **1**
Harvey's, **7**
Kendricks, **6**
Restaurant Bacchus, **5**
Rum Runners, **8**
Savant, **2**

Lodging
Hotel Caravelle, **8**
Hotel on the Cay, **4**
King Christian Hotel, **3**
Pink Fancy Hotel, **9**

Exploring
Danish Customs House, **3**
D. Hamilton Jackson Park, **5**
Fort Christiansværn, **4**
Government House, **7**
Post Office Building, **2**
Scale House, **6**
Steeple Building, **1**

Gallows Bay

Christiansted Harbor

D. Hamilton Jackson Park

Boardwalk

Kings Walk
Kings Alley Wk.
Comanche Wk.
PanAm Pavillion
Caravelle Arcade

Hospital St.
Church St.
Queen Cross St.
King Cross St.
Fisher St.
East St.
Hill St.
Queen St.
Company St.
Prince St.
King St.
Strand St.
North St.
Watergut St.
West St.
Smith St.
Market St.
Company Cross

★ Fodor'sChoice **Fort Christiansvaern.** The large, yellow fortress
❹ dominates the waterfront. Because it's so easy to spot, it
🐾 makes a good place to begin a walking tour. In 1749 the
Danish built the fort to protect the harbor, but the structure was repeatedly damaged by hurricane-force winds and
had to be partially rebuilt in 1771. It's now a national historic site, the best preserved of the few remaining Danish-
built forts in the Virgin Islands. The park's visitor center
is here. Rangers are on hand to answer questions. Hours
are. ⊠*Hospital St.* ☎*340/773–1460* ⊕*www.nps.gov/chri*
☉ *Weekdays 8 to 4:30 and weekends 9 to 4:30* 🖃 *$3
(includes Steeple Building).*

❺ **D. Hamilton Jackson Park.** When you're tired of sightseeing,
stop at this shady park on the street side of Fort Christiansvaern for a rest. It's named for a famed labor leader, judge,
and journalist who started the first newspaper not under
the thumb of the Danish crown (his birthday, November 1,
is a territorial holiday celebrated with much fanfare in St.
Croix). ⊠*Between Fort Christiansvaern and Danish Customs House.*

❸ **Danish Customs House.** Built in 1830 on foundations that
date from a century earlier, the historic building, which is
near Fort Christiansvaern, originally served as both a customs house and a post office. In 1926 it became the Christiansted Library, and it's been a national park facility since
1972. It's closed to the public, but the sweeping front steps
make a nice place to take a break. ⊠*King St.* ☎*340/773–
1460* ⊕*www.nps.gov/chri.*

❻ **Scale House.** Constructed in 1856, this was once the spot
where goods passing through the port were weighed and
inspected. Park staffers now sell a good selection of books
about St. Croix history and its flora and fauna. ⊠*King St.*
☎*340/773–1460* ⊕*www.nps.gov/chri* ☉ *Weekdays 8 to
4:30 and weekends 9 to 4:30.*

❶ **Steeple Building.** Built by the Danes in 1753, the former
church was the first Danish Lutheran church on St. Croix.
It's now a national park museum and contains exhibits that
document the island's Indian inhabitants. It's worth the
short walk to see the building's collection of archaeologi-
cal artifacts, displays on plantation life, and exhibits on the
architectural development of Christiansted, the early history of the church, and Alexander Hamilton, the first secre-
tary of the U.S. Treasury, who grew up in St. Croix. Hours

are irregular, so ask at the visitor center. ✉*Church St.* ☎*340/773–1460* ✐ *$3 (includes Fort Christiansvaern).*

❷ **Post Office Building.** Built in 1749, Christiansted's former post office was once the Danish West India & Guinea Company warehouse. It now serves as the park's administrative building. ✉*Church St.*

❼ **Government House.** One of the town's most elegant structures was built as a home for a Danish merchant in 1747. Today it houses offices. If you're here weekdays from 8 to 4:30, slip into the peaceful inner courtyard to admire the still pools and gardens. A sweeping staircase leads you to a second-story ballroom, still used for official government functions. ✉*King St.* ☎*340/773–1404*

EAST END BEYOND CHRISTIANSTED

An easy drive (roads are flat and well marked) to St. Croix's eastern end takes you through some choice real estate. Ruins of old sugar estates dot the landscape. You can make the entire loop on the road that circles the island in about an hour, a good way to end the day. If you want to spend a full day exploring, you can find some nice beaches and easy walks with places to stop for lunch.

Buck Island Reef National Monument. Buck Island has pristine beaches that are just right for sunbathing, but there's also some shade for those who don't want to fry. The snorkeling trail set in the reef allows close-up study of coral formations and tropical fish. Overly warm seawater temperatures have led to a condition called coral bleaching that has killed some of the coral. The reefs are starting to recover, but how long it will take is anyone's guess. There's an easy hiking trail to the island's highest point, where you can be rewarded for your efforts by spectacular views of St. John. Charter-boat trips leave daily from the Christiansted waterfront or from Green Cay Marina, about 2 mi (3 km) east of Christiansted. Check with your hotel for recommendations. ✉*Off north shore of St. Croix* ☎*340/773–1460* ⊕*www.nps.gov/buis*

❽ **Point Udall.** This rocky promontory, the easternmost point in the United States, is about a half-hour drive from Christiansted. A paved road takes you to an overlook with glorious views. More adventurous folks can hike down to the pristine beach below. On the way back, look for the castle, an enormous mansion that can only be described as a cross between a Moorish mosque and the Taj Mahal. It was

Turtles on St. Croix

CLOSE UP

Like creatures from the earth's prehistoric past, green, leatherback, and hawksbill turtles crawl ashore during the annual April-to-November turtle nesting season to lay their eggs. They return from their life at sea every two to seven years to the beach where they were born. Since turtles can live for up to 100 years, they may return many times to nest in St. Croix.

The leatherbacks like Sandy Point National Wildlife Refuge and other spots on St. Croix's western end, but the hawksbills prefer Buck Island and the East End. Green turtles are also found primarily on the East End.

All are endangered species that face numerous natural and man-made predators. Particularly in the Frederiksted area, dogs and cats prey on the nests and eat the hatchlings.

Occasionally a dog will attack a turtle about to lay its eggs, and cats train their kittens to hunt at turtle nests, creating successive generations of turtle-egg hunters. In addition, turtles have often been hit by fast-moving boats that leave large slices in their shells if they don't kill them outright.

The leatherbacks are the subject of a project by the international group Earthwatch. Each summer, teams arrive at Sandy Point National Wildlife Refuge to ensure that poachers, both natural and human, don't attack the turtles as they crawl up the beach. The teams also relocate nests that are laid in areas prone to erosion. When the eggs hatch, teams stand by to make sure the turtles make it safely to the sea, and scientists tag them so they can monitor their return to St. Croix.

built by an extravagant recluse known only as the Contessa. Point Udall is sometimes a popular spot for thieves. Residents advise taking your valuables with you and leaving your car unlocked so they won't break into your car to look inside. ⊠*Rte. 82, Et Stykkeland.*

BETWEEN CHRISTIANSTED & FREDERIKSTED

A drive through the countryside between these two towns will take you past ruins of old plantations, many bearing whimsical names (Morningstar, Solitude, Upper Love) bestowed by early owners. The traffic moves quickly—by island standards—on the main roads, but you can pause and poke around if you head down some side lanes. It's easy to find your way west, but driving from north to south requires good navigation. Don't leave your hotel without a map. Allow an entire day for this trip, so you'll have enough time for a swim at a north-shore beach. Although you can find lots of casual eateries on the main roads, pick up a picnic lunch if you plan to head off the beaten path.

⑬ **Cruzan Rum Distillery.** A tour of the company's factory, established in 1760, culminates in a tasting of its products, all sold here at bargain prices. It's worth a stop to look at the distillery's charming old buildings even if you're not a rum connoisseur. ⊠ *West Airport Rd., Estate Diamond* ☎ *340/692-2280* ⊕ *www.cruzanrum.com* ☞ *$4* ☉ *Weekdays 9–11:30 and 1–4:15.*

⑩ **Judith's Fancy.** In this upscale neighborhood are the ruins of an old greathouse and tower of the same name, both remnants of a circa-1750 Danish sugar plantation. The "Judith" comes from the first name of a woman buried on the property. From the guardhouse at the neighborhood entrance, follow Hamilton Drive past some of St. Croix's loveliest homes. At the end of Hamilton Drive the road overlooks Salt River Bay, where Christopher Columbus anchored in 1493. On the way back, make a detour left off Hamilton Drive onto Caribe Road for a close look at the ruins. The million-dollar villas are something to behold, too. ⊠ *Turn north onto Rte. 751, off Rte. 75.*

⑨ **Little Princess Estate.** If the old plantation ruins scattered around St. Croix intrigue you, a visit to this Nature Conservancy project will give you even more of a glimpse into the past. The staff has carved walking paths out of the bush that surrounds what's left of a 19th-century plantation. It's easy to stroll among well-labeled fruit trees and see the ruins of the windmill, the sugar and rum factory, and the laborers' village. This is the perfect place to reflect on St. Croix's agrarian past fueled with labor from African slaves. ⊠ *Off Rte. 75; turn north at Five Corners traffic light* ☎ *340/773-5575* ☞ *Donations accepted* ☉ *Weekdays 9–5.*

⑫ **Mt. Eagle.** At 1,165 feet, this is St. Croix's highest peak. Leaving Cane Bay and passing North Star Beach, follow the coastal road that dips briefly into a forest; then turn left on Route 69. Just after you make the turn, the pavement is marked with the words THE BEAST and a set of giant paw prints. The hill you're about to climb is the famous Beast of the St. Croix Half Ironman Triathlon, an annual event during which participants must cycle up this intimidating slope. ⊠ *Rte. 69.*

⓫ Salt River Bay National Historical Park & Ecological Pre-serve. This joint national and local park commemorates the area where Christopher Columbus's men skirmished with the Carib Indians in 1493 on his second visit to the New World. The peninsula on the bay's east side is named for the event: Cabo de las Flechas (Cape of the Arrows). Although the park is just in the developing stages, it has several sights with cultural significance. A ball court, used by the Caribs in religious ceremonies, was discovered at the spot where the taxis park. Take a short hike up the dirt road to the ruins of an old earthen fort for great views of Salt River Bay. The area also encompasses a coastal estuary with the region's largest remaining mangrove forest, a sub-marine canyon, and several endangered species, including the hawksbill turtle and the roseate tern. A visitor center sits just uphill to the west. The water at the beach can be on the rough side, but it's a nice place for sunning. ⊠*Rte. 75 to Rte. 80, Salt River* ☎*340/773–1460* ⊕*www.nps.gov/sari* ⊗*Tues.–Thurs 9–4.*

⓳ St. George Village Botanical Gardens. At this 17-acre estate, fragrant flora grows amid the ruins of a 19th-century sugar-cane plantation village. There are miniature versions of each ecosystem on St. Croix, from a semiarid cactus grove to a verdant rain forest. ⊠*Rte. 70, turn north at sign, St. George* ☎*340/692–2874* ⊕*www.sgvbg.org* ⊠*$8* ⊗*Daily 9–5.*

FREDERIKSTED & ENVIRONS

St. Croix's second-largest town, Frederiksted, was founded in 1751. While Christiansted is noted for its Danish build-ings, Frederiksted is better known for its Victorian archi-tecture. One long cruise-ship pier juts into the sparkling sea. It's the perfect place to start a tour of this quaint city. A stroll around its historic sights will take you no more than an hour. Allow a little more time if you want to duck into the few small shops. The area just outside town has old plantations, some of which have been preserved as homes or historic structures that are open to the public.

Visitor Center. Across from the pier, Frederiksted's visitor center has brochures from numerous St. Croix businesses, as well as a few exhibits on St. Crois. You can stop in weekdays from 8 to 5 to view exhibits on St. Croix. ⊠*200 Strand St.* ☎*340/772–0357* ⊗ *Weekdays 8 to 5.*

⓴ Caribbean Museum Center for the Arts. Sitting across from the waterfront in a historic building, this small museum hosts an always-changing roster of exhibits. Many are cut-

KEY

1 Exploring Sights

1 Hotel & Restaurants

Frederiksted

Dining
Blue Moon, **32**
Le St. Tropez, **34**
Turtles Deli, **33**

Lodging
Sandcastle on the Beach, **35**

Exploring
Caribbean Center for the Arts, **20**
Fort Frederick, **21**

ting-edge multimedia efforts that you might be surprised to find in such an out-of-the way location. The openings are popular events. ⊠*10 Strand St.* ☏*340/772–2622* ⊕*www. cmcarts.org* ⊠*Free* ⊙*Wed.–Fri. noon–6, Sat. 10–4.*

⑯ **Carl & Marie Lawaetz Museum.** For a trip back in time, tour this circa-1750 farm. Owned by the prominent Lawaetz family since 1896, just after Carl Lawaetz arrived from Denmark, the lovely two-story house is in a valley at La Grange. A Lawaetz family member shows you the four-poster mahogany bed Carl and Marie shared, the china Marie painted, the family portraits, and the fruit trees that fed the family for several generations. Initially a sugar plantation, it was subsequently used to raise cattle and grow produce. ⊠*Rte. 76, Mahogany Rd., Estate Little La Grange* ☏*340/772–1539* ⊕*www.stcroixlandmarks.com* ⊠*$10* ⊙*Tues., Thurs., and Sat. 10–4.*

⑱ **Estate Mount Washington Plantation.** Several years ago, while surveying the property, the owners discovered the ruins of a sugar plantation beneath the rain-forest brush. The grounds have since been cleared and opened to the public. You can take a self-guided walking tour of the mill, the rum factory, and other ruins. ⊠*Rte. 63, Mount Washington* ☎*340/772–1026* ⊙*Ruins open daily dawn–dusk.*

㉑ Fort Frederik. On July 3, 1848, 8,000 slaves marched on
⟳ the redbrick to demand their freedom. Danish governor Peter von Scholten, fearing they would burn the town to the ground, stood up in his carriage parked in front of the fort and granted their wish. The fort, completed in 1760, houses a number of interesting historical exhibits and an art gallery. It's within earshot of the visitor center. ⊠*Waterfront* ☎*340/772–2021* ⊠*$3* ⊙*Weekdays 8:30 to 4.*

⑰ St. Croix Leap. This workshop sits in the heart of the rain forest, about a 15-minute drive from Frederiksted. It sells mirrors, tables, bread boards, and mahogany jewelry boxes crafted by local artisans. ⊠*Rte. 76, Brooks Hill* ☎*340/772–0421* ⊙*Weekdays 9–5, Sat. 10–5.*

⑮ West End Salt Pond. A bird-watcher's delight, this salt pond attracts a large number of winged creatures, including flamingos. ⊠*Veteran's Shore Dr., Hesselberg.*

⑭ Whim Plantation Museum. The lovingly restored estate, with
⟳ a windmill, cook house, and other buildings, will give you
★ a sense of what life was like on St. Croix's sugar plantations in the 1800s. The oval-shape greathouse has high ceilings and antique furniture and utensils. Notice its fresh, airy atmosphere—the waterless stone moat around the greathouse was used not for defense but for gathering cooling air. If you have kids, the grounds are the perfect place for them to run around, perhaps while you browse in the museum gift shop. It's just outside of Frederiksted. ⊠*Rte. 70, Estate Whim* ☎*340/772–0598* ⊕*www.stcroix-landmarks.com* ⊠*$10* ⊙*Mon.–Sat. 10–4.*

WHERE TO EAT

St. Croix has restaurants scattered from one end to the other, so it's usually not hard a place to stop when you're exploring the island. Most travelers eat dinner near their hotel to avoid long drives on dark, unfamiliar roads. Christiansted has the island's widest selection of restaurants. Don't rule out Frederiksted, especially if you're out exploring the island. It has a handful of delightful restaurants. *For approximate costs, see the dining and lodging price chart on the U.S. Virgin Islands Planner, at the beginning of this chapter.*

Marching on Frederiksted

On July 3, 1848, more than 8,000 slaves demanding their freedom marched half a mile from LaGrange to Frederiksted. Their actions forever changed the course of history. Gov. General Peter von Scholten stood up in his carriage in front of Fort Frederick to declare: "You are now free. You are hereby emancipated. Go home peacefully."

Von Scholten was relieved of his position and charged with dereliction of duty by the Danish government. He departed St. Croix on July 14, leaving behind his lover, a free black woman named Anna Heegaard. He never returned and died in Denmark in 1852.

The revolt had its roots in the 1834 emancipation of slaves in Great Britain's Caribbean colonies, including in what is now called the British Virgin Islands. The Danish government, sensing what was coming, began to improve the working conditions for its slaves. These efforts, however, failed to satisfy the slaves who wanted full freedom.

On July 28, 1847, Danish King Christian VIII ruled that slavery would continue a dozen more years, but those born during those 12 years would be free. This further angered the island's slaves. On July 2, 1848, a conch shell sounded, signifying that the slaves should start gathering. The die was cast, and the rest, as they say, is history.

After emancipation, the former slaves were forced to sign yearly contracts with plantation owners. Those contracts could only be renegotiated on October 1, still called Contract Day. This angered the plantation workers and sparked other uprisings throughout the late 1800s.

CHRISTIANSTED

CARIBBEAN

¢–$$ ✕ **Harvey's.** The dining room is plain, even dowdy, and plastic lace tablecloths constitute the sole attempt at decor—but who cares? The food is delicious. Daily specials, such as mouthwatering goat stew and tender whelks in butter, served with big helpings of rice and vegetables, are listed on the blackboard. Genial owner Sarah Harvey takes great pride in her kitchen, bustling out from behind the stove to chat and urge you to eat up. ✉ *11B Company St.* ☎ *340/773–3433* ⊟ *No credit cards* ✆ *Closed Sun. No dinner.*

CONTINENTAL

$$$–$$$$ ✕**Kendricks.** The chef at this open-air restaurant—a long-
★ time favorite among locals—conjures up creative contem-
porary cuisine. To start, try the Alaskan king crab cakes
with lemon–black pepper aioli or the warm chipotle pepper
with garlic and onion soup. Move on to the house spe-
cialty: pecan-crusted roast pork loin with ginger mayon-
naise. ✉*Company St. and King Cross St.* ☎*340/773–9199*
🍴*MC, V* ⊘*Closed Sun. No lunch.*

$$–$$$$ ✕**Restaurant Bacchus.** On the chic side, this restaurant is as
★ notable for its extensive wine list as it is for its food. The
menu changes regularly but often includes favorites like
chopped tuna in a soy-sesame dressing served over crispy
wontons. Such entrées as local lobster and fresh fish, steak
swimming in mushroom sauce, and pasta with Parmesan
cheese and truffle oil are always popular. For dessert, try
the rum-drenched sourdough-bread pudding. ✉*Queen
Cross St., off King St.* ☎*340/692–9922* 🍴*AE, D, MC, V*
⊘*Closed Mon. No lunch.*

$$–$$$$ ✕**Savant.** Savant is one of those small but special spots that
★ locals love. The cuisine is a fusion of Mexican, Thai, and
Caribbean—an unusual combination that works surpris-
ingly well. You can find anything from fresh fish to enchila-
das stuffed with chicken to maple-teriyaki pork tenderloin
coming out of the kitchen. With 20 tables crammed into
the indoor dining room and small courtyard, this little
place can get crowded. Call early for reservations. ✉*4C
Hospital St.* ☎*340/713–8666* 🍴*AE, MC, V* ⊘*Closed Sun.
No lunch.*

$$–$$$ ✕**Rum Runners.** The view is as stellar as the food at this
☾ highly popular local standby. Sitting right on Christiansted
★ Boardwalk, Rum Runners serves everything, including a
to-die-for salad of crispy romaine lettuce and tender grilled
lobster drizzled with a lemongrass vinaigrette. More hearty
fare includes baby back ribs cooked with the restaurant's
special spice blend and Guinness stout. ✉*Hotel Caravelle,
44A Queen Cross St.* ☎*340/773–6585* 🍴*AE, MC, V.*

ECLECTIC

¢–$$ ✕**Avocado Pitt.** Locals gather at this Christiansted waterfront spot for the breakfast and lunch specials as well
as for a bit of gossip. Breakfast runs to stick-to-the-ribs
dishes like oatmeal and pancakes. Lunches include such
dressed-up basics as the Yard Bird on a Bun, a chicken
breast sandwich tarted up with a liberal dose of hot sauce.
The yellowfin tuna sandwich is made from fresh fish and

gives a new taste to a standard lunchtime favorite. ⊠*King Christian Hotel, 59 Kings Wharf* ☎*340/773–9843* ▤*AE, MC, V* ⊗*No dinner.*

FRENCH

$-$$ ✕**Café Christine.** A favorite with the professionals who work
★ in downtown Christiansted, Café Christine's presentation is as dazzling as the food. The small menu changes daily, but look for dishes like shrimp salad drizzled with a lovely vinaigrette or a vegetarian plate with quiche, salad, and lentils. Desserts are perfection. If the pear pie topped with chocolate is on the menu, don't hesitate. This tiny restaurant has tables in both the air-conditioned dining room and the outside porch that overlooks historic buildings. ⊠*Apothecary Hall Courtyard, 4 Company St.* ☎*340/713– 1500* ▤*No credit cards* ⊗*Closed weekends and July–mid Nov. No dinner.*

OUTSIDE CHRISTIANSTED

ECLECTIC

$$-$$$ ✕**Breezes.** This aptly named restaurant is poolside at Club
☯ St. Croix condominiums. Visitors and locals are drawn by its reasonable prices and good food. This is *the* place on the island to be for Sunday brunch, where the menu includes Caesar salad, burgers, and blackened prime rib with Cajun seasonings and a horseradish sauce. For dessert, try the flourless chocolate torte—a wedge of rich chocolate served with a river of chocolate sauce. ⊠*Club St. Croix, 3220 Golden Rock, off Rte. 752, Golden Rock* ☎*340/773–7077* ▤*AE, D, MC, V.*

★ Fodor'sChoice✕**Elizabeth's.** With a lovely beachfront location
$$-$$$ and stellar food, this restaurant has developed quite a following. Dinner entrées include a tasty pistachio-crusted Chilean sea bass with jasmine rice and a lemongrass glaze. Lunch brings out lots of locals for the generous helping of curried chicken salad and a crab cake wrapped in a flavorful tortilla. The piquant horseradish sauce adds a tasty touch. ⊠*The Palms at Pelican Cove, off Rte. 752, Estate Princess* ☎*340/719–0735* ▤*AE, D, MC, V.*

¢-$ ✕**Anna's Café.** Stop by this cozy spot in a popular shopping center for light fare. Lunch runs to wraps and sandwiches filled with veggies, cheeses, and sliced meats. If you can't decide, try the restaurant's famous chicken salad, or a personal-sized pizza. For breakfast, the chef cooks up French toast, croissants, and eggs cooked any way you like. Smoothies are a

house specialty. ⊠*Gallows Bay Market Pl.* ☎*340/773–6620*
▤*No credit cards* ⊙*Closed Sun. No dinner.*

ITALIAN

$$–$$$$ ×**Tutto Bene.** Its muraled walls, brightly striped cushions,
and painted trompe-l'oeil tables make Tutto Bene look
more like a sophisticated Mexican cantina than an Ital-
ian cucina. One bite of the food, however, will clear up
any confusion. Written on hanging mirrors is the daily
menu, which includes such specialties as veal saltimbocca
and scallopine of veal with prosciutto and sage. Desserts,
including a decadent tiramisu, are on the menu as well.
⊠*Hospital St., in Boardwalk shopping center* ☎*340/773–
5229* ▤*AE, MC, V* ⊙*No lunch.*

EAST END

ECLECTIC

$$$–$$$$ ×**The Galleon.** This popular dockside restaurant is always
busy. Start with the Caesar salad or perhaps a flaky lay-
ered duck napoleon. The chef's signature dish is a tender
filet mignon topped with fresh local lobster. Pasta lovers
should sample the linguine with shrimp, mussels, and fish
tossed with fresh tomatoes, spinach, and olive oil. Take
Route 82 out of Christiansted; then turn left at the sign
for Green Cay Marina. ⊠*Annas Hope* ☎*340/773–9949*
▤*MC, V* ⊙*No lunch.*

$$–$$$ ×**The Deep End.** A favorite with locals and vacationers, this
poolside restaurant serves up terrific crab-cake sandwiches,
London broil with onions and mushrooms, and delicious
pasta in various styles. To get here from Christiansted, take
Route 82 and turn left at the sign for Green Cay Marina.
⊠*Tamarind Reef Hotel, Annas Hope* ☎*340/713–7071*
▤*MC, V.*

FREDERIKSTED

ECLECTIC

★ Fodor'sChoice ×**Blue Moon.** This terrific little bistro, which has
$$$ a loyal local following, offers a changing menu that draws
on Cajun and Caribbean flavors. Try the spicy gumbo with
andouille sausage or crab cakes with a spicy aioli for your
appetizer. Chicken, shrimp, sausage, and peppers served
over pasta makes a good entrée. The Almond Joy sun-
dae should be your choice for dessert. There's live jazz on
Wednesday and Friday. ⊠*7 Strand St.* ☎*340/772–2222*
▤*AE, MC, V* ⊙*Closed Mon.*

¢–$ ✕**Turtles Deli.** Eat outside at this tiny spot just as you enter
♻ downtown Frederiksted. Lunches are as basic as a corned
beef on rye or as imaginative as "The Raven" (turkey
breast with bacon, tomato, and melted cheddar cheese on
French bread). Also good is "The Beast," named after the
grueling hill that challenges bikers in the annual triathlon.
It's piled high with hot roast beef, raw onion, and melted
Swiss cheese with horseradish and mayonnaise. Early ris-
ers stop by for cinnamon buns and espresso. ✉*625 Strand
St., at Prince Passage* ☎*340/772–3676* ▭*No credit cards*
⊘*Closed Sun. No dinner.*

FRENCH

$$$ ✕**Le St. Tropez.** A ceramic-tile bar and soft lighting set the
mood at this Mediterranean-style bistro tucked into a
courtyard one block from the waterfront. Seated either
inside or on the adjoining patio, you can enjoy grilled meats
in delicate sauces. The menu changes daily, often taking
advantage of local seafood. The fresh basil, tomato, and
mozzarella salad is heavenly. ✉*227 King St.* ☎*340/772–
3000* ▭*AE, MC, V* ⊘*Closed Sun. No lunch Sat.*

OUTSIDE FREDERIKSTED

$$–$$$ ✕**Sunset Grill.** As you would expect, this alfresco restaurant
♻ is a hot spot for sunset watchers, as well as a social hub
for locals. The ever-changing menu features fish, fish, and
more fish. Try the almond-crusted grouper in a soy-butter
sauce or whatever else the chef whipped up that day. Those
who aren't fond of seafood can pick from dishes like a rib-
eye steak for dinner. Desserts might include fresh blueber-
ries and strawberries in a rum sauce. It's about 2 km (i mi)
north of Frederiksted. ✉*Rte. 63* ☎*340/772–5855* ▭*MC,
V* ⊘*Closed Mon.*

NORTH SHORE

ECLECTIC

$–$$ ✕**Off the Wall.** Divers fresh from a plunge at the north
shore's popular Cane Bay Wall gather at this breezy spot
on the beach. If you want to sit a spell before you order,
a hammock beckons. Deli sandwiches, served with deli-
cious chips, make up most of the menu. Pizza and salads
are also available. ✉*Rte. 80, Cane Bay* ☎*340/778–4771*
▭*AE, MC, V.*

WHERE TO STAY

Although a stay right in historic Christiansted may mean putting up with a little urban noise, you probably won't have trouble sleeping. Christiansted rolls up the sidewalks fairly early, and air-conditioners drown out any noise. Solitude is guaranteed at hotels and inns outside Christiansted and those on the outskirts of sleepy Frederiksted.

For approximate costs, see the dining and lodging price chart on the U.S. Virgin Islands Planner, at the beginning of this chapter.

3

CHRISTIANSTED

$$ **Hotel Caravelle.** Near the harbor, at the waterfront end of a pleasant shopping arcade, the Caravelle's in-town location puts you steps away from shops and restaurants. Rooms are tasteful and tropical, with white walls and floral-print bedspreads and curtains; most have ocean views. A small pool provides a swimming and sunning option. The ever-popular Rum Runners restaurant sits just off the lobby. Pro: good restaurant, convenient location, plenty of parking. Con: no beach, rundown neighborhood. ⊠44A Queen Cross St., 00820 ☎340/773–0687 or 800/524–0410 ☎340/778–7004 ⊕www.hotelcaravelle.com ☞43 rooms, 1 suite ♿In-room: refrigerator, Ethernet, Wi-Fi. In-hotel: restaurant, bar, pool, public Internet, no elevator ☰AE, D, DC, MC, V ⧉EP.

$–$$ **Pink Fancy Hotel.** Offering a connection to the island's elegant past, the venerable hotel is listed on the National Register of Historic Places. Dating from 1780, it became a hotel in 1948. Rooms are filled with antiques, mahogany furnishings, and colorful Oriental rugs. Lush gardens meander around the fenced-in compound, creating a comfortable base for folks who like to get out and about. Guests gather poolside for breakfast and conversation. Pros: homey rooms, lovely gardens, friendly atmosphere. Cons: rundown neighborhood, no parking lot. ⊠27 Prince St., 00820 ☎340/773–8460 or 800/524–2045 ☎340/773–6448 ⊕www.pinkfancy.com ☞12 rooms ♿In-room: kitchen, dial-up. In-hotel: no elevator, public Wi-Fi, no-smoking rooms ☰AE, MC, V ⧉CP.

$ **Hotel on the Cay.** Hop on the free ferry to reach this lodging in the middle of Christiansted Harbor. Although the island location sounds a bit inconvenient, the ferry ride takes no time at all. The captain zips over to the water-front whenever he sees someone waiting. Rooms are pleasantly furnished and have harbor views, balconies or patios, and kitchenettes for times when you don't want to eat at the hotel's restaurant. In addition to sunning at the small beach, chatting with fellow travelers, and strolling the lushly planted grounds, you can try snorkeling and other water sports. Keep an eye out for one of the endangered St. Croix ground lizards that call the island home. Pros: quiet atmosphere, convenient location, lovely beach. Cons: accessible only by ferry, no parking lot ⊠*Protestant Cay 00820-4441* ☎*340/773-2035 or 800/524-2035* 🖷*340/773-7046* ⊕*www.hotelonthecay.com* 🛏*53 rooms* ♿*In-room: kitchen. In-hotel: restaurant, pool, beachfront, water sports, no elevator, public Internet, public Wi-Fi* ▭*AE, D, MC, V* ⎮⎮*EP.*

$ 🖳**King Christian Hotel.** A stay at the King Christian puts you right in the heart of Christiansted's historic district. Parts of the building date back to the mid-1700s, but numerous renovations have brought it up to modern standards. Rooms are a bit on the pedestrian side, but floral spreads and pastel walls brighten things up considerably. Unless you're on a rock-bottom budget, don't opt for the depressing rooms in the back. You can hop a ferry to nearby Protestant Cay for an afternoon at the beach when you tire of the pool. You're a quick walk to restaurants, shops, and water-sports excursions. Pros: waterfront rooms, car rental in lobby, convenient location. Cons: no beach, need taxi at night, no parking lot. ⊠*57 King St., Box 24467, 00824-0467* ☎*340/773-6330 or 800/524-2012* 🖷*340/773-9411* ⊕*www.kingchristian.com* 🛏*39 rooms* ♿*In-room: safe (some), refrigerator. In-hotel: pool, diving, public Internet, public Wi-Fi* ▭*AE, MC, V* ⎮⎮*EP.*

OUTSIDE CHRISTIANSTED

★ Fodor'sChoice 🖳**Carringtons Inn.** Hands-on owners Claudia
$ and Roger Carrington are the real reason to stay here, and they conjure up delicious breakfasts—rum-soaked French toast is a house specialty—dole out advice, and make you feel right at home. Formerly a private home, the comfy bed-and-breakfast is a 10-minute drive from Christiansted. Each room is different, with a decorating theme that reflects a namesake flower. Wicker furniture, handwoven carpets, and balconies in some rooms, colorful spreads, and sea or pool views create an inviting atmosphere. The hillside sub-

urban location means you need a rental car if you stay. Pros: welcoming hosts, tasteful rooms, great breakfasts. Cons: no beach, need car to get around. ⊠*4001 Estate Hermon Hill, Christiansted 00820* ☎*340/713–0508 or 877/658–0508* 🖷*340/719–0841* ⊕*www.carringtonsinn. com* ⇄*5 rooms* ⚘*In-room: kitchen (some), refrigerator, no TV. In-hotel: pool, no elevator, public Internet, public Wi-Fi, no-smoking rooms* ⊟*AE, MC, V* ⍩*BP.*

EAST END

$$$–$$$$ ⊞**The Buccaneer.** For travelers who want everything at their
♨ fingertips, this resort has sandy beaches, swimming pools, and extensive sports facilities. A palm-tree-lined main drive leads to the large, pink main building atop a hill; the rest of the resort sits on the grounds of a 300-acre former sugar plantation, where shops, restaurants, and guest quarters are scattered about the manicured lawns. Spacious rooms are tropical in style, with tile floors, four-poster beds, massive wardrobes of pale wood, marble baths, and local art. Beachside doubloon rooms are the largest and are steps from the sand, but you can be perfectly comfortable no matter where you stay. Pros: beachfront location, numerous activities, nice golf course. Cons: expensive rates, insular environment, need car to get around. ⊠*Rte. 82, Box 25200, Shoys 00824* ☎*340/712–2100 or 800/255–3881* 🖷*340/712–2104* ⊕*www.thebuccaneer.com* ⇄*138 rooms* ⚘*In-room: safe, refrigerator, Wi-Fi. In-hotel: 4 restaurants, bar, golf course, tennis courts, pools, gym, spa, beachfront, water sports, children's programs (ages 4–12), no elevator, public Internet, no-smoking rooms* ⊟*AE, D, MC, V* ⍩*BP.*

$$$–$$$$ ⊞**Chenay Bay Beach Resort.** The seaside setting and compli-
♨ mentary tennis and water-sports equipment make this resort a real find, particularly for families with active kids. Rooms have ceramic-tile floors, tropical color schemes, rattan furnishings, and front porches. Gravel paths meander among terraced wood or stucco cottages. Other facilities include a large L-shape pool, a protected beach, a picnic area, and a casual restaurant. There's also a reasonably priced shuttle to grocery stores and shopping areas. Pros: beachfront location, good children's program, wide array of water sports. Cons: need car to get around, lacks pizzazz. ⊠*Rte. 82, Green Cay* ⚲*Box 24600, Christiansted 00824* ☎*340/773–2918 or 800/548–4457* 🖷*340/773– 6665* ⊕*www.chenaybay.com* ⇄*50 rooms* ⚘*In-room: kitchen, dial-up. In-hotel: restaurant, bar, tennis courts,*

pool, beachfront, water sports, no elevator, children's programs (ages 4–12), public Wi-Fi ⊟AE, D, MC, V ﴾O﴿EP.

$$$ ⊡**Divi Carina Bay Resort.** An oceanfront location puts most rooms at the Divi Carina Bay Resort close to the beach, but the villas are across the road, behind the main building. Because it has the island's only casino and regular evening entertainment, this resort is your best choice if you enjoy nonstop nightlife. The rooms have rattan and wicker furniture, white-tile floors, and sapphire and teal colors. Although its location on the island's East End puts you a long way from anywhere, the hotel provides a fair amount of activities to keep you busy. Pros: on-site casino, spacious beach, good restaurant. Cons: need car to get around, many stairs to climb, staff seems disinterested. ✉*25 Rte. 60, Estate Turner Hole 00820* ☎*340/773–9700 or 877/773–9700* 🖷*340/773–9479* ⊕*www.divicarina.com* ↪*146 rooms, 2 suites, 20 villas* ☖*In-room: safe, refrigerator, dial-up, Wi-Fi (some). In-hotel: 2 restaurants, bars, tennis courts, pool, gym, beachfront, water sports, public Internet, public Wi-Fi* ⊟*AE, D, DC, MC, V* ﴾O﴿*EP.*

$$ ⊡**Tamarind Reef Hotel.** Spread out along a sandy beach, these low-slung buildings offer casual comfort. Independent travelers who want the option to eat in or out will enjoy the rooms with basic kitchenettes. The spacious modern rooms have rattan furniture, tropical-print fabrics, and either a terrace or a deck with views of St. Croix's sister islands. Snorkelers can explore a nearby reef, but shallow water makes serious swimming difficult. There's a snack bar just off the beach, and the Galleon Restaurant is next door at Green Cay Marina. Pros: good snorkeling, tasty restaurant, rooms have kitchenettes. Cons: need car to get around, motel-style rooms. ✉*5001 Tamarind Reef, off Rte. 82, Annas Hope 00820* ☎*340/773–4455 or 800/619–0014* 🖷*340/773–3989* ⊕*www.usvi.net/hotel/ tamarind* ↪*39 rooms* ☖*In-room: refrigerator, Wi-Fi. In-hotel: restaurant, pool, water sports, no elevator, no-smoking rooms* ⊟*AE, DC, MC, V* ﴾O﴿*EP.*

FREDERIKSTED

$–$$$ ⊡**Sandcastle on the Beach.** Right on a gorgeous stretch of white beach, this hotel caters primarily to gay men and lesbians, but anyone is welcome. The hotel has a tropical charm that harkens back to a simpler time in the Caribbean; proximity to Frederiksted's interesting dining scene is also a plus. Rooms, which have contemporary decor, tile floors, and bright fabrics, come in several sizes and locations. All have kitchens or kitchenettes, and most have sea views. Packages that include a car and bar privileges are a good value. Although some people bring their kids, the hotel caters more to singles and couples, especially during the winter season. Pros: lovely beach, close to restaurants, gay-friendly vibe. Cons: neighborhood sketchy at night, need car to get around, no children's activities. ⊠127 *Smithfield, Rte. 71, Frederiksted 00840* ☎340/772–1205 *or 800/524–2018* 🖷340/772–1757 ⊕*www.sandcastleon-thebeach.com* 🛏8 rooms, 8 suites, 6 villas ♿*In-room: no phone, safe, kitchen (some), VCRs (some). In-hotel: restaurant, pools, gym, beachfront, water sports, no elevator, laundry facilities, public Internet, public Wi-Fi* ▤AE, D, MC, V ⊙CP.

NORTH SHORE

★ Fodor'sChoice 🏨**Villa Greenleaf.** This spacious B&B is all
$$–$$$$ about the details—four-poster beds with elegant duvets, towels folded just so, hand-stenciled trim on the walls, and gardens tastefully planted. Staying here is like visiting a well-heeled relative who happens to have home in the Caribbean. The house was built in the 1950s but was totally renovated in 2004. You'll want to spend your days gazing at the lovely view of St. Croix's north shore or relaxing beside the sparkling pool. A car is included in the rates for trips around the island. Pros: tasteful decor, convivial atmosphere, car included in rate. Cons: no beach, no restaurants nearby, need car to get around. ⊠*Island Center Rd., Montpelier* ⊙*Box 675, Christiansted 00821* ☎340/719–1958 *or 888/282–1001* 🖷340/772–5425 ⊕*www.villagreenleaf.com* 🛏5 rooms ♿*In-room: safe, refrigerator, Wi-Fi. In-hotel: pool, no elevator, public Wi-Fi* ▤AE, D, MC, V ⊙BP.

$$–$$$ 🏨**Cane Bay Reef Club.** These modestly sized lodgings sit seaside in the peaceful community of Cane Bay. They're perfect for folks who don't need every amenity but want to be right at the water's edge. All the rooms in the two-story buildings have no-frills kitchenettes, the usual rattan furniture with tropical accents, and balconies or porches that put you almost on the beach. You can rent dive gear nearby to explore St. Croix's famous Cane Bay Wall. Pros: near Cane Bay Beach, restaurants nearby, nice views. Cons: need car to get around, decor dated, on main road. ⊠*Rte. 80, Cane Bay* ⊙*Box 1407, Kingshill 00851* ☎340/778–

2966 ☎*800/253–8534* ⊕*www.canebay.com* ⇘*9 units* ♿*In-room: kitchen. In-hotel: restaurant, pool, no elevator, public Internet, public Wi-Fi* ☐*AE, D, DC, MC, V* ⊚*EP.*

$$–$$$ ⊞**Renaissance Carambola Beach Resort.** We like this resort's stellar beachfront setting and peaceful ambience. As of this writing the hotel was in the midst of a massive renovation. The refurbished rooms are lovely, with attractive palm-theme accessories that match the resort's atmosphere. All have terra-cotta floors, ceramic lamps, mahogany ceilings and furnishings, and rocking chairs. Each has a patio and a huge bathroom (shower only). Lushly planted walkways connect the rooms and the hotel's restaurants and pool. Pros: lovely beach, relaxing atmosphere, close to golf. Cons: some dated rooms, need car to get around. ✉*Rte. 80, Davis Bay* ⌖*Box 3031, Kingshill 00851* ☎*340/778–3800 or 888/503–8760* ☐*340/778–1682* ⊕*www.carambola beach.com* ⇘*151 rooms* ♿*In-room: safe, kitchen (some), dial-up. In-hotel: 3 restaurants, tennis courts, pool, gym, spa, beachfront, diving, water sports, no elevator, public Internet, public Wi-Fi* ☐*AE, D, DC, MC, V* ⊚*EP.*

$$ ⊞**Hibiscus Beach Hotel.** This hotel is on a lovely beach—the best reason to stay here. Rooms, each named for a tropical flower, show obvious wear and tear, but all have spacious balconies and are decorated with brightly colored fabrics. Bathrooms are clean but nondescript—both the shower stalls and the vanity mirrors are on the small side. You'll need a car to get around, as the surrounding neighborhood isn't a great place for walking. Pros: nice beach, good restaurant, close to Christiansted. Cons: dated decor, sketchy neighborhood, need car to get around. ✉*4131 Estate La Grande Princesse, off Rte. 752, La Grande Princesse 00820-4441* ☎*340/773–4042 or 800/442–0121* ☐*340/773–7668* ⊕*www.hibiscusbeachresort.com* ⇘*37 rooms* ♿*In-room: safe, refrigerator, dial-up. In-hotel: restaurant, pool, beachfront, water sports, no elevator, public Internet, public Wi-Fi* ☐*AE, D, MC, V* ⊚*CP.*

$$ ⊞**Waves at Cane Bay.** St. Croix's famed Cane Bay Wall is just offshore from this resort, giving it an enviable location. It's a good bet for divers, as there's a dive shop just down the road. Although the hotel's stretch of beach is rocky, you can sunbathe at a small patch of sand beside the pool. Two blue-and-white buildings are where you can find large, balconied rooms decorated in soft pastels. Pros: great diving, restaurants nearby, beaches nearby. Cons: need car to get around, on main road, bland decor. ✉*Rte. 80, Cane Bay* ⌖*Box 1749, Kingshill 00851* ☎*340/778–*

1805 or 800/545–0603 ☎*340/778–4945* ⊕*www.canebay stcroix.com* ⤢*12 rooms* ⚒*In-room: safe, kitchen, Wi-Fi. In-hotel: restaurant, bar, pool, water sports, no elevator* ⊟*AE, MC, V* ⦿*EP.*

$–$$ 🏠**Villa Margarita.** This quiet retreat is along a tranquil north-shore beach, about 20 minutes from Christiansted's shops and restaurants. It provides a particularly good base if you want to admire the dramatic views of the wind-swept coast. Units vary in size, but all come with kitch-enettes, tropical furnishings, private balconies, and those spectacular views. Swimming in front of the hotel is diffi-cult because of the shallow water, but other sandy beaches are steps away. The snorkeling nearby is excellent. Pros: friendly host, great views, snorkeling nearby. Cons: iso-lated location, need car to get around, limited amenities. ✉*Off Rte. 80, Salt River* ⌂*9024 Salt River, Christiansted 00820* ☎*340/713–1930 or 866/274–8811* ☎*340/719–3389* ⊕*www.villamargarita.com* ⤢*3 units* ⚒*In-room: no phone, kitchen, refrigerator. In-hotel: pool, no elevator, no kids under 18* ⊟*AE, D, MC, V* ⦿*EP.*

CONDOMINIUMS

If you want to be close to the island's restaurants and shopping, look for a condominium in the hills above Christiansted or on either side of the town. An East End location gets you out of Christiansted's hustle and bustle, but you're still only 15 minutes from town. North Shore locations are lovely, with gorgeous sea views and lots of peace and quiet.

$$–$$$$ 🏠**Sugar Beach.** With all the conveniences of home, Sugar Beach has apartments that are immaculate and breezy. Each unit has a full kitchen and a large patio or balcony with an ocean view; larger ones also have washers and dryers. Although the exteriors are drab stucco, the interiors are enliv-ened by tropical furnishings. The pool occupies the ruins of a 250-year-old sugar mill. A lovely beach is just steps away, and Christiansted's conveniences are an easy 10-minute drive. It's one of a string of condominium complexes near a public-housing project, so don't walk in the neighborhood at night. Pros: pleasant beach, full kitchens, space to spread out. Cons: sketchy neighborhood, need car to get around. ✉*Rte. 752, Estate Golden Rock 00820* ☎*340/773–5345 or 800/524–2049* ☎*340/773–1359* ⊕*www.sugarbeachstcroix. com* ⤢*46 apartments* ⚒*In-room: kitchen, Wi-Fi (some).*

In-hotel: tennis courts, pool, beachfront, no elevator, public Internet, public Wi-Fi ⊟AE, D, MC, V ⦿EP.

$$–$$$ ⚏**Club St. Croix.** Sitting beachfront just outside Chris-
☾ tiansted, this modern condominium complex faces a lovely sandy beach. You have easy access to shopping and restaurants in nearby Christiansted, but you need a car to get there. Breezes restaurant provides full meal service if you tire of cooking in your fully equipped kitchen. Spacious condos come in different sizes: studios, one-, and two-bedrooms; all have balconies or patios. Rooms have rattan furniture and bright accents. The location near public housing doesn't encourage strolls through the neighborhood. Pros: beachfront location, good restaurant, full kitchens. Cons: need car to get around, sketchy neighborhood. ⊠*Rte. 752, Estate Golden Rock 00824* ☎*340/773–9150 or 800/524–2025* 🖷*340/778–4009* ⊕*www.antillesresorts.com* ⇔*53 apartments* ⚸*In-room: kitchen, Wi-Fi. In-hotel: restaurant, tennis courts, pool, beachfront, no elevator, public Internet, public Wi-Fi ⊟AE, D,MC, V ⦿EP.*

$$–$$$ ⚏**Villa Madeleine.** If you like privacy, we think you'll like
★ Villa Madeleine. The two-story villas flow downhill from this condominium resort's centerpiece, a West Indian plantation greathouse. Each villa has a full kitchen and its own pool. The decor evokes the property's natural surroundings: rattan furniture with plush cushions, rocking chairs, and, in some, bamboo four-poster beds. Special touches include pink-marble showers and hand-painted floral wall borders. You definitely need a car for sightseeing. Pros: pleasant decor, full kitchens, private pools. Cons: lower units may not have views, need car to get around. ⊠*Off Rte. 82, Teague Bay* ⊅*5014 Villa Madeleine, Christiansted 00820* ☎*340/713–0923 or 800/237–1959* ⊕*www.rentonstcroix.com* ⇔*43 villas* ⚸*In-room: kitchen. In-hotel: tennis court, pools, no elevator, public Wi-Fi ⊟AE, MC, V ⦿EP.*

$$ ⚏**Colony Cove.** In a string of condominium complexes,
☾ Colony Cove lets you experience comfortable beachfront living. Units all have two bedrooms, two bathrooms, and washer–dryer combos, making it a good choice for families. They have typical tropical furnishings with most furniture made of rattan and wicker. Floors are tile. The neighborhood isn't the best, so don't plan on strolling too far at night. Pros: beachfront location, comfortable units, good views. Cons: sketchy neighborhood, need car to get around. ⊠*Rte. 752, Estate Golden Rock 00824* ☎*340/773–1965 or 800/524–2025* ⊕*www.antillesresorts.*

com ⊃62 *apartments* ⅏*In-room: kitchen, dial-up, Wi-Fi. In-hotel: pool, beachfront, no elevator, public Wi-Fi* ═*AE, D, MC, V* ◦⃝*EP.*

PRIVATE VILLAS

St. Croix has villas scattered all over the island, but most are in the center or on the East End. Renting a villa gives you all the convenience of home as well as top-notch amenities. Many have pools, hot tubs, and deluxe furnishings. Most companies meet you at the airport, arrange for a rental car, and provide helpful information about the island.

RENTAL AGENTS

Island Villas (☎340/772–0420 *or* 800/626–4512 ⊕*www. stcroixislandvillas.com*) has a supply of villas across the island. **Teague Bay Properties** (☎800/237–1959 ⊕*www. rentonstcroix.com*) specializes in villas and condominiums across the island, with many on the eastern end. **Vacation St. Croix** (☎340/778–0361 *or* 877/788–0361 ⊕*www.vaca-tionstcroix.com*) has villas all around the island.

CAMPING

☾ ⚠**Mount Victory Camp.** A remarkable quietude distinguishes this out-of-the-way spread on 8 acres in the island's rain forest. If you really want to commune with nature, you'll be hard-pressed to find a better way to do it on St. Croix. Hosts Bruce and Mathilde Wilson are on hand to explain the environment. You sleep in screened-in tent-cottages perched on a raised platform and covered by a roof. Each has electricity and a rudimentary outdoor kitchen. The shared, spotlessly clean bathhouse is an easy stroll away. The location feels remote, but a lovely sand beach and the Sunset Grill restaurant are a 2-mi (3-km) drive down the hill. In another 10 minutes you're in Frederiksted. Pros: quiet location, friendly hosts, clean bathrooms. Cons: need car to get around, basic facilities. ⅏*Flush toilets, drinking water, showers, picnic tables* ⊃5 *tents* ⊠*Creque Dam Rd., Frederiksted 00841* ☎340/772–1651 *or* 866/772–1651 ⊕*www.mtvictorycamp.com* ⚑*Reservations essential* ═*No credit cards.*

BEACHES

★ **Buck Island.** A visit to this island beach, part of Buck Island
Reef National Monument, is a must. The beach is beautiful, but its finest treasures are those you can see when you
plop off the boat and adjust your mask, snorkel, and fins
to swim over colorful coral and darting fish. Don't know
how to snorkel? No problem—the boat crew will have you
outfitted and in the water in no time. Take care not to step
on those black-pointed spiny sea urchins or touch the mus-
tard-color fire coral, which can cause a nasty burn. Most
charter boat trips start with a snorkel over the lovely reef
before a stop at the island's beach. An easy 20-minute hike
leads uphill to an overlook for a bird's-eye view of the reef
below. Find rest rooms at the beach. Buck Island is 5 mi (8
km) north of St. Croix.

Cane Bay. The waters aren't always gentle at this breezy
north-shore beach, but there are seldom many people
around, and the scuba diving and snorkeling are won-
drous. You can see elkhorn and brain corals, and less than
200 yards out is the drop-off called Cane Bay Wall. Cane
Bay can be an all-day destination. You can rent kayaks
and snorkeling and scuba gear at water-sports shops across
the road, and a couple of casual restaurants beckon when
the sun gets too hot. The beach has no public rest rooms.
⊠*Rte. 80, about 4 mi (6 km) west of Salt River.*

West End Beaches. There are several unnamed beaches along
the coast road north of Frederiksted, but it's best if you
don't stray too far from civilization. For safety's sake, most
vacationers plop down their towel near one of the casual
restaurants spread out along Route 63. The beachfront
Sunset Grill makes a nice spot for lunch. The beach at the
Rainbow Beach Club, a five-minute drive outside Frederiksted, has a bar, a casual restaurant, water sports, and volleyball. If you want to be close to the cruise-ship pier, just
stroll on over to the adjacent sandy beach in front of Fort
Frederik. On the way south out of Frederiksted, the stretch
near Sandcastle on the Beach hotel is also lovely. ⊠*Rte. 63,
north and south of Frederiksted.*

SPORTS & THE OUTDOORS

BOAT TOURS

Almost everyone takes a day trip to Buck Island aboard a charter boat. Most leave from the Christiansted waterfront or from Green Cay Marina and stop for a snorkel at the island's eastern end before dropping anchor off a gorgeous sandy beach for a swim, a hike, and lunch. Sailboats can often stop right at the beach; a larger boat might have to anchor a bit farther offshore. A full-day sail runs about $90, with lunch included on most trips. A half-day sail costs about $60. **Big Beard's Adventure Tours** (☎340/773–4482 ⊕*www.bigbeards.com*) takes you on catamarans, either the *Renegade* or the *Flyer,* from the Christiansted waterfront to Buck Island for snorkeling before dropping anchor at a private beach for a barbecue lunch. **Caribbean Sea Adventures** (☎340/773–2628 ⊕*www.caribbeansea adventures.com*) departs from the Christiansted waterfront for half- and full-day trips. The **Teroro Charters** (☎340/773–3161 ⊕*www.visitstcroix.com/captainheinz.html*) trimaran *Teroro II* leaves Green Cay Marina for full- or half-day sails. Bring your own lunch.

DIVING & SNORKELING

At **Buck Island,** a short boat ride from Christiansted or Green Cay Marina, the reef is so nice that it's been named a national monument. You can dive right off the beach at **Cane Bay,** which has a spectacular drop-off called the Cane Bay Wall. Dive operators also do boat trips along the Wall, usually leaving from Salt River or Christiansted. **Frederiksted Pier** is home to a colony of sea horses, creatures seldom seen in the waters of the Virgin Islands. At **Green Cay,** just outside Green Cay Marina in the east end, you can see colorful fish swimming around the reefs and rocks. Two exceptional north-shore sites are **North Star** and **Salt River,** which you can reach only by boat. At Salt River you can float downward through a canyon filled with colorful fish and coral.

The island's dive shops take you out for one- or two-tank dives. Plan to pay about $65 for a one-tank dive and $85 for a two-tank dive, including equipment and an underwater tour. All companies offer certification and introductory courses called resort dives for novices.

Which dive outfit you pick usually depends on where you're staying. Your hotel may have one on-site. If so, you're just a short stroll away from the dock. If not, other companies are close by. Where the dive boat goes on a particular day depends on the weather, but in any case, all St. Croix's dive sites are special. All shops are affiliated with PADI, the Professional Association of Diving Instructors.

If you're staying in Christiansted, **Dive Experience** (✉*1111 Strand St., Christiansted* ☎*340/773–3307 or 800/235–9047* ⊕*www.divexp.com*) has PADI five-star status and runs trips to the north-shore walls and reefs in addition to offering the usual certification and introductory classes. **St. Croix Ultimate Bluewater Adventures** (✉*Queen Cross St., Christiansted* ☎*340/773–5994 or 877/567–1367* ⊕*www. stcroixscuba.com*) can take you to your choice of more than 75 sites; it also offers a variety of packages that include hotel stays.

Folks staying in the Judith's Fancy area are closest to **Anchor Dive Center** (✉*Salt River Marina, Rte. 801, Salt River* ☎*340/778–1522 or 800/532–3483* ⊕*www.anchor divestcroix.com*). The company also has facilities at the Buccaneer hotel. Anchor takes divers to more than 35 sites, including the wall at Salt River Canyon.

Cane Bay Dive Shop (✉*Rte. 80, Cane Bay* ☎*340/773–9913 or 800/338–3843* ⊕*www.canebayscuba.com*) is the place to go if you want to do a beach dive or boat dive along the north shore. The famed Cane Bay Wall is 150 yards from the five-star PADI facility. This company also has shops at Pan Am Pavilion in Christiansted, on Strand Street in Frederiksted, at the Carambola Beach Resort, and at the Divi Carina Bay hotel.

In Frederiksted, **Scuba Shack** (✉*Frederiksted Beach, Rte. 631, Frederiksted* ☎*340/772–3483 or 888/789–3483* ⊕*www. stcroixscubashack.com*) takes divers right off the beach near Coconuts restaurant, on night dives off the Frederiksted Pier, or on boat trips to wrecks and reefs. **Scuba West** (✉*330 Strand St., Frederiksted* ☎*340/772–3701 or 800/352–0107* ⊕*www. divescubawest.com*) runs trips to reefs and wrecks from its base in Frederiksted but specializes in showing divers the sea horses that live around the Frederiksted Pier.

FISHING

Since the early 1980s, some 20 world records—many for blue marlin—have been set in these waters. Sailfish, skip-jack, bonito, tuna (allison, blackfin, and yellowfin), and wahoo are abundant. A charter runs about $100 an hour per person, with most boats going out for four-, six- or eight-hour trips. **Caribbean Sea Adventures** (⊠*59 Kings Wharf, Christiansted* ☎*340/773–2628* ⊕*www.caribbean seaadventures.com*) will take you out on a 38-foot power-boat called the *Fantasy.*

GOLF

★ St. Croix's courses welcome you with spectacular vistas and well-kept greens. Check with your hotel or the tour-ist board to determine when major celebrity tournaments will be held. There's often an opportunity to play with the pros. The **Buccaneer** (⊠*Rte. 82, Shoys* ☎*340/712–2144* ⊕*www.thebuccaneer.com*) has an 18-hole course. It's close to Christiansted, so it's convenient for those staying in or near town. Greens fees are $85 with an additional $20 for cart rental. The spectacular 18-hole course at **Carambola Golf Club** (⊠*Rte. 80, Davis Bay* ☎*340/778–5638* ⊕*www. golfcarambola.com*), in the northwest valley, was designed by Robert Trent Jones Sr. It sits near Carambola Beach Resort. Greens fees are $99 for 18 holes, which includes the use of a golf cart. The **Reef Golf Course** (⊠*Teague Bay* ☎*340/773–8844*), a public course on the island's east end, has 9 holes. Greens fees are $20, and cart rental is $12.

HIKING

Although you can set off by yourself on a hike through a rain forest or along a shore, a guide will point out what's important and tell you why. **Ay-Ay Eco Hike & Tours Associa-tion** (⊠*Box 2435, Kingshill 00851* ☎*340/772–4079*), run by Ras Lumumba Corriette, takes hikers up hill and down dale in some of St. Croix's most remote places, including the rain forest and Mount Victory. Some hikes include stops at places like the Carl and Marie Lawaetz Museum and old ruins. The cost is $50 per person for a three- or four-hour hike. There's a three-person minimum. A full-day jeep tour through the rain forest runs $120 per person.

HORSEBACK RIDING

Well-kept roads and expert guides make horseback riding on St. Croix pleasurable. At Sprat Hall, just north of Frederiksted, Jill Hurd runs **Paul & Jill's Equestrian Stables** (⊠*Rte. 58, Frederiksted* ☎*340/772–2880 or 340/772–2627* ⊕*www.paulandjills.com*). She will take you clip-clopping through the rain forest, across the pastures, along the beaches, and over the hilltops—explaining the flora, fauna, and ruins on the way. A 1½-hour ride costs $75.

KAYAKING

Caribbean Adventure Tours (⊠*Salt River Marina, Rte. 80, Salt River* ☎*340/778–1522* ⊕*www.stcroixkayak.com*) takes you on trips through Salt River Bay National Historical Park and Ecological Preserve, one of the island's most pristine areas. All tours run $45. **Virgin Kayak Tours** (⊠*Rte. 80, Cane Bay* ☎*340/778–0071* ⊕*www.kayakstcroix.com*) runs guided kayak trips through the Salt River and rents kayaks so you can tour around the Cane Bay area by yourself. All tours run $45. Kayak rentals are $15 an hour or $40 for the entire day.

SHOPPING

AREAS & MALLS

Although the shopping on St. Croix isn't as varied or extensive as that on St. Thomas, the island does have several small stores with unusual merchandise. In Christiansted the best shopping areas are the **Pan Am Pavilion** and **Caravelle Arcade,** off Strand Street, and along **King** and **Company streets.** These streets give way to arcades filled with boutiques. **Gallows Bay** has a blossoming shopping area in a quiet neighborhood. St. Croix shop hours are usually Monday through Saturday 9 to 5, but there are some shops in Christiansted open in the evening. Stores are often closed on Sunday.

The best shopping in Frederiksted is along **Strand Street** and in the side streets and alleyways that connect it with **King Street.** Most stores close Sunday except when a cruise ship is in port. One caveat: Frederiksted has a reputation for muggings, so for safety's sake stick to populated areas of Strand and King streets, where there are few—if any—problems.

SPECIALTY ITEMS

ART

Danica Art Gallery. Modern paintings by owner Danica David, as well as jewelry, pottery, and other works by various artists, fill this gallery. ⊠*54 Kings St., Christiansted* ☎*340/719–6000.*

BOOKS

Undercover Books. For Caribbean books or the latest good read, try this bookstore across from the post office in the Gallows Bay shopping area. ⊠*5030 Anchor Way, Gallows Bay* ☎*340/719–1567.*

CLOTHING

★ FodorsChoice **Coconut Vine.** Pop into this store at the start of your vacation, and you'll leave with enough comfy cotton or rayon batik men's and women's clothes to make you look like a local. Although the tropical designs and colors originated in Indonesia, they're perfect for the Caribbean. ⊠*1111 Strand St., Christiansted 00820* ☎*340/773–1991.*

From the Gecko. Come here for the hippest clothes on St. Croix, including superb hand-painted sarongs and other items. ⊠*1233 Queen Cross St., Christiansted* ☎*340/778–9433.*

Hot Heads. Hats, hats, and more hats perch on top of cotton shifts, comfortable shirts, and other tropical wear at this small store. If you forgot your bathing suit, this store has a good selection. ⊠*Kings Alley Walk, Christiansted* ☎*340/773–7888.*

Pacificotton. Round out your tropical wardrobe with something from this store. Shifts, tops, and pants in Caribbean colors as well as bags and hats fill the racks. ⊠*1110 Strand St., Christiansted* ☎*340/773–2125.*

Quiet Storm. With brands that include Fresh Produce, Tommy Bahama, Tori Richard, Roxy, and Quick Silver, shop here for upmarket resort wear and beach accessories. ⊠*1108 King St., Christiansted* ☎*340/773–7703.*

FOOD

If you've rented a condominium or a villa, you'll appreciate St. Croix's excellent stateside-style supermarkets. Fresh vegetables, fruits, and meats arrive frequently. Try the open-air stands strung out along Route 70 for island produce.

Cost-U-Less. This warehouse-type store is great for visitors because it doesn't charge a membership fee. It's east of Sunny Isle Shopping Center. ⊠*Rte. 70, Sunny Isle* ☎*340/719–4442.*

Plaza Extra. Shop here for Middle Eastern foods in addition to the usual grocery-store items. ⊠*United Shopping Plaza, Rte. 70, Sion Farm* ☎*340/778–6240* ⊠*Rte. 70, Mount Pleasant* ☎*340/719–1870.*

Pueblo. This stateside-style market has branches all over the island. ⊠*Orange Grove Shopping Center, Rte. 75, Christiansted* ☎*340/773–0118* ⊠*Villa La Reine Shopping Center, Rte. 75, La Reine* ☎*340/778–1272.*

Schooner Bay Market. Although it's on the smallish side, Schooner Bay has good-quality deli items. ⊠*Rte. 82, Mount Welcome* ☎*340/773–3232.*

GIFTS

Gone Tropical. Whether you're looking for inexpensive souvenirs or a special gift, you can probably find it here. On her travels about the world, Margo Meacham keeps her eye out for special delights for her shop—from tablecloths and napkins in bright Caribbean colors to carefully crafted wooden birds. ⊠*5 Company St., Christiansted* ☎*340/773–4696.*

Many Hands. Pottery in bright colors, paintings of St. Croix and the Caribbean, prints, and maps—all made by local artists—make perfect take-home gifts. If your purchase is too cumbersome to carry, the owners ship all over the world. ⊠*21 Pan Am Pavilion, Strand St., Christiansted* ☎*340/773–1990.*

Mitchell-Larsen Studio. Carefully crafted glass plates, suncatchers, and more grace the shelves of this interesting store. All made on-site by a St. Croix glassmaker, the pieces are often whimsically adorned with tropical fish, flora, and fauna. ⊠*58 Company St., Christiansted* ☎*340/719–1000.*

★ Fodor'sChoice **Royal Poinciana.** This attractive shop is filled with island seasonings and hot sauces, West Indian crafts, bath gels, and herbal teas. Shop here for tablecloths and paper goods in tropical brights. ⊠*1111 Strand St., Christiansted 00820* ☎*340/773–9892.*

Tesoro. The colors are bold and the merchandise eclectic at this crowded store. Shop for metal sculptures made from retired steel pans, mahogany bowls, and hand-painted place mats in bright tropical colors. ⊠*36C Strand St., Christiansted* ☎*340/773–1212.*

Tradewinds Shop. Whatever the wind blew in seems to land here. Glass sailboats glide across the shelves while metal fish sculptures swim nearby. Candles with tropical motifs, note cards, and costume jewelry jostle for space with Naot sandals. ⊠*53 King St., Christiansted* ☎*340/719–3918.*

HOUSEWARES

Designworks. If a mahogany armoire or cane-back rocker catches your fancy, the staff will arrange to have it shipped to your home at no charge from its mainland warehouse. Furniture aside, this store has one of the largest selections of local art, along with Caribbean-inspired bric-a-brac in all price ranges. ⊠*6 Company St., Christiansted* ☎*340/713–8102.*

JEWELRY

Crucian Gold. This store carries the unique gold creations of St. Croix native Brian Bishop. His trademark piece is the Turk's Head ring (a knot of interwoven gold strands), but the chess sets with Caribbean motifs as the playing pieces are just lovely. ⊠*1112 Strand St., Christiansted* ☎*340/773–5241.*

Gold Worker. In silver and gold, the handcrafted jewelry at this tiny store will remind you of the Caribbean. Hummingbirds dangle from silver chains, and sand dollars adorn gold necklaces. The sugar mills in silver and gold speak of St. Croix's past. ⊠*3 Company St., Christiansted* ☎*340/773–5167.*

ib Designs. This small shop showcases the handcrafted jewelry of local craftsman Whealan Massicott. In silver and gold, the designs are simply elegant. ⊠*Company St. at Queen Cross St., Christiansted* ☎*340/773–4322.*

Nelthropp and Low. Specializing in gold jewelry, this store also carries diamonds, emeralds, rubies, and sapphires. Jewelers will create one-of-a-kind pieces to your design. ⊠*1102 Strand St., Christiansted* ☎*340/773–0365 or 800/416–9078.*

Sonya's. Sonya Hough invented the hook bracelet, popular among locals as well as visitors. With hurricanes hitting the island so frequently, she has added an interesting decoration to these bracelets: the swirling symbol used in weather forecasts to indicate these storms. ✉*1 Company St., Christiansted* ☎*340/778–8605.*

LIQUOR & TOBACCO

Baci Duty Free Liquor and Tobacco. A walk-in humidor with a good selection of Arturo Fuente, Partagas, and Macanudo cigars is the centerpiece of this store, which also carries sleek Danish-made watches and Lladró figurines. ✉*1235 Queen Cross St., Christiansted* ☎*340/773–5040.*

Kmart. The two branches of this discount department store—a large one in the Sunshine Mall and a smaller one mid-island at Sunny Isle Shopping Center—carry a huge line of discounted, duty-free liquor. ✉*Sunshine Mall, Rte. 70, Frederiksted* ☎*340/692–5848* ✉*Sunny Isle Shopping Center, Rte. 70, Sunny Isle* ☎*340/719–9190.*

PERFUMES

Violette Boutique. Perfumes, cosmetics, and skin-care products are the draws here. ✉*Caravelle Arcade, 38 Strand St., Christiansted* ☎*340/773–2148.*

NIGHTLIFE & THE ARTS

The island's nightlife is ever-changing, and its arts scene is eclectic—ranging from Christmastime performances of *The Nutcracker* to any locally organized shows. Folk-art traditions, such as quadrille dancers, are making a comeback. To find out what's happening, pick up the local newspapers—*V. I. Daily News* and *St. Croix Avis*—available at newsstands. Christiansted has a lively and eminently casual club scene near the waterfront. Frederiksted has a couple of restaurants and clubs offering weekend entertainment.

NIGHTLIFE

Hotel on the Cay (✉*Protestant Cay, Christiansted* ☎*340/773–2035*) has a West Indian buffet on Tuesday nights in the winter season, when you can watch a broken-bottle dancer (a dancer who braves a carpet of shattered glass) and mocko jumbie characters. Although you can gamble at the island's only casino, it's the nightly music that draws big crowds to **Divi Carina Bay Casino** (✉*Rte. 60, Estate Turner Hole* ☎*340/773–9700*). **Moonraker** (✉*43A Queen Cross St., Christiansted* ☎*340/713–8025*) attracts a youthful crowd for DJ music on Wednesday through Saturday night.

Blue Moon (⊠*7 Strand St., Frederiksted* ☎*340/772–2222*), a waterfront restaurant, is the place to be for live jazz on Wednesday and Friday.

THE ARTS

Sunset Jazz (⊠*Waterfront, Frederiksted* ☎*340/277–0692*), has become the hot event in Frederiksted, drawing crowds of both visitors and locals at 6 PM on the third Friday of every month to watch the sun go down and hear good music.

The **Whim Plantation Museum** (⊠*Rte. 70, Estate Whim* ☎*340/772–0598*), outside of Frederiksted, hosts classical music concerts in winter.

ST. CROIX ESSENTIALS

To research prices, get advice from other travelers, and book travel arrangements, visit www.fodors.com.

TRANSPORTATION

BY AIR

While St. Croix is not as well served as St. Thomas when it comes with nonstop flights from the U.S., you will still be able to fly nonstop from Atlanta (on Delta) or Miami (on American Airlines). You can also get connecting service through San Juan or St. Thomas. Cape Air flies from San Juan and St. Thomas and offers code-share arrangements with all major airlines, so your luggage can transfer seamlessly. Seaborne Airlines flies between St. Thomas, St. Croix, and San Juan.

BY BOAT & FERRY

A ferry run by V.I. Sea Trans connects St. Thomas and St. Croix Friday through Monday. It leaves St. Thomas from the Charlotte Amalie Waterfront at 9:30 AM and 6:45 PM. Trips leave Gallows Bay, St. Croix, at 7:30 AM and 4:30 PM.

Information **V.I. SeaTrans** (☎*340/776-5494* ⊕*www.govisea trans.com).*

144 < **St. Croix**

BY BUS

Privately owned taxi vans crisscross St. Croix regularly,
providing reliable service between Frederiksted and Christiansted along Route 70. This inexpensive ($1.50 one-way)
mode of transportation is favored by locals, and though
the many stops on the 20-mi (32-km) drive between the
two main towns make the ride slow, it's never dull. Vitran public buses aren't the quickest way to get around the
island, but they're comfortable and affordable. The fare
is $1 between Christiansted and Frederiksted or to places
in between.

BY CAR

Unlike St. Thomas and St. John, where narrow roads wind
through hillsides, St. Croix is relatively flat, and it even
has a four-lane highway. The speed limit on the Melvin H.
Evans Highway is 55 mph (88 kph) and between 35 to 40
mph (55 to 65 kph) elsewhere. Roads are often unmarked,
so be patient—sometimes getting lost is half the fun. On
St. Croix, where the big HOVENSA refinery is located,
gas prices are much closer to what you might expect to
pay stateside.

CAR RENTALS

Atlas is outside Christiansted but provides pickups at
hotels. Avis is at Henry Rohlsen Airport and at the seaplane ramp in Christiansted. Budget has branches at the
airport, in the King Christian Hotel in Christiansted, and
at the Renaissance Carambola Beach Resort. Judi of Croix
delivers vehicles to your hotel. Midwest is outside Frederiksted but arranges pick-up at hotels. Olympic and Thrifty
are outside Christiansted but will pick up at hotels.

Information **Atlas** (☎340/773-2886 or 800/426-6009). **Avis**
(☎340/778-9355 ⊕www.avis.com). **Budget** (☎340/778-9636
⊕www.budgetstcroix.com). **Judi of Croix** (☎340/773-2123 or
877/903-2123 ⊕www.judiofcroix.com). **Midwest** (☎340/772-
0438 or 877/772-0438 ⊕www.midwestautorental.com). **Olympic**
(☎340/773-8000 or 888/878-4227 ⊕www.stcroixcarrentals.com).
Thrifty (☎340/773-7200 ⊕www.thrifty.com).

BY TAXI

Taxis, generally station wagons or minivans, are a phone
call away from most hotels and are available in downtown
Christiansted, at the Henry E. Rohlsen Airport, and at the
Frederiksted pier during cruise-ship arrivals. In Frederiksted all the shops are a short walk away, and you can swim

off the beach. Most ship passengers visit Christiansted on a tour; a taxi will cost $24 for one or two people.

Information **Antilles Taxi Service** (☎ 340/773–5020). **St. Croix Taxi Association** (☎ 340/778–1088).

CONTACTS & RESOURCES

BANKS
St. Croix has branches of Banco Popular in Orange Grove and Sunny Isle shopping centers. V.I. Community Bank is in Orange Grove Shopping Center and in downtown Christiansted. Scotia Bank has branches in Sunny Isle, Frederiksted, Christiansted, and Sunshine Mall.

EMERGENCIES
Coast Guard **Marine Safety Detachment** (☎ 340/772–5557). **Rescue Coordination Center** (☎ 787/289–2041 in San Juan, PR).

Emergency Services **Air Ambulance Network** (☎ 800/327–1966). **Ambulance and fire emergencies** (☎ 911). **Medical Air Services** (☎ 340/777–8580 or 800/643–9023). **Police emergencies** (☎ 911).

Hospitals **Gov. Juan F. Luis Hospital and Health Center** (✉ 6 Diamond Ruby, north of Sunny Isle Shopping Center on Rte. 79, Christiansted ☎ 340/778–6311). **Ingeborg Nesbitt Clinic** (✉ 516 Strand St., Frederiksted ☎ 340/772–0260).

Pharmacy **Kmart Pharmacy** (✉ Sunshine Mall, Cane Estate ☎ 340/692–2622).

Scuba-Diving Emergencies **Roy L. Schneider Hospital** (✉ Sugar Estate, St. Thomas ☎ 340/776–8311).

INTERNET, MAIL & SHIPPING
There are post offices at Christiansted, Frederiksted, Gallows Bay, and Sunny Isle on St. Croix. Postal rates are the same as if you were in the mainland United States, but Express Mail and Priority Mail aren't as quick. The FedEx office on St. Croix is in Peter's Rest Commercial Center; try to drop off your packages before 5:30 PM. On St. Croix, check your e-mail, make phone calls, and buy postage stamps at Surf the Net Internet Café in Christiansted. Rates run $5 for a half hour of Internet time.

Internet Cafes **Surf the Net** (✉ Pan Am Pavilion, 1102 Strand St., Christiansted, St. Croix ☎ 340/719–6245).

Shipping **FedEx** (✉ Peter's Rest Commercial Center, Rte. 708, Peter's Rest, St. Croix ☎ 800/463–3339).

SAFETY

Don't wander the streets of Christiansted or Frederiksted alone at night. If you plan to carry things around, rent a car—not an open-air vehicle—and lock possessions in the trunk. Keep your rental car locked wherever you park. Don't leave cameras, purses, and other valuables lying on the beach while you snorkel for an hour (or even for a minute).

TOUR OPTIONS

St. Croix Safari Tours offers van tours of St. Croix. Excursions depart from Christiansted and last about five hours. Costs run from $45 per person, including admission fees to attractions. St. Croix Transit offers van tours of St. Croix. Tours depart from Carambola Beach Resort, last about three hours, and cost from $45 per person plus admission fees to attractions.

Information **St. Croix Safari Tours** (☎340/773-6700 ⊕www. gotostcroix.com/safaritours). **St. Croix Transit** (☎340/772-3333).

WEDDINGS

Superior Court Offices **In St. Croix** (✍Box 929, Christiansted 00820 ☎340/778-9750).

Tortola

WORD OF MOUTH

"Tortola is such a great destination; it is one of my favorite islands. I did stay at Cane Garden Bay for few days...very cute hotels and a nice beach. The best was actually chartering a boat out of Tortola and being able to visit a different island every day."

—Sunshine_Lee

By Lynda Lohr

Once a sleepy backwater, Tortola is definitely busy these days, particularly when several cruise ships tie up at the Road Town dock. Passengers crowd the streets and shops, and open-air jitneys filled with cruise-ship passengers create bottlenecks on the island's byways. That said, most folks visit Tortola to relax on its deserted sands or linger over lunch at one of its many delightful restaurants. Beaches are never more than a few miles away, and the steep green hills that form Tortola's spine are fanned by gentle trade winds. The neighboring islands glimmer like emeralds in a sea of sapphire. It can be a world far removed from the hustle of modern life, but it simply doesn't compare to Virgin Gorda in terms of beautiful beaches—or even luxury resorts, for that matter.

Still a British colonial outpost, the island's economy depends on tourism and its offshore financial services businesses. With a population of around 19,000 people, most people work in those industries or for the local government. You'll hear lots of crisp British accents thanks to a large number of expats who call the island home, but the melodic West Indian accent still predominates.

Initially settled by Taino Indians, Tortola saw a string of visitors over the years. Christopher Columbus sailed by in 1493 on his second voyage to the new world, with Spain, Holland, and France making periodic visits about a century later. Sir Francis Drake arrived in 1595, leaving his name on the passage between Tortola and St. John. Pirates and buccaneers followed, with the British finally laying claim to the island in the late 1600s. In 1741, John Pickering became the first lieutenant governor of Tortola and the seat of the British government moved from Virgin Gorda to Tortola. As the agrarian economy continued to grow, slaves were imported from Africa. The slave trade was abolished in 1807, but slaves in Tortola and the rest of the BVI did not gain their freedom until August 1, 1834, when the Emancipation Proclamation was read at Sunday Morning Well in Road Town. That date is celebrated every year with the island's annual Carnival.

Visitors have a choice of accommodations, but most fall into the small and smaller still category. Only Long Bay Resort on Tortola's North Shore qualifies as a resort, but even some of the smaller properties add amenities occasionally add an amenity or two. A couple of new hotel projects are in the works, so look for more growth in the island's hotel industry over the next decade.

EXPLORING TORTOLA

Tortola doesn't have many historic sights, but it does have lots of beautiful natural scenery. Although you could explore the island's 10 square mi (26 square km) in a few hours, opting for such a whirlwind tour would be a mistake. There's no need to live in the fast lane when you're surrounded by some of the Caribbean's most breathtaking panoramas. Also, the roads are extraordinarily steep and twisting, making driving demanding. The best strategy is to explore a bit of the island at a time. For example, you might try Road Town (the island's tiny metropolis) one morning and a drive to Cane Garden Bay and West End (a little town on, of course, the island's west end) the next afternoon. Or consider a visit to East End, a *very* tiny town located exactly where its name suggests. The north shore is where all the best beaches are found.

ABOUT THE RESTAURANTS

Local seafood is plentiful on Tortola, and although other fresh ingredients are scarce, the island's chefs are a creative lot who apply their skills to whatever the boat delivers. Contemporary American dishes with Caribbean influences are very popular, but you can find French and Italian fare as well. The more expensive restaurants have dress codes: long pants and collared shirts for men and elegant but casual resort wear for women. Prices are often a bit higher than you'd expect to pay back home and the service can sometimes be a tad on the slow side, but enjoy the chance to linger over the view.

ABOUT THE HOTELS

Luxury on Tortola is more about a certain state of mind—serenity, seclusion, gentility, and a bit of Britain in the Caribbean—than about state-of-the-art amenities and fabulous facilities. Some properties, especially the vacation villas, are catching up with current trends, but others seem stuck in the 1980s. But don't let a bit of rust on the screen door or a chip in the paint on the balcony railing mar your appreciation of the ambience. You will likely spend most of your time outside, so the location, size, or price of a hotel should be more of a factor to you than the decor.

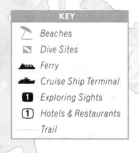

0 _____ 2 mi

0 _____ 2 km

The Chikuzen

Little Jost
Van Dyke

Green Cay

Jost Van Dyke

Little Harbour

Sandy Cay

A T L A N T I C   O C E A N

Rough Pt.

Shark Bay   Hell Hole

Brewers Bay
Pinnacle

Brewers
Bay

Brewers Bay

Mt. Healthy
10 **National Park**

Dubois Pt.

Skyworld

9 **22**

Todman Pk.

21

Cane Garden
Bay Rd.

Ridge Rd.

20

Joe's Hill Rd.

Cane Garden Bay **8**

Leonard's

Road
Town

Windy
Hill

Road Town

1 – **3**

Wickh

Carrot Bay

Apple Bay

Sage Mountain
National Park

7

Ridge Rd.

1 – **10**

see detail map

4

Dolphin
Discove

17

18

Sea Cows
Bay

Long Bay
West

Smuggler's
Cove

Lower
Belmont
Bay

15 **16**

Zion Hill Rd.

West
End

Mt. Sage

Sea Cows
Bay

19

Great Thatch
Island

Steele
Pt.

14

Soper's Hole

Freshwater
Pond

13 **12**

Little Thatch
Island

6

Soper's
Hole

Frenchman's
Cay

5 **11**

Fort Recovery

← TO
ST. THOMAS

ST. JOHN

KEY	
🏖	*Beaches*
🔷	*Dive Sites*
⛴	*Ferry*
🚢	*Cruise Ship Terminal*
1	*Exploring Sights*
①	*Hotels & Restaurants*
......	*Trail*

The Indians

NORMAN
ISLAND

Tortola

TO ANEGADA ↗

Wash
Ballock Pt.

Longman's
Pt.

Muskmellon
Bay

North
Bay

Great
Camanoe

Guana Island

White
Bay

Lee
Bay

Kitto
Ghut

Scrub
Island

Monkey Pt.

Little
Camanoe

Marina
Cay

Rogue's Pt.

Elizabeth
Beach
23

Long Bay,
Beef Island

Trellis
Bay

idge Rd.

Buta Mt.

Long Look

Parham
Town

East End

Beef Island
International
Airport
24
25

Bluff
Bay

Beef
Island

Mt. Belle-Vue

Long Swamp

Fat Hogs
Bay

Ft. Shirley

26

Buck
Island

TO →
VIRGIN GORDA

Road
Harbour

27

Paraquita
Bay

Sir Francis
Drake Channel

Alice in
Wonderland

Blonde Rock
Painted Walls
RMS Rhone

PETER ISLAND

Hotels
Fort Recovery Beach
Front Villas, **11**
Frenchman's Cay Hotel, **12**
Hodge's Creek
Marina Hotel, **26**
Lambert Beach Resort, **23**
Long Bay Beach Resort, **15**
Myett's, **20**
Nanny Cay Hotel, **19**
Sebastian's on the Beach, **16**
Sugar Mill Hotel, **17**
Surfsong Villa, **24**

Restaurants
Brandywine Bay, **27**
CalaMaya, **26**
Eclipse, **25**
Jolly Roger, **14**
Mountain View, **18**
Myett's, **20**
Palm Terrace, **15**
Pusser's Landing, **13**
Quito's Gazebo, **21**
Sebastian's Beach, **16**
Skyworld, **22**
Sugar Mill, **17**
Turtles, **23**

TORTOLA TOP 5

Charter a Boat: Tortola is a popular destination for boaters. Newcomers usually opt for a boat with captain and crew. Of course, you can take the wheel and help in the galley if you're so inclined.

Hit the Road: You'll get the real flavor of the still-rural island by heading out in whatever direction you choose. The views are dramatic, and the traffic is light enough to allow for easy driving.

Shop in Road Town: The island's largest community is also home to an eclectic collection of stores selling everything from made-on-

the-island arts and crafts to comfortable tropical wear by famous designers.

Hit the Trail: Tortola is home to Sage Mountain National Park, a small but quite nice nature reserve. It's home to several rare and endangered species as well as some trees that normally grow only in rain forests.

Get Wet: Dive trips to spectacular locations leave from Tortola. If you're not certified to dive, an introductory course can teach you the basics and whet your appetite for more adventures under the sea.

Hotels in Road Town don't have beaches, but they do have pools and are within walking distance of restaurants, bars, and shops. Accommodations outside Road Town are relatively isolated, but most face the ocean. Tortola resorts are intimate—only a handful have more than 50 rooms. Guests are treated as more than just room numbers, and many return year after year. This can make booking a room at popular resorts difficult, even off-season, despite the fact that more than half the island's visitors stay aboard their own or chartered boats.

A few hotels lack air-conditioning, relying instead on ceiling fans to capture the almost constant trade winds. Nights are cool and breezy, even in midsummer, and never reach the temperatures or humidity levels that are common in much of the United States. You may assume that all accommodations listed here have air-conditioning unless we mention otherwise. Remember that some places may be closed during the peak of hurricane season—August through October—to give their owners a much-needed break.

WHAT IT COSTS IN DOLLARS				
$$$$	**$$$**	**$$**	**$**	**¢**
RESTAURANTS				
OVER $30	$20–$30	$12–$20	$8–$12	UNDER $8
HOTELS				
* OVER $350	$250–$350	$150–$250	$80–$150	UNDER $80
** OVER $450	$350–$450	$250–$350	$125–$250	UNDER $125

*EP, BP, CP; **AI, FAP, MAP; Restaurant prices are for a main course at dinner, excluding 10% service charge. Hotel prices are for two people in a double room during high season, excluding 7% BVI tax, 10% service charge, and meal plans (except for all-inclusives).

TIMING

Tortola celebrates Carnival on and around August 1 to mark the anniversary of the end of slavery in 1834. A slew of activities culminating with a parade through the streets take place in Road Town. Hotels fill up fast, so make sure to reserve your room and rental car rental well in advance.

ROAD TOWN

Numbers in the margin correspond to points of interest on the Road Town map.

The bustling capital of the BVI looks out over Road Harbour. It takes only an hour or so to stroll down Main Street and along the waterfront, checking out the traditional West Indian buildings painted in pastel colors and with corrugated-tin roofs, bright shutters, and delicate fretwork trim. For sightseeing brochures and the latest information on everything from taxi rates to ferry schedules, stop in the BVI Tourist Board office. Or just choose a seat on one of the benches in Sir Olva Georges Square, on Waterfront Drive, and watch the people come and go from the ferry dock and customs office across the street.

WHAT TO SEE

❸ **Fort Burt.** The most intact historic ruin on Tortola was built by the Dutch in the early 17th century to safeguard Road Harbour. It sits on a hill at the western edge of Road Town and is now the site of a small hotel and restaurant. The

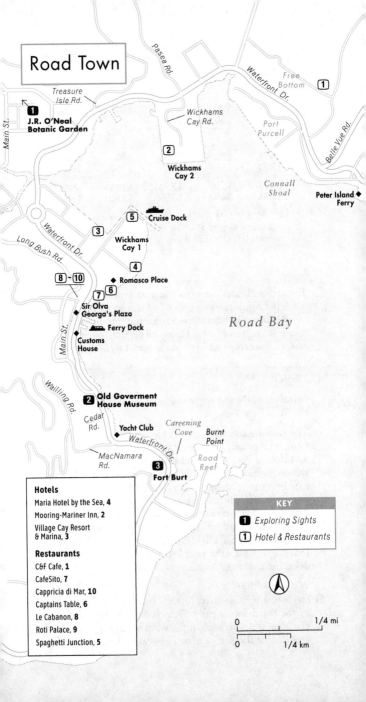

Road Town

Treasure Isle Rd.

Pasea Rd.

Waterfront Dr.

Free Bottom

1

Main St.

1
J.R. O'Neal Botanic Garden

Wickhams Cay Rd.

Port Purcell

Belle Vue Rd.

2
Wickhams Cay 2

Connall Shoal

Peter Island ◆ Ferry

Waterfront Dr.

Long Bush Rd.

5 ⛴ **Cruise Dock**

3

Wickhams Cay 1

4

8 – **10**

◆ **Romasco Place**

7 **6**

◆ **Sir Olva Georga's Plaza**

Road Bay

Main St.

🚢 **Ferry Dock**

◆ **Customs House**

Wailling Rd.

2 **Old Goverment House Museum**

Cedar Rd.

◆ **Yacht Club**

Careening Cove

Burnt Point

MacNamara Rd.

Waterfront Dr.

Road Reef

3 **Fort Burt**

Hotels
Maria Hotel by the Sea, **4**

Mooring-Mariner Inn, **2**

Village Cay Resort & Marina, **3**

Restaurants
C&F Cafe, **1**

CafeSito, **7**

Cappricia di Mar, **10**

Captains Table, **6**

Le Cabanon, **8**

Roti Palace, **9**

Spaghetti Junction, **5**

KEY

1 *Exploring Sights*

1 *Hotel & Restaurants*

0 _____ 1/4 mi

0 _____ 1/4 km

CLOSE UP

Ferry Confusion

The ferry situation is mindboggling for newcomers to the British Virgin Islands. Ferries depart from Road Town, West End, and Beef Island, so make sure you get to the right place at the correct time. Sometimes boats bound for Jost Van Dyke, Virgin Gorda, Anegada, St. Thomas, and St. John depart minutes apart, other times the schedule is skimpy. Departures can be suddenly canceled, particularly in the summer season. Sometimes ferries make stops not on the schedule. To avoid being stranded, call in the morning to make sure the ferry you want is actually going that day.

4

foundations and magazine remain, and the structure offers a commanding view of the harbor. ⊠ *Waterfront Dr., Road Town* ☎*No phone* ☑*Free* ⊙*Daily dawn–dusk.*

❶ **J. R. O'Neal Botanic Gardens.** Take a walk through this 4-
★ acre showcase of lush plant life. There are sections devoted to prickly cacti and succulents, hothouses for ferns and orchids, gardens of medicinal herbs, and plants and trees indigenous to the seashore. From the tourist office in Road Town, cross Waterfront Drive and walk one block over to Main Street and turn right. Keep walking until you see the high school. The gardens are on your left. ⊠*Botanic Station, Road Town* ☎*284/494–3904* ☑*$3* ⊙*Mon.–Sat. 9–4:30.*

❷ **Old Government House Museum.** The seat of government
★ until 1987, this gracious building now displays a nice collection of items from Tortola's past. The rooms are filled with period furniture, hand-painted china, books signed by Queen Elizabeth II on her 1966 and 1977 visits, and numerous items reflecting Tortola's seafaring legacy. ⊠ *Waterfront Dr., Road Town* ☎*284/494–3701* ☑*Free* ⊙*Weekdays 8:30–4:30.*

AROUND THE ISLAND

Other than spectacular views and some beautiful beaches, Tortola has few must-see attractions. That said, you came to relax, read in the hammock and spend hours at dinner, not to dash madly around the island ticking yet another site off your list. Except for the Dolphin Discovery, where advance

No Parking

CLOSE UP

Road Town's traffic and parking can be horrific. Try to avoid driving along the Waterfront Drive at morning and afternoon rush hours. It's longer, but often quicker, to take a route through the hills above Road Town. (You'll also be treated to some lovely views along the way.) Parking can be very difficult in Road Town, particularly during the busy winter season. There's parking along the waterfront and on the inland side on the eastern end of downtown, but if you're planning a day of shopping, go early to make sure you get a parking space.

booking is recommended, the others are best seen when you stumble upon them on your round-the-island drive.

Numbers in the margin correspond to points of interest on the Tortola map.

WHAT TO SEE

⑧ **Cane Garden Bay.** Once a sleepy village, Cane Garden Bay is growing into one of Tortola's most important destinations. Stay here at a small hotel or guesthouse or stop by for lunch, dinner, or drinks at a seaside restaurant. You can find a few small stores selling clothing and basics like suntan lotion, and, of course, one of Tortola's most popular beaches is at your feet. The roads in and out of this area are dauntingly steep, so use caution when driving.

④ **Dolphin Discovery.** Get up close and personal with dolphins as they swim in a spacious seaside pen. There are two different programs that provide a range of experiences. In the Royal Swim, dolphins tow participants around the pen. The less expensive Encounter allows you to touch the dolphins. ⊠*Prospect Reef Resort, Road Town* ☎*284/494–7675* ⊕*www.dolphindiscovery.com* ☜*Royal Swim $139, Encounter $79* ⊙*Daily, by appointment only.*

⑤ **Fort Recovery.** The unrestored ruins of a 17th-century Dutch fort sit amid a profusion of tropical greenery on the grounds of Villas of Fort Recovery Estates. There's not much to see here, and there are no guided tours, but you're welcome to stop by and poke around. ⊠*Waterfront Dr., Road Town* ☎*284/485–4467* ☜*Free.*

⑩ **Mount Healthy National Park.** The remains of an 18th-century sugar plantation can be seen here. The windmill structure has been restored, and you can see the ruins of a mill, a factory with boiling houses, storage areas, stables, a hospital, and many dwellings. It's a nice place to picnic. ⊠*Ridge Rd., Todman Peak* ☎*No phone* ⊕*www.bvinationalparkstrust.org* ᴢ*Free* ⊙*Daily dawn–dusk.*

❼ **Sage Mountain National Park.** At 1,716 feet, Sage Mountain
★ is the highest peak in the BVI. From the parking area, a trail leads you in a loop not only to the peak itself (and extraordinary views) but also to a small rain forest that is sometimes shrouded in mist. Most of the forest was cut down over the centuries to clear land for sugarcane, cotton, and other crops; to create pastureland; or simply to utilize the stands of timber. In 1964 this park was established to preserve what remained. Up here you can see mahogany trees, white cedars, mountain guavas, elephant-ear vines, mamey trees, and giant bullet woods, to say nothing of such birds as mountain doves and thrushes. Take a taxi from Road Town or drive up Joe's Hill Road and make a left onto Ridge Road toward Chalwell and Doty villages. The road dead-ends at the park. ⊠*Ridge Rd., Sage Mountain* ☎*284/494–3904* ⊕*www.bvinationalparkstrust.org* ᴢ*$3* ⊙*Daily dawn–dusk.*

❾ **Skyworld.** Drive up here and climb the observation tower
★ for a stunning 360-degree view of numerous islands and cays. On a clear day you can even see St. Croix (40 mi [64½ km] away) and Anegada (20 mi [32 km] away). ⊠*Ridge Rd., Joe's Hill* ☎*No phone* ᴢ*Free.*

❻ **Soper's Hole.** On this little island connected by a causeway to Tortola's western end, you can find a marina and a captivating complex of pastel West Indian–style buildings with shady balconies, shuttered windows, and gingerbread trim that house art galleries, boutiques, and restaurants. Pusser's Landing is a lively place to stop for a cold drink (many are made with Pusser's famous rum) and a sandwich and to watch the boats in harbor.

WHERE TO EAT

Restaurants are scattered from one end of the island to another, so you're never far from a good meal. Cane Garden Bay, with a handful of restaurants along the beach, is a popular dining destination. Eateries in Road Town are a short stroll from each other, making it easy to find a place that pleases everyone. Most hotels have restaurants that welcome nonguests.

ROAD TOWN

CARIBBEAN

$$–$$$$ ✕**C&F Restaurant.** Crowds head to this casual spot for the best barbecue in town (chicken, fish, and ribs), fresh local fish and lobster, and excellent curries. Sometimes there's a wait for a table, but it's worth it. The restaurant is just outside Road Town, on a side street past the Moorings. ⊠*Off Canaan Rd., Purcell Estate* ☎*284/494–4941* ⌸*Reservations not accepted* ⊟*AE, D, MC, V* ⊘*No lunch.*

$–$$$ ✕**Roti Palace.** You might be tempted to pass this tiny spot
★ on Road Town's Main Street when you see the plastic tablecloths and fake flowers, but owner Jean Leonard's reputation for dishing up fantastic roti is known far and wide. This flatbread is filled with curried potatoes, onions and lobster, chicken, beef, conch, goat, or vegetables. Ask for the bone out if you order the chicken to save yourself the trouble of fishing them out of your mouth. ⊠*Main St., Road Town* ☎*284/494–4196* ⊟*No credit cards* ⊘*Closed Sun.*

ECLECTIC

$$–$$$ ✕**CafeSito.** Don't be put off by the pedestrian decor. The chef at this shopping-center spot conjures up delicious dishes that run the gamut from burgers to lobster to chicken alfredo. It's the place to go for pizza smothered with everything from the standard cheese and tomato to the more unusual chicken and bacon. In winter, the staff will deliver anything from its menu straight to your hotel. ⊠*Wickham's Cay I, Waterfront Dr.* ☎*284/494–7412* ⊟*MC, V.*

FRENCH

$$$–$$$$ ✕**Le Cabanon.** Birds and bougainvillea brighten the patio of this breezy French restaurant and bar, a popular gathering spot for locals and visitors alike. French onion soup and herring salad are good appetizer choices. From there, move on to the grilled tuna with foie gras, monkfish in rosemary sauce, or beef tenderloin with green peppercorn sauce. Save room for such tasty desserts as chocolate cake and crème brûlée, or opt for a platter of French cheeses. ⊠*Waterfront Dr.* ☎*284/494–8660* ⊟*D, MC, V* ⊘*Closed Sun.*

ITALIAN

$–$$ ×**Capriccio di Mare.** The owners of the well-known Bran-
★ dywine Bay restaurant also run this authentic Italian outdoor café. Stop by for an espresso, fresh pastry, a bowl of
perfectly cooked penne, or a crispy tomato and mozzarella
pizza. Drink specialties include a mango Bellini, an adapta-
tion of the famous cocktail served at Harry's Bar in Ven-
ice. ⊠*Waterfront Dr.* ☎*284/494–5369* ⚓*Reservations not
accepted* ▤*MC, V* ⊘*Closed Sun.*

$–$$ ×**Spaghetti Junction.** Popular with the boating crowd,
★ this longtime favorite serves up such West Indian dishes
as stewed oxtail along with Italian favorites like penne
smothered in a spicy tomato sauce, spinach-mushroom
lasagna, and angel-hair pasta with shellfish. For something
that combines a bit of both, try the spicy jambalaya pasta.
You can also find old-fashioned favorites like lobster ther-
midor on the menu. ⊠*Blackburn Hwy., Baughers Bay*
☎*284/494–4880* ▤*AE, MC, V* ⊘*Closed Sun.*

SEAFOOD

$$–$$$ ×**The Captain's Table.** Select the lobster you want from the
pool, but be careful not to fall in—it's in the floor right in
the middle of the dining room. The menu also includes
traditional conch fritters, steak with red wine sauce, duck-
ling with a mango chutney sauce, and creative daily specials that usually include freshly caught fish. Ceiling fans
keep the dining room cool, but there are also tables on a
breezy terrace overlooking the harbor. ⊠*Wickham's Cay I*
☎*284/494–3885* ▤*MC, V* ⊘*No lunch Sat.*

OUTSIDE ROAD TOWN

AMERICAN–CASUAL

$$$ ×**Pusser's Landing.** Yachters navigate their way to this
☾ waterfront restaurant. Downstairs, from late morning
to well into the evening, you can belly up to the outdoor
mahogany bar or sit downstairs for sandwiches, fish-and-
chips, and pizzas. At dinnertime head upstairs for a harbor
view and a quiet alfresco meal of grilled steak or local fish.
⊠*Soper's Hole* ☎*284/495–4554* ▤*AE, MC, V.*

CARIBBEAN

$$–$$$$ ×**Myett's Garden & Grille.** Right on the beach, this bi-level
restaurant and bar is hopping day and night. Chowder
made with fresh conch is the specialty here, although the
menu includes everything from vegetarian dishes to grilled
shrimp, steak, and tuna. There's live entertainment every

night in winter. ⊠*Cane Garden Bay* ☎*284/495–9649* ⊟*AE, MC, V.*

$$–$$$$ ✕**Quito's Gazebo.** This rustic beachside bar and restaurant is owned and operated by island native Quito Rymer, a multitalented recording star who plays and sings solo on Tuesday and Thursday and performs with his reggae band on Friday and Saturday. The menu is Caribbean, with an emphasis on fresh fish. Try the conch fritters or the chicken roti. ⊠*Cane Garden Bay* ☎*284/495–4837* ⊟*AE, MC, V* ⊘*Closed Mon.*

CONTINENTAL

$$$–$$$$ ✕**Skyworld.** The top of a mountain is the location for this casually elegant dining room. The menu changes constantly, but look for imaginative dishes such as New York strip steak with a brandy and mustard sauce and grilled yellowfin tuna with a pineapple-mango glaze. Other specialties include grilled local fish, roast duck, rack of lamb, and key lime pie. The lunch menu runs to hamburgers and sandwiches with some interesting additions such as a goat cheese tartlet. The restaurant can be crowded at midday when cruise ships dock. ⊠*Ridge Rd., Joe's Hill* ☎*284/494–3567* ⊟*AE, D, DC, MC, V.*

$$$ ✕**Palm Terrace Garden Restaurant.** Relax over dinner in this open-air eatery at Long Bay Beach Resort. Tables are well spaced, offering enough privacy for intimate conversations. The menu changes daily, but several dishes show up regularly. Start your meal with cheese ravioli with wild mushrooms in a garlic cream sauce, Caribbean-style fish and potato chowder, and shrimp cocktail. Entrées include snapper crusted with cornmeal, pan-seared tuna with a mango-caper coulis, and T-bone steak seasoned with peppercorns. There are always at least five desserts to choose from, which might include Belgian chocolate mousse, strawberry cheesecake, or a fluffy lemon and coconut cake. ⊠*Long Bay Beach Resort, Long Bay* ☎*284/495–4252* ⊟*AE, D, MC, V* ⊘*No lunch.*

ECELCTIC

$$$–$$$$ ✕**Eclipse.** This popular waterfront spot isn't much more ★ than a terrace filled with tables, but you can be caressed by the soft ocean breezes while you're impressed with the cuisine. With dishes from all over the globe, the menu is certainly well traveled. The garden lounge serves lighter fare—try the coconut shrimp, the seafood linguine, or maybe a slice or two of freshly baked pizza. In the main dining room, you can find dishes like filet mignon with a

spicy wasabi sauce and chicken with a Parmesan cheese and marsala wine sauce, and tuna dusted with seaweed, soy, and ginger. ⊠*Fat Hog's Bay, East End* ☎*284/495–1646* ▭*MC, V* ⊘*No lunch.*

★ Fodor'sChoice✕**Sugar Mill Restaurant.** Candles gleam, and the background music is peaceful in this romantic restaurant inside a 17th-century sugar mill. Well-prepared selections on the à la carte menu, which changes nightly, include some pasta and vegetarian entrées. Lobster bisque with basil croutons and a creamy conch chowder are good starters. Favorite entrées include fresh fish baked in banana leaves, filet mignon topped with an herb-cream sauce, pan-roasted quail, and pumpkin and black bean lasagna. ⊠*Sugar Mill Hotel, Apple Bay* ☎*284/495–4355* ▭*AE, MC, V* ⊘*No lunch.*

$$$–$$$$

$$–$$$$ ✕**Jolly Roger Restaurant.** This casual, open-air restaurant near the ferry terminal is as popular with locals as it is with visitors. The menu ranges from burgers to rib-eye steak to the island favorite, local lobster. Try the savory fritters filled with tender local conch and herbs for a good start to your dinner. End it with a slice of sweet key lime pie. ⊠*West End* ☎*284/495–4559* ▭*D, MC, V.*

★ Fodor'sChoice✕**Mountain View.** It's worth the drive up Sage Mountain for lunch or dinner at this casual restaurant. The view is spectacular—one of the best on Tortola. The small menu includes dishes like veal with a ginger sauce and grilled mahimahi in a lime-onion sauce. The lobster salad sandwich is the house lunch specialty. If it's on the menu, don't pass up the chicken roti. ⊠*Sage Mountain* ☎*284/495–9536* ▭*MC, V.*

$$–$$$$

$$–$$$$ ✕**Sebastian's Beach Bar & Restaurant.** The waves practically lap at your feet at this beachfront restaurant on Tortola's northern shore. The menu runs to seafood—especially lobster, conch, and local fish—but you can also find dishes like ginger chicken and filet mignon. It's a perfect spot to stop for lunch on your around-the-island tour. Try the grilled dolphinfish sandwich, served on a soft roll with an oniony tartar sauce. Finish off with a cup of Sebastian's coffee spiked with home-brewed rum. ⊠*North Coast Rd., Apple Bay* ☎*284/494–4212* ▭*AE, D, MC, V.*

$$$ ✕**CalaMaya.** Casual fare is what you can find at this waterfront restaurant. You can always order a burger or lobster salad; the grilled Kaiser sandwich—shrimp, cheese, and pineapple on a crisp roll—is a tasty alternative. For dinner, try the snapper with onions, peppers, and thyme.

4

✉ *Hodge's Creek Marina, Blackburn Hwy.* ☎ *284/495–2126* ⊟ *AE, MC, V.*

$$$ ✕ **Turtles.** If you're touring the island, Turtles is a good place to stop for lunch or dinner. Sitting near the ocean at Lambert Beach Resort, this casual place provides a relaxing respite from the rigors of navigating mountain roads. At dinner you might find tiger shrimp in a curry sauce or rack of lamb with a raspberry glaze. Lunch favorites include fried shrimp, fresh tuna on a bun, and pasta dishes. ✉ *Lambert Beach Resort, Lambert Bay, East End* ☎ *284/495–2877* ⊟ *AE, D, MC, V.*

ITALIAN

★ **Fodor's**Choice ✕ **Brandywine Bay.** At this restaurant in Bran-
$$$$ dywine Bay, candlelit outdoor tables have sweeping views of neighboring islands. Owner Davide Pugliese prepares foods the Tuscan way: grilled with lots of fresh herbs. The remarkable menu may include duck with a berry sauce, beef carpaccio, grilled swordfish, and veal chop with ricotta and sun-dried tomatoes. The homemade mozzarella is another standout. The wine list is excellent, and the lemon tart and the tiramisu are irresistible. ✉ *Sir Francis Drake Hwy., east of Road Town, Brandywine Bay* ☎ *284/495–2301* ⚓ *Reservations essential* ⊟ *AE, MC, V* ⊙ *Closed Sun. No lunch.*

WHERE TO STAY

A stay at any one of the hotels and guesthouses on Tortola's north side will put you closer to the beach, but not to worry: it doesn't take that long to get from one side of the island to the other. Visitors who want to be closer to Road Town's restaurants and shops can find a handful of places in and around the island's main town.

HOTELS & INNS

ROAD TOWN

$$–$$$ ⌂ **Moorings-Mariner Inn.** If you enjoy the camaraderie of a busy marina, this inn on the edge of Road Town may appeal to you. It's a hot spot for charter boaters—usually a lively group—heading out for weeklong sails around the islands. Rooms are spacious and have balconies or porches that are perfect for an afternoon's relaxing. All have pastel accents that complement the peach exteriors. Pros: good dining options, friendly guests, excellent spot to charter boats. Cons: busy location, long walk to Road Town, need

American or British?

CLOSE UP

Yes, the Union Jack flutters overhead in the tropical breeze, schools operate on the British system, place names have British spellings, Queen Elizabeth II appoints the governor—and the queen's picture hangs on many walls. Indeed, residents celebrate the queen's birthday every June with a public ceremony. You can overhear that charming English accent from a good handful of expats when you're lunching at Road Town restaurants, and you can buy British biscuits—which Americans call cookies—in the supermarkets.

But you can pay for your lunch and the biscuits with American money, because the U.S. dollar is legal tender here. The unusual circumstance is a matter of geography. The practice started in the mid-20th century, when BVI residents went to work in the nearby USVI. On trips home, they brought their U.S. dollars with them. Soon, they abandoned the barter system, and in 1959, the U.S. dollar became the official form of money. Interestingly, the government sells stamps for use only in the BVI that often carry pictures of Queen Elizabeth II and other royalty with the monetary value in U.S. dollars and cents.

The American influence continued to grow when Americans began to open businesses in the BVI because they preferred its quieter ambience to the hustle and bustle of St. Thomas. Inevitably, cable and satellite TV's U.S.–based programming, along with Hollywood-made movies, further influenced life in the BVI. And most goods are shipped from St. Thomas in the USVI, meaning you can find more American-made Oreos than British-produced Peak Freens on the supermarket shelves.

car to get around ⊠*Waterfront Dr., Box 139, VG1110* ☎*284/494–2333 or 800/535–7289* 🖷*284/494–2226* 🖘*36 rooms, 4 suites* ⚒*In-room: kitchen (some), refrigerator, dial-up. In-hotel: restaurant, bar, pool, diving, no elevator, public Internet* ☐*MC, V* ⊙*EP.*

$$ 🗹 **Maria's Hotel by the Sea.** Sitting near the water in busy Road Town, Maria's Hotel by the Sea is perfect for budget travelers who want to be near shops and restaurants but who don't need many frills. The least expensive rooms don't have ocean views, but all have bright tropical fabrics and rattan furniture to remind you that you're on an island. Pros: good location, spacious rooms, walk to shops and restaurants. Cons: busy street, little parking, need

car to get around. ✉ *Waterfront Dr., Box 2364, VG1110* ☎*284/494–2595* 🖷*284/494–2420* ⊕*www.mariasbythesea. com* 🖙*41 rooms* ⚐*In-room: refrigerator, dial-up. In-hotel: restaurant, bar, pool, public Wi-Fi* ☰*AE, MC, V* ❏*EP.*

$$ 🏨**Village Cay Resort & Marina.** If you want to be able to walk to restaurants and shops, you simply can't beat the prime location in the heart of Road Town. It's perfect for charter-yachters who want a night or two in town before heading out to sea, but land-based vacationers like it equally well. Rooms and suites are done in tropical style with tile floors, rattan furniture, and town or marina views. You'll need a car to get to the beach. Otherwise, a tiny pool will have to suffice for your morning swim. Pros: good location, shops and restaurants nearby, nautical ambience. Cons: little parking, busy street, need car to get around. ✉ *Wickham's Cay I, Box 145, VG1110* ☎*284/494–2771* 🖷*284/494–2773* ⊕*www.villagecay.com* 🖙*21 rooms* ⚐*In-room: refrigerator, Ethernet. In-hotel: restaurant, bar, pool, spa, no elevator, public Internet, public Wi-Fi* ☰*AE, MC, V* ❏*EP.*

OUTSIDE ROAD TOWN

$$$$ 🏨**Frenchman's Cay Hotel.** Tucked away down a narrow road near busy Soper's Hole, Frenchman's Cay provides a quiet oasis for folks who want the option of eating in or out and a bit more space than you'd find in a typical hotel room. All accommodations are villa style, with separate bedrooms and kitchens. We like this place for its get-away-from-it-all feel. That said, you can easily walk to Soper's Hole to expand your dining horizons and to do some shopping. At this writing, the rooms were all getting a makeover. Pros: varied activities, secluded location, walk to shops and restaurants. Cons: small beach, need car to get around. ✉*Frenchman's Cay, Box 1054, West End VG1130* ☎*284/495–4844 or 800/235–4077* 🖷*284/495–4056* ⊕*www.frenchmans.com* 🖙*9 villas* ⚐*In-room: kitchen, no TV. In-hotel: restaurant, bar, tennis court, pool, beachfront, water sports, no elevator* ☰*AE, D, MC, V* ❏*EP.*

★ **Fodor'sChoice** 🏨**Sugar Mill Hotel.** Though it's not a sprawling
$$$$ resort, this is our favorite resort on Tortola. The rooms are attractively decorated with more than the usual floral spreads and have balconies with good views, kitchens or kitchenettes, and even some sofa beds. The grounds get accolades for their lovely gardens, but many say the real reason to stay here is the easy access to the excellent restaurant, which has both superb food and a stunning setting in

the property's old sugar mill. The owners, food and travel writers Jeff and Jinx Morgan, have brought all their expertise to this well-run small resort. The north-shore location puts you across the road from a nice beach, but you need a car to do anything more than enjoy the sun and sand. Pros: lovely rooms, excellent restaurant, nice views. Cons: on busy road, small beach, need car to get around ⊠*Apple Bay* ✆*Box 425, Road Town VG1130* ☎*284/495–4355 or 800/462–8834* 🖷*284/495–4696* ⊕*www.sugarmillhotel. com* ⇆*19 rooms, 2 suites, 1 villa, 1 cottage* ⌂*In-room: safe, kitchen (some), no TV (some), Wi-Fi. In-hotel: 2 restaurants, bars, pool, beachfront, water sports, no elevator, public Internet* ═*AE, MC, V* ⊨*EP.*

★ Fodor'sChoice ⛯ **Surfsong Villa Resort.** Nested in lush foliage
$$$$ right at the water's edge, this small resort on Beef Island provides a pleasant respite for vacationers who want a villa atmosphere with some hotel amenities. The hotel has a chef who whips up meals for an extra charge. A studio villa with minimal kitchen facilities is tucked up in the trees, but the one- and two-bedroom villa are right at the water's edge. It takes about a minute to walk to Sandy Well Bay Beach. Wood furniture and attractive tile floors provide a comfortable ambience. The public spaces are equally cozy, with pergolas providing shade. Service such as massage as well as yoga and Pilates classes are available. Pros: lovely rooms, beautiful beach, chef on call. Cons: need a car to get around, no restaurants nearby. ⊠*Beef Island* ✆*Box 606, Road Town VG1110* ☎*284/495–1864* 🖷*284/495–0089* ⊕*www.surfsong.net* ⇆*1 suite, 3 villas* ⌂*In-room: no a/c (some,) safes, gym, kitchen, DVD, Ethernet. In-hotel: beachfront, water sports, bicycles, no elevator, laundry service, concierge, public Internet, public Wi-Fi, airport shuttle, no children under 8* ═*MC, V* ⊨*EP.*

$$$–$$$$ ⛯**Fort Recovery Beachfront Villas.** This is one of those small
☾ but special properties, distinguished by friendly service
★ and the chance to get to know your fellow guests rather than the poshness of the rooms and the upscale amenities. Villas come in several sizes, and all are quaint—though not fancy—and have good views across the water toward St. John. A sandy beach stretches seaside, providing calm waters perfect for kids. The emphasis on wellness is a welcome touch, and beachside yoga classes are a specialty. The staff is helpful and will arrange day sails and scuba-diving trips. Pros: beautiful beach, spacious units, historic site. Cons: need car to get around, isolated location. ⊠*Waterfront Dr., Box 239, Pockwood Pond VG1110* ☎*284/495–4354*

or 800/367–8455 ≈284/495–4036 ⊕www.fortrecovery. com ⟿29 suites, 1 villa ⌂In-room: kitchen, dial-up, Wi-Fi. In-hotel: pool, gym, beachfront, water sports, no elevator, laundry service, public Internet ⊟AE, MC, V ⊚EP.

$$$–$$$$ 🏨 **Long Bay Beach Resort.** Although the service draws an occasional complaint, the management has been addressing the frosty attitude of some staff members. Long Bay Beach Resort is still Tortola's only choice if you want all the resort amenities, including a beach, scads of water sports, tennis courts, and even a pitch-and-putt golf course. Accommodations range from traditional hotel rooms to three-bedroom villas, with lots of choices in between. All have a modern tropical feel with rattan furniture and brightly colored fabrics. Given its relative isolation on the northwest shore, you may not be inclined to make many excursions. Luckily, the Palm Terrace Garden Restaurant serves romantic dinners. Pros: resort atmosphere, good restaurants, many activities. Cons: need car to get around, sometimes curt staff, uphill hike to some rooms. ⊠*Long Bay ⌖Box 433, Road Town VG1130 ≈284/495–4252 or 800/345–0271 ≈284/495–4677 ⊕www.longbay.com ⟿53 rooms, 37 suites, 26 villas ⌂In-room: safe, kitchen (some), dial-up. In-hotel: 3 restaurants, bars, tennis courts, pool, gym, spa, beachfront, diving, water sports, no elevator, public Internet, public Wi-Fi ⊟AE, MC, V ⊚EP.*

$$–$$$ 🏨 **Lambert Beach Resort.** Although this isolated location on the northeast coast puts you far from Road Town, Lambert Bay is one of the island's loveliest stretches of sand and the main reason to recommend this resort. Rooms are tucked back in the foliage, but you're a few steps away from an afternoon of sunning and swimming. A handful of restaurants in and around nearby Fat Hogs Bay are within easy reach if you have to get off that gorgeous beach. At this writing, construction was set to begin on a complete renovation. Ask about their progress if you fear construction noise will be a problem. Pros: lovely beach, beautiful setting, good restaurant. Cons: bland rooms, isolated location, need car to get around. ⊠*Lambert Bay, Box 534, East End VG1120 ≈284/495–2877 ≈284/495–2876 ⊕www.lambertresort.com ⟿38 rooms, 2 villas, 27 condos ⌂In-room: kitchen (some), refrigerator, dial-up (some). In-hotel: restaurant, bar, tennis court, pool, spa, beachfront, water sports, no elevator, public Internet ⊟AE, D, MC, V ⊚EP.*

$$ 🏨 **Hodge's Creek Marina Hotel.** Sitting marina-side on the island's East End, this hotel puts you in the middle of the

nautical action. If you're heading out on a chartered sail-boat or if you especially enjoy the marine scene, this is defi-nitely the place for you. Rooms are carpeted and have tiny balconies, but brightly colored spreads and curtains give them a tropical feel. There's a small pool and the CalaMaya Restaurant in the complex. Pros: marina atmosphere, good restaurant, some shopping. Cons: bland rooms, need car to get around. ⊠*Hodge's Creek* ⌖*Box 663, Road Town VG1110* ☎*284/494–5000* ⊟*284/494–7676* ⊕*www.hodg-escreek.com* ⥽*24 rooms* ⌂*In-hotel: restaurant, pool, no elevator, public Internet* ⊟*AE, MC, V* ⦿*EP.*

$$ ⊡**Myett's.** Tucked away in a beachfront garden, this tiny hotel puts you right in the middle of Cane Garden Bay's busy nightlife. The restaurant is one of the area's hot spots. Rooms have a typical tropical feel, thanks to the tile floors and rattan furniture. Although you might be content to lounge at the beach and stroll around the bay, you'll need a car to get out and about. Pros: beautiful beach, good restaurant, shops nearby. Cons: busy location, loud music, need car to get around. ⊠*Cane Garden Bay* ⌖*Box 556, Cane Garden Bay VG1130* ☎*284/495–9649* ⊟*284/495–9579* ⊕*www.myettent.com* ⥽*6 rooms* ⌂*In-room: refrig-erator. In-hotel: restaurant, spa, beachfront, no elevator, public Internet, public Wi-Fi* ⊟*AE, MC, V* ⦿*EP.*

$$ ⊡**Nanny Cay Hotel.** This quiet oasis is far enough from Road Town to give it a secluded feel but close enough to make shops and restaurants convenient. You're just steps from the hotel's restaurant, boat charters, and the chance to stroll the busy boatyard to gawk at the yachts under repair, but you still have to drive a good 20 minutes to get to the clos-est beach at Cane Garden Bay. The cheerful rooms, which have tile floors, are enlivened by lots of bright Caribbean colors. Pros: nearby shops and restaurant, pleasant rooms, marina atmosphere. Cons: busy location, need car to get around. ⊠*Nanny Cay* ⌖*Box 281, Road Town VG1110* ☎*284/494–2512* ⊟*284/494–0555* ⊕*www.nannycay.com* ⥽*38 rooms* ⌂*In-room: kitchen (some), refrigerator. In-hotel: 2 restaurants, tennis court, pool, diving, no elevator, public Internet, public Wi-Fi* ⊟*MC, V* ⦿*EP.*

$–$$ ⊡**Sebastian's on the Beach.** Sitting on the island's north coast, Sebastian's definitely has a beachy feel, and that's its primary charm. Rooms vary in amenities and price, with the remodeled beachfront rooms a bit more up-to-date than those that the hotel calls "beach rear." The beach-front rooms have the best views and put you right on the sand. The less expensive rooms are basic, across the street

from the ocean, and lack views. Those nearest the intersection of North Coast Road and Zion Hill Road suffer
from traffic noise. Although you can eat all your meals at
the resort's enjoyable restaurant, the wonderful Sugar Mill
Restaurant is just a short drive east. Pros: nice beach, good
restaurants, beachfront rooms. Cons: on busy road, some
rooms nicer than others, need car to get around. ✉*Apple
Bay* ⌂*Box 441, Road Town VG1110* ☎*284/495–4212
or 800/336–4870* 🖷*284/495–4466* ⊕*www.sebastiansbvi.
com* ↪*26 rooms, 9 villas* ♿*In-room: refrigerator, no TV
(some). In-hotel: restaurant, bar, beachfront, no elevator,
public Internet, public Wi-Fi* ⊟*AE, D, MC, V* ◉*EP.*

VILLAS

Renting a villa is growing in popularity. Vacationers like
the privacy, the space to spread out, and the opportunity
to cook meals. As is true everywhere, the most important
thing is location. If you want to be close to the beach, opt
for a villa on the North Shore. If you want to dine out in
Road Town every night, a villa closer to town may be a
better bet. Prices per week during the winter season run
from around $2,000 for a one- or two-bedroom villa up
to $10,000 for a five-room beachfront villa. Rates in sum-
mer are substantially less. Most, but not all, villas accept
credit cards.

RENTAL AGENCIES

Areana Villas (⌂*Box 263, Road Town VG1110* ☎*284/494–
5864* 🖷*284/494–7626* ⊕*www.areanavillas.com*) represents top-of-the-line properties. Pastel-color villas with one
to six bedrooms can accommodate up to 10 guests. Many
have pools, whirlpool tubs, and tiled courtyards.

The St. Thomas–based **McLaughlin-Anderson Luxury Villas** (⌂*1000 Blackbeard's Hill, Suite 3, St. Thomas USVI
00802-6739* ☎*340/776–0635 or 800/537–6246* ⊕*www.
mclaughlinanderson.com*) manages nearly three dozen
properties around Tortola. Villas range in size from one to
six bedrooms and come with full kitchens and stellar views.
Most have pools. The company can hire a chef and stock
your kitchen with groceries.

Purple Pineapple Villa Rentals (⌂*95167 Bermuda Dr., Fernan-
dina Beach, FL 32034* ☎*904/415–1231 or 866/867–8652
🖷*305/723–0855* ⊕*www.purplepineapple.com*) manages
seven luxury homes in locations all over the island. Most

have pools, hot tubs, and other amenities. Villas range in size from one to six bedrooms.

Smiths Gore (✆Box 135, Road Town VG1110 ☎284/494–2446 ᕍ284/494–2141 ⊕www.smithsgore.com) has properties all over the island, but many are in the Smuggler's Cove area. They range in size from two to five to bedrooms. They all have stellar views, lovely furnishings, and lush landscaping.

BEACHES

Beaches in the BVI are less developed than those on St. Thomas or St. Croix, but they are also less inviting. The best BVI beaches are on deserted islands reachable only by boats, so take a snorkeling or sailing trip at least once. Tortola's north side has several perfect palm-fringed, white-sand beaches that curl around turquoise bays and coves, but none really achieves greatness. Nearly all are accessible by car (preferably a four-wheel-drive vehicle), albeit down bumpy roads that corkscrew precipitously. Some of these beaches are lined with bars and restaurants as well as water-sports equipment stalls; others have absolutely nothing.

Apple Bay. If you want to surf, the area including Little Apple Bay and Capoon's Bay is the spot—although the white, sandy beach itself is narrow. Sebastian's, a casual hotel, caters to those in search of the perfect wave. The legendary Bomba's Surfside Shack—a landmark festooned with all manner of flotsam and jetsam—serves drinks and casual food. Otherwise, there's nothing else in the way of amenities. Good waves are never a sure thing, but you're more apt to find them in January and February. If you're swimming and the waves are up, take care not to get dashed on the rocks. ⊠North Shore Rd. at Zion Hill Rd.

Brewers Bay. The water here is good for snorkeling, and you can find a campground with showers and bathrooms and beach bar tucked in the foliage right behind the beach. An old sugar mill and ruins of a rum distillery are off the beach along the road. The beach is easy to find, but the paved roads leading down the hill to it can be a bit daunting. You can get there from either Brewers Bay Road East or Brewers Bay Road West. ⊠Brewers Bay Rd. E off Cane Garden Bay Rd., or Brewers Bay Rd. W off Ridge Rd.

Cane Garden Bay. This silky stretch of sand has exceptionally calm, crystalline waters—except when storms at sea turn the water murky. Snorkeling is good along the edges. Casual guesthouses, restaurants, bars, and even shops are steps from the beach in the growing village of the same name. The beach is a laid-back, even somewhat funky place to put down your towel. It's the closest beach to Road Town—one steep uphill and downhill drive—and one of the BVI's best-known anchorages (unfortunately, it can be very crowded). Water-sports shops rent equipment. ⊠*Cane Garden Bay Rd. off Ridge Rd.*

Elizabeth Beach. Home to Lambert Beach Resort, the palm-lined, wide, and sandy beach has parking on its steep downhill access road. Other than at the hotel, which welcomes nonguests, there are no amenities aside from peace and quiet. Turn at the sign for Lambert Beach Resort. If you miss it, you wind up at Her Majesty's Prison. ⊠*Lambert Rd. off Ridge Rd., on eastern end of island.*

Long Bay, Beef Island. The scenery here is superlative: the beach stretches seemingly forever, and you can catch a glimpse of Little Camanoe and Great Camanoe islands. If you walk around the bend to the right, you can see little Marina Cay and Scrub Island. Long Bay is also a good place to search for seashells. Swim out to wherever you see a dark patch for some nice snorkeling. There are no amenities, so come prepared with your own drinks and snacks. Turn left shortly after crossing the bridge to Beef Island. ⊠*Beef Island Rd., Beef Island.*

Long Bay West. Have your camera ready to snap the breathtaking approach to this stunning, mile-long stretch of white sand. Although Long Bay Resort sprawls along part of it, the entire beach is open to the public. The water isn't as calm here as at Cane Garden or Brewers Bay, but it's still swimable. Rent water-sports equipment and enjoy the beachfront restaurant at the resort. Turn left at Zion Hill Road; then travel about half a mile. ⊠*Long Bay Rd.*

Smuggler's Cove. After bouncing your way down a pot-hole-filled dirt road to this beautiful, palm-fringed beach, you'll feel as if you've found a hidden piece of the island. You probably won't be alone on weekends, though, when the beach fills with snorkelers and sunbathers. There's a fine view of Jost Van Dyke from the shore. The beach is popular with Long Bay Resort guests who want a change of scenery, but there are no amenities. Follow Long Bay Road past Long Bay Resort, keeping to the roads nearest the water until you reach the beach. It's about a mile past the resort. ⊠*Long Bay Rd.*

SPORTS & THE OUTDOORS

BOATING

Rent a 23-, 25- or 30-foot powerboat for a day trip to offshore cays. Prices range from $250 for a half day on a smaller boat to $850 for a full day on a larger boat. Count on paying about $80 for gas and oil. Call **Sunshine Pleasure Boats** (⊠*C Dock, Village Cay Marina* ☎*284/494–8813* ⊕*www.sunshinepowerboats.com*).

DIVING & SNORKELING

Clear waters and numerous reefs afford some wonderful opportunities for underwater exploration. In some spots visibility reaches 100 feet, but colorful reefs teeming with fish are often just a few feet below the sea surface. The BVI's system of marine parks means the underwater life visible through your mask will stay protected.

There are several popular dive spots around the islands. **Alice in Wonderland** is a deep dive south of Ginger Island with a wall that slopes gently from 15 feet to 100 feet. It's an area overrun with huge mushroom-shape coral, hence its name. Crabs, lobsters, and shimmering fan corals make their homes in the tunnels, ledges, and overhangs of **Blonde Rock**, a pinnacle that goes from 15 feet below the surface to 60 feet deep. It's between Dead Chest and Salt Island. When the currents aren't too strong, **Brewers Bay Pinnacle** (20 to 90 feet down) teems with sea life. At the **Indians**, near Pelican Island, colorful corals decorate canyons and grottoes created by four large, jagged pinnacles that rise 50 feet from the ocean floor. The **Painted Walls** is a shallow dive site where corals and sponges create a kaleidoscope of colors on the walls of four long gullies. It's northeast of Dead Chest.

The *Chikuzen,* sunk northwest of Brewers Bay in 1981, is a 246-foot vessel in 75 feet of water; it's home to thousands of fish, colorful corals, and big rays. In 1867 the **RMS** *Rhone,* a 310-foot royal mail steamer, split in two when it sank in a devastating hurricane. It's so well preserved that it was used as an underwater prop in the movie *The Deep.*

You can see the crow's nest and bowsprit, the cargo hold in the bow, and the engine and enormous propeller shaft in the stern. Its four parts are at various depths from 30 to 80 feet. Get yourself some snorkeling gear and hop aboard a dive boat to this wreck near Salt Island (across the channel from Road Town). Every dive outfit in the BVI runs scuba and snorkel tours to this part of the BVI National Parks Trust; if you only have time for one trip, make it this one. Rates start at around $60 for a one-tank dive and $90 for a two-tank dive.

Your hotel probably has a dive company right on the premises. If not, the staff can recommend one nearby. Using your hotel's dive company makes a trip to the offshore dive and snorkel sites a breeze. Just stroll down to the dock and hop aboard. All dive companies are certified by PADI, the Professional Association of Diving Instructors, which ensures your instructors are qualified to safely take vacationers diving. The boats are also inspected to make sure they're seaworthy. If you've never dived, try a short introductory dive, often called a resort course, which teaches you enough to get you under water. In the unlikely event you get a case of the bends, a condition that can happen when you rise to the surface too fast, your dive team will whisk you to the decompression chamber at Roy L. Schneider Regional Medical Center Hospital in nearby St. Thomas.

Blue Waters Divers (⊠*Nanny Cay* ☎*284/494–2847* ⊠*Soper's Hole, West End* ☎*284/495–1200* ⊕*www.bluewaterdiversbvi.com*) teaches resort, open-water, rescue, and advanced diving courses, and also makes daily dive trips. If you're chartering a sailboat, the company's boat will meet your boat at Peter, Salt, or Cooper Island for a rendezvous dive. Rates include all equipment as well as instruction. Reserve two days in advance. **Dive Tortola** (⊠*Prospect Reef* ☎*284/494–9200* ⊕*www.divetortola.com*) offers beginner and advanced diving courses and daily dive trips. Trainers teach open-water, rescue, advanced diving, and resort courses. Dive Tortola also offers a rendezvous diving option for folks on charter sailboats.

FISHING

Most of the boats that take you deep-sea fishing for bluefish, wahoo, swordfish, and shark leave from nearby St. Thomas, but local anglers like to fish the shallower water for bonefish. A half day runs about $480, a full day around

$850. Call **Caribbean Fly Fishing** (⊠*Nanny Cay* ☎*284/494–4797* ⊕*www.caribflyfishing.com*).

HIKING

♻ Sage Mountain National Park attracts hikers who enjoy the quiet trails that crisscross the island's loftiest peak. There are some lovely views and the chance to see rare species that grow only at higher elevations.

SAILING

★ **Fodor'sChoice** The BVI are among the world's most popular
♻ sailing destinations. They're clustered together and surrounded by calm waters, so it's fairly easy to sail from one anchorage to the next. Most of the Caribbean's biggest sailboat charter companies have operations in Tortola. If you know how to sail, you can charter a bareboat (perhaps for your entire vacation); if you're unschooled, you can hire a boat with a captain. Prices vary depending on the type and size of the boat you wish to charter. In season, a weekly charter runs from $1,500 to $35,000. Book early to make sure you get the boat that fits you best. Most of Tortola's marinas have hotels, which give you a convenient place to spend the nights before and after your charter.

If a day-sail to some secluded anchorage is more your spot of tea, the BVI have numerous boats of various sizes and styles that leave from many points around Tortola. Prices start at around $80 per person for a full-day sail, including lunch and snorkeling equipment.

BVI Yacht Charters (⊠*Port Purcell, Road Town* ☎*284/494–4289 or 888/615–4006* ⊕*www.bviyachtcharters.com*) offers 31-foot to 71-foot sailboats for charter—with or without a captain and crew, whichever you prefer. **Catamaran Charters** (⊠*Nanny Cay Marina, Nanny Cay* ☎*284/494–6661 or 800/262–0308* ⊕*www.catamarans.com*) charters catamarans with or without a captain. The **Moorings** (⊠*Wickham's Cay II, Road Town* ☎*284/494–2331 or 800/535–7289* ⊕*www.moorings.com*), considered one of the world's best bareboat operations, has a large fleet of well-maintained, mostly Beneteau sailing yachts. Hire a captain or sail the boat yourself. If you prefer a powerboat, call **Regency Yacht Vacations** (⊠*Wickham's Cay I, Road Town* ☎*284/495–1970 or 800/524–7676* ⊕*www.regencyvacations.com*) for both bareboat and captained sail and powerboat charters.

Sunsail (✉ *Wickham's Cay II, East End* ☎ *284/495–4740 or 800/327–2276* ⊕ *www.sunsail.com*) offers a full fleet of boats to charter with or without a captain. **Voyages** (✉ *Soper's Hole Marina, West End* ☎ *284/494–0740 or 888/869–2436* ⊕ *www.voyagecharters.com*) offers a variety of sailboats for charter with or without a captain and crew.

Aristocat Charters (✉ *West End* ☎ *284/499–1249* ⊕ *www. aristocatcharters.com*) sets sail daily to the Indians and Peter Island aboard a 48-foot catamaran. **White Squall II** (✉ *Village Cay Marina, Road Town* ☎ *284/494–2564* ⊕ *www.whitesquall2.com*) takes you on regularly scheduled day sails to the Baths at Virgin Gorda, Jost Van Dyke, or the Caves at Norman Island on an 80-foot schooner.

WINDSURFING

Steady trade winds make windsurfing a breeze. Three of the best spots for sailboarding are Nanny Cay, Slaney Point, and Trellis Bay on Beef Island. Rates for sailboards start at about $25 an hour or $75 for a two-hour lesson.

Boardsailing BVI (✉ *Trellis Bay, Beef Island* ☎ *284/495–2447* ⊕ *www.windsurfing.vi*) rents equipment and offers private and group lessons.

SHOPPING

The BVI aren't really a shopper's delight, but there are many shops showcasing original wares—from jams and spices to resort wear to excellent artwork.

SHOPPING AREAS

Many shops and boutiques are clustered along and just off Road Town's **Main Street.** You can shop in Road Town's **Wickham's Cay I** adjacent to the marina. The **Crafts Alive Market** on the Road Town waterfront is a collection of colorful West Indian–style buildings with shops that carry items made in the BVI. You might find pretty baskets or interesting pottery or perhaps a bottle of home-brewed hot sauce. There's an ever-growing number of art and clothing stores at **Soper's Hole** in West End.

SPECIALTY STORES

ART

The **Allamanda Gallery** (⊠*124 Main St., Road Town* ☎*284/494–6680*) carries art by owner Lisa Gray and other Tortola artists. **Sunny Caribbee** (⊠*Main St., Road Town* ☎*284/494–2178*) has many paintings, prints, and watercolors by artists from around the Caribbean.

CLOTHES & TEXTILES

Arawak (⊠*On dock, Nanny Cay* ☎*284/494–5240* ⊠*Hodge's Creek Marina, Hodge's Creek* ☎*284/495–1106* ⊠*Soper's Hole Marina, West End* ☎*284/495–4262*) carries batik sundresses, sportswear, and resort wear for men and women. There's also a selection of children's clothing. **Hucksters** (⊠*Main St., Road Town* ☎*284/495–7165* ⊠*Soper's Hole Marina, West End* ☎*284/495–3087*) carries nifty souvenirs as well as unusual items for the home. **Latitude 18°** (⊠*Main St., Road Town* ⊠*Soper's Hole Marina, West End* ☎*284/494–7807 for both stores*) sells Maui Jim, Smith, Oakley, and Revo sunglasses; Freestyle and Reactor watches; and a fine collection of beach towels, sandals, sundresses, and sarongs. **Pusser's Company Store** (⊠*Main St. at Waterfront Rd., Road Town* ☎*284/494–2467* ⊠*Soper's Hole Marina, West End* ☎*284/495–4599*) sells nautical memorabilia, ship models, and marine paintings. There's also an entire line of clothing for both men and women, handsome decorator bottles of Pusser's rum, and gift items bearing the Pusser's logo. **Zenaida's of West End** (⊠*Soper's Hole Marina, West End* ☎*284/495–4867*) displays the fabric finds of Argentine Vivian Jenik Helm, who travels through South America, Africa, and India in search of batiks, hand-painted and hand-blocked fabrics, and interesting weaves that can be made into pareus (women's wraps) or wall hangings. The shop also sells unusual bags, belts, sarongs, scarves, and ethnic jewelry.

FOODSTUFFS

Ample Hamper (⊠*Inner Harbour Marina, Road Town* ☎*284/494–2494* ⊠*Frenchman's Cay Marina, West End* ☎*284/495–4684* ⊕*www.amplehamper.com*) has an outstanding collection of cheeses, wines, fresh fruits, and canned goods from the United Kingdom and the United States. The staff will your yacht or rental villa. **Best of British** (⊠*Wickham's Cay I, Road Town* ☎*284/494–3462*) has lots of nifty British food you won't find elsewhere. Shop here for Marmite, Vegemite, shortbread, frozen meat pies, and delightful Christmas crackers filled with surprises. **RiteWay** (✉*Waterfront Dr., at Pasea Estate, Road Town* ☎*284/494–2263* ✉*Fleming St., Road Town* ☎*284/494–2263* ⊕*www.rtwbvi.com*) carries a good selection of the usual supplies, but don't expect an inventory like your hometown supermarket. RiteWay will stock villas and yachts.

GIFTS

Bamboushay (✉*Nanny Cay Marina, Nanny Cay* ☎*284/494–0393*) sells handcrafted Tortola-made pottery in shades that reflect the sea. In a brightly painted West Indian house, **Sunny Caribbee** (✉*Main St., Road Town* ☎*284/494–2178*) packages its own herbs, teas, coffees, vinegars, hot sauces, soaps, skin and suntan lotions, and exotic concoctions—Arawak Love Potion and Island Hangover Cure, for example.

JEWELRY

Colombian Emeralds International (✉*Wickham's Cay I, Road Town* ☎*284/494–7477*), a Caribbean chain catering to the cruise-ship crowd, is the source for duty-free emeralds and other gems, gold, crystal, and china. **D'Zandra's** (✉*Wickham's Cay I, Road Town* ☎*284/494–8330*) carries mostly black coral items set in gold and silver. Many pieces reflect Caribbean and sea themes. **Samarkand** (✉*Main St., Road Town* ☎*284/494–6415*) crafts charming gold-and-silver pendants, earrings, bracelets, and pins, many with island themes like seashells, lizards, pelicans, and palm trees. There are also reproduction Spanish pieces of eight (old Spanish coins) that were found on sunken galleons.

PERFUMES & COSMETICS

Flamboyance (✉*Palm Grove Shopping Center, Waterfront Dr., Road Town* ☎*284/494–4099*) carries designer fragrances and upscale cosmetics.

STAMPS

The **BVI Post Office** (✉*Main St., Road Town* ☎*284/494–3701*) is a philatelist's dream. It has a worldwide reputation for exquisite stamps in all sorts of designs. Although the stamps carry U.S. monetary designations, they can be used for postage only in the BVI.

NIGHTLIFE & THE ARTS

NIGHTLIFE

Like any other good sailing destination, Tortola has watering holes that are popular with salty and not-so-salty dogs. Many offer entertainment; check the weekly *Limin' Times* for schedules and up-to-date information. Bands change like the weather, and what's hot today can be old news tomorrow. The local beverage is the Painkiller, an innocent-tasting mixture of fruit juices and rums. It goes down smoothly but packs quite a punch, so give yourself time to recover before you order another.

By day **Bomba's Surfside Shack** (⊠ *Apple Bay* ☎ *284/495– 4148*), which is covered with everything from crepe-paper leis to ancient license plates to spicy graffiti, looks like a pile of junk; by night it's one of Tortola's liveliest spots. There's a fish fry and a live band every Wednesday and Sunday. People flock here from all over on the full moon, when bands play all night long. At the **Jolly Roger** (⊠ *West End* ☎ *284/495–4559*) an ever-changing roster of local and down-island bands plays everything from rhythm and blues to reggae and rock every Friday and Saturday—and sometimes Sunday—starting at 8. Local bands play at **Myett's** (⊠ *Cane Garden Bay* ☎ *284/495–9649*) most nights, and there's usually a lively dance crowd. At the **Pub** (⊠ *Waterfront St., Road Town* ☎ *284/494–2608*) there's a happy hour from 5 to 7 every day and live blues on Thursday. Courage is what people are seeking at **Pusser's Road Town Pub** (⊠ *Waterfront St., Road Town* ☎ *284/494–3897*)— John Courage by the pint. Other nights try Pusser's famous mixed drinks, called Painkillers, and snack on the excellent pizza. BVI recording star Quito Rhymer sings island ballads and love songs at **Quito's Gazebo** (⊠ *Cane Garden Bay* ☎ *284/495–4837*), his rustic beachside bar-restaurant. Solo shows are on Tuesday and Thursday at 8:30; on Friday and Saturday nights at 9:30 Quito performs with his band. There's often live music at **Sebastian's** (⊠ *Apple Bay* ☎ *284/495–4212*) on Thursday and Sunday evenings, and you can dance under the stars.

4

CLOSE UP

Rocking the Bay

Cane Garden Bay is the place to go for live music, with Quito Rhymer frequently delighting the crowds at his Quito's Restaurant. Myett's is also a happening place some nights. The entire village really jams come May when the BVI Music Fest gets going. Thousands of people arrive from around the Caribbean and around the world to listen to the best of the Caribbean's reggae, blues, and socca musicians.

Cane Garden Bay is a small but growing community on Tortola's North Shore. There are no chain hotels or sprawling resorts here—all of the places to stay are small and locally owned. In addition to the handful of properties on the beach, there are plenty of others tucked up in the hillsides that have eye-popping views. The area has plenty of places to eat, with lobster the specialty on many a menu.

The area fairly bustles on cruise-ship days as busload after busload of round-the-island tour groups disembark to snap a few pictures. Once they're gone, however, a modicum of peace returns to the village.

THE ARTS

Musicians from around the world take to the stage during the **Performing Art Series** (⊠*H. Lavity Stoutt Community College, Paraquita Bay* ☎*284/494–4994* ⊕*www.hlscc. edu.vg*), held from October to March each year. Past artists have included Britain's premier a cappella group, Black Voices; the Leipzig String Quartet; and Keith Lockhart and the Serenac Quartet (from the Boston Pops Symphony).

Every May, hordes of people head to Tortola for the three-day **BVI Music Festival** (⊠*Cane Garden Bay* ☎*284/495–3378* ⊕*www.bvimusicfest.net*) to listen to reggae, gospel, blues, and salsa music by musicians from around the Caribbean and the U.S. mainland.

SIDE TRIPS FROM TORTOLA

There are several islands that make great side trips from Tortola, including lovely Marina Cay and tony Peter's Island. Both have great accommodations, so you might want to spend the night.

MARINA CAY

♻ Beautiful little Marina Cay is in Trellis Bay, not far from Beef Island. Sometimes you can see it and its large J-shape coral reefs—a most dramatic sight—from the air soon after takeoff from the airport on Beef Island. Covering 8 acres, this islet is considered small even by BVI standards. On it there's a restaurant, Pusser's Store, and a six-unit hotel. Ferry service is free from the dock on Beef Island.

WHERE TO STAY & EAT

$$ ⊞**Pusser's Marina Cay Hotel & Restaurant.** If getting away from it all is your priority, this may be the place for you, because there's nothing to do on this beach-rimmed island other than swim, snorkel, and soak up the sun—there's not even a TV to distract you. Rooms, decorated in simple wicker and wood with floral-print fabrics, are on a hilltop facing the trade winds; two villas look right out to the morning sunrise. The laid-back tempo picks up at 4:30 PM, when charter boaters come ashore to hear local musicians entertain in the bar during happy hour. The restaurant, open for breakfast, lunch, and dinner, offers a menu that ranges from fish and lobster to steak, chicken, and barbecued ribs. Pusser's Painkiller Punch is the house specialty. There's free ferry service from the Beef Island dock for anyone visiting the island, though ferry times and frequency vary with the seasons. ⊠ *West side of Marina Cay* ⌂ *Box 76, Road Town, Tortola* ☎ *284/494–2174* 🖶 *284/494–4775* ⊕ *www.pussers.com* ↪ *4 rooms, 2 2-bedroom villas* ⚐ *In-room: no a/c, no phone, no TV. In-hotel: restaurant, bar, beachfront, no elevator, public Wi-Fi* ⊟ *AE, MC, V* ⏍ *CP.*

PETER ISLAND

Although Peter Island is home to the resort of the same name, it's also a popular anchorage for charter boaters and a destination for Tortola vacationers. The scheduled ferry trip from Peter Island's shoreside base outside Road Town runs $15 round-trip for nonguests. The island is lush, with forested hillsides sloping seaward to meet white sandy beaches. There are no roads other than those at the resort, and there's nothing to do but relax at the lovely beach set aside for day-trippers. You're welcome to dine at the resort's restaurants.

WHERE TO STAY & EAT

$$$$ ✕⬚ **Peter Island Resort.** Total pampering and the prices to match are the ticket at this luxury resort. If you want to while away your days at the beach, enjoy a morning at the spa, stroll the lushly planted grounds, and relax over dinner with other like-minded guests—and have the money to afford the steep rates—this is a good place to do it. For more active types, there are tennis courts and water sports galore. Peter Island is a half-hour ferry ride from Tortola, but once you arrive, you're in another world. The rooms are gorgeous, with thoughtful touches like showers with a view. A couple of villas sit above the hotel rooms. ⬚*Peter Island* ⬚*Box 211, Road Town, Tortola* ☎*284/495–2000 or 800/346–4451* ⬚*284/495–2500* ⬚*www.peterisland. com* ⬚*52 rooms, 3 villas* ⬚*In-room: safe, no TV. In-hotel: 2 restaurants, bar, pool, gym, spa, beachfront, diving, water sports, no elevator, public Internet, public Wi-Fi* ⬚*AE, MC, V* ⬚*FAP.*

TORTOLA ESSENTIALS

To research prices, get advice from other travelers, and book travel arrangements, visit www.fodors.com.

TRANSPORTATION
BY AIR

There's no nonstop service from the continental United States to Tortola; connections are usually made through San Juan, Puerto Rico, or St. Thomas. Tortola's airport, Terrence B. Lettsome Airport terminal at Beef Island (TOC), can get crowded when several departures are scheduled close together.

BY BOAT & FERRY

Frequent daily ferries connect the Tortola with St. Thomas, where many vacationers decide to use as their main air gateway. Ferries go to and from both Charlotte Amalie and Red Hook. There's huge competition among the Tortola-based ferry companies on the St. Thomas–Tortola runs, with boats leaving close together. As you enter the ferry terminal to buy your ticket, crews may try to convince you to take their ferry. Ferries also link Tortola to St. John, and if this is your destination you should know that all Red Hook–bound ferries stop in Cruz Bay to clear customs and immigration.

Ferries also link Tortola with Jost Van Dyke, Peter Island, and Virgin Gorda. Tortola has two ferry terminals—one at West End and one in Road Town—so make sure you hop a ferry that disembarks closest to where you want to go. Ferry schedules vary, and not all companies make daily trips. The BVI Tourist Board Web site *(⇨see By Boat & Ferry in Virgin Island Essentials)* has links to all the ferry companies, which are the best up-to-date sources of information for specific routes and schedules.

BY CAR

Tortola's main roads are well paved, for the most part, but there are exceptionally steep hills and sharp curves; driving demands your complete attention. A main road circles the island, and several roads cross it, almost always through mountainous terrain.

Contacts Avis (⊠*Opposite Police Station, Road Town, Tortola* ☎*284/494–3322*). **D&D** (⊠*West End Rd., West End, Tortola* ☎*284/495–4765*). **Hertz** (⊠*West End, Tortola* ☎*284/495–4405* ⊠*Airport, Tortola* ☎*284/495–6600* ⊠*Road Town, Tortola* ☎*284/494–6228*). **Itgo Car Rental** (⊠*Wickham's Cay I, Road Town, Tortola* ☎*284/494–2639*).

BY TAXI

Taxi rates aren't set on Tortola, so you should negotiate the fare with your driver before you start your trip. Fares are per destination, not per person here, so it's cheaper to travel in groups because the fare will be the same whether you have one, two, or three passengers. On Tortola, the BVI Taxi Association has stands in Road Town near Wickham's Cay I. The Waterfront Taxi Association picks up passengers from the Road Town ferry dock. The Beef Island Taxi Association operates at the Beef Island–Tortola airport. You can also usually find a West End Taxi Association ferry at the West End ferry dock.

Information Airport Taxi Association (⊠*Beef Island Airport, Tortola* ☎*284/495–1982*). **BVI Taxi Association** (⊠*Near ferry dock, Road Town, Tortola* ☎*284/494–3942*). **West End Taxi Association** (⊠*West End ferry terminal, Tortola* ☎*284/495–4934*). **Waterfront Taxi Association** (⊠*Road Town* ☎*284/494–6362*).

CONTACTS & RESOURCES

BANKS

On Tortola, banks are near the Waterfront at Wickham's Cay I. All have ATM machines. Look for First Caribbean International Bank, First Bank, and Scotia Bank, among others.

EMERGENCIES

Ambulance, Fire & Police **General emergencies** (☎999).

Hospitals & Clinics **Peebles Hospital** (✉ *Road Town, Tortola* ☎ *284/494–3497*).

Marine Emergencies **VISAR** (☎ *767 from phone or Marine Radio Channel 16*).

Pharmacies **J.R. O'Neal Drug Store** (✉ *Road Town, Tortola* ☎ *284/494–2292*). **Medicure Pharmacy** (✉ *Road Town, Tortola* ☎ *284/494–6189*).

INTERNET, MAIL & SHIPPING

There's a post office in Road Town on Tortola. For a small fee, Rush It, in Road Town, offers most U.S. mail and UPS services (via St. Thomas the next day). If you wish to write to an establishment in the BVI, be sure to include the specific island in the address.

Many hotels have Internet access for their guests. Internet cafés, however, are harder to find. On Tortola, try Trellis Bay Cybercafé.

Contacts **Rush It** (✉ *Road Town, Tortola* ☎ *284/494–4421*). **Trellis Bay Cybercafé** (✉ *Trellis Bay, Tortola* ☎ *284/495–2447*).

SAFETY

Although crime is rare, use common sense: don't leave your camera on the beach while you take a dip or your wallet on a hotel dresser when you go for a walk.

TOUR OPTIONS

Romney Associates/Travel Plan Tours can arrange island tours, boat tours, snorkeling and scuba-diving trips, dolphin swims, and yacht charters from its Tortola base.

Information **Romney Associates/Travel Plan Tours** (☎ *284/494–4000*).

WEDDINGS

Contacts **BVI Wedding Planners & Consultants** (☎ *284/494–5306* ⊕ *www.bviweddings.com*).

Virgin Gorda

WORD OF MOUTH

"When we arrived at the Top of the Baths we were immediately awestruck, despite the fact that we had seen hundreds of photos before the fact. The enormity of some of the boulders within our limited beginning view is something that just can't be captured on film."

—Maggi

By Lynda
Lohr

Lovely Virgin Gorda sits at the end of the chain that
stretches eastward from St. Thomas. Virgin Gorda, or "Fat
Virgin," received its name from Christopher Columbus.
The explorer envisioned the island as a reclining pregnant
woman, with Virgin Gorda Peak being her belly and the
boulders of the Baths her toes.

While nearby Tortola positively bustles some days, Virgin Gorda has a slower pace. Goats still wander across
the roads in places like North Sound. But that's changing.
Virgin Gorda Yacht Harbour, the center of commerce and
activity in Spanish Town, is expanding. More hotels and
condominium developments are in the works, and pricey
villas are going up all over the island. That said, budget
travelers can still find modest villas and guesthouses all
over the island to while away a few days or more.

Virgin Gorda isn't all that easy to get to, but once you're
here you can find enough diversions to make getting out of
your chaise lounges worthwhile. You can drive from one
end of the island to the other in about 20 minutes, but
make sure to take time to visit Copper Mine Point to learn
about the island's history or to hike up Virgin Gorda Peak
to survey the surroundings. At numerous spots with stellar
views, the local government has thoughtfully built viewing
platforms with adjacent parking. It's worth a stop to snap
some photos.

The scenery on the northeastern side of the island is the
most dramatic, with a steep road ending at Leverick
Bay and Gun Creek in North Sound. For lunch you can
hop aboard a ferry to Biras Creek Resort, the Bitter End
Yacht Club, or Saba Rock Resort. Head to the other end
of the island for views of the huge boulders that spill
over from the Baths into the southwest section of Virgin
Gorda. You can find several restaurants dotted around
this end of the island.

In truth, though, it's the beaches that make Virgin Gorda
special. Stretches of talcum-powder sand fringe aquama-
rine waters. Popular places like the Baths see hordes of
people, but just a quick walk down the road brings you to
quieter beaches like Spring Bay. On the other side of Spanish Town, you may be the only person at such sandy spots
as Savannah Bay.

If shopping's on your agenda, you can find stores in Virgin
Gorda Yacht Harbour selling items perfect for rounding

VIRGIN GORDA TOP 5

Beautiful Beaches: Virgin Gorda's stunning white sandy beaches are the number one reason to visit. While you can join the crowds at the Baths, it's easy to find your own place in the sun at any one of the island's stretches of sand.

The Baths: The ever-popular Baths, an area strewn with giant boulders—many are as big as houses—draws hordes of visitors. Go early or late to enjoy the solitude that comes from splashing or snorkeling among the rocks

Vacation Villas: Virgin Gorda villas come in all sizes and price ranges. Some are so spectacular they grace the pages of glossy magazines. These get top dollar, of course. Others are more modest, with prices that are comparable to what you'd pay for a hotel room.

North Sound: Even if you aren't a guest at one of North Sound's handful of resorts, you still should visit. Ferries depart frequently for the short trip along the island's beautiful coastline. Stay for lunch, or just enjoy an afternoon drink.

Solitude: You don't go to Virgin Gorda for the nightlife (although there is some here and there) or endless activities (but you might want to rent a kayak). Instead, go to relax on your terrace as you watch the sun slip below the horizon.

5

out your tropical wardrobe or tucking into your suitcase to enjoy when you get home.

Virgin Gorda has very little crime and hardly any frosty attitudes among its more than 3,100 permanent residents. In short, the island provides a welcome respite in a region that's changing rapidly.

EXPLORING VIRGIN GORDA

One of the most efficient ways to see Virgin Gorda is by sailboat. There are few roads, and most byways don't follow the scalloped shoreline. The main route sticks resolutely to the center of the island, linking the Baths on the southern tip with Gun Creek and Leverick Bay at North Sound. The craggy coast, scissored with grottoes and fringed by palms and boulders, has a primitive beauty. If you drive, you can hit all the sights in one day. The best plan is to explore the area near your hotel (either Spanish Town or North Sound) first, then take a day to drive to the other end. Stop to

Virgin Gorda

Mountain Pt.

Cockroach Island

George Dog

Coastal Islands
6

Great Dog

West Dog

Sir Francis Drake Channel

Nail Bay Point 13

Mango Bay

Virgin Gorda Peak National Park 5

Mahoe Bay 12

11

Pond Bay

Little Dix Bay

Savannah Bay

Colison Pt.

9

St. Thomas Bay

10

Handsome Bay

← TO TORTOLA

Spanish Town 7

Virgin Gorda Airport

Fort Pt. 2 1

5 6

8

The Valley

Copper Mine Bay

Spring Bay Beach 1

3

Devil's Bay

4 **Copper Mine Point**

The Baths 3 2

Crook's Bay

4

Stoney Bay

Fallen Jerusalem

6 **Coastal Islands**

KEY

- Beaches
- Ferry
- Cruise Ship Terminal
- 1 Exploring Sights
- 1 Hotels & Restaurants
- .... Trail

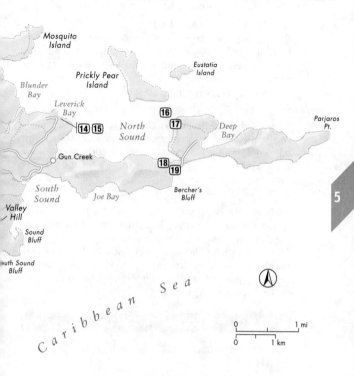

↑ TO
NECKER ISLAND

↑ TO
ANEGADA

Mosquito
Island

Prickly Pear
Island

Eustatia
Island

Blunder
Bay

Leverick
Bay

14 15

16

17

North
Sound

Deep
Bay

Parjaros
Pt.

Gun Creek

18

19

South
Sound

Joe Bay

Bercher's
Bluff

Valley
/ Hill

Sound
Bluff

uth Sound
Bluff

Caribbean Sea

5

0 ———————— 1 mi

0 ———————— 1 km

Hotels	**Restaurants**
Biras Creek Resort, **21**	The Bath and Turtle, **8**
Bitter End Yacht Club, **19**	Biras Creek, **22**
Fischer's Cove Beach Hotel, **6**	Chez Bamboo, **9**
Guavaberry Spring Bay Vacation Homes, **4**	The Clubhouse, **20**
Leverick Bay Resort & Marina, **16**	The Fat Virgins Cafe, **23**
Little Dix Bay, **11**	The Flying Iguana, **10**
Mango Bay Resort, **14**	Giorgio's Table, **13**
Nail Bay Resort, **15**	Little Dix Bay Pavilion, **11**
Olde Yard Village, **12**	LSL Restaurant, **7**
Saba Rock Resort, **18**	Mad Dog's, **3**
	The Mine Shaft Café, **5**
	The Restaurant at Leverick Bay, **17**
	The Rock Café, **1**
	Top of the Baths, **2**

climb Gorda Peak, which is in the island's center. Signage is erratic, so come prepared with a map.

ABOUT THE RESTAURANTS

Restaurants range from simple to elegant. Hotels that are accessible only by boat will arrange transport in advance upon request from nonguests who wish to dine at their restaurants. It's wise to make dinner reservations almost everywhere except really casual spots.

TIMING

Easter is also Carnival on Virgin Gorda. The celebration is smaller than you'll find on more heavily touristed islands, but people visiting family and friends do come from around the Caribbean. If you're heading to Virgin Gorda during the three-day annual event, make sure you've booked your room well in advance.

ABOUT THE HOTELS

Virgin Gorda's charming hostelries appeal to a select, appreciative clientele; repeat business is extremely high. Those who prefer Sheratons, Marriotts, and the like may feel they get more for their money on other islands, but the peace and pampering offered on Virgin Gorda are priceless to the discriminating traveler.

WHAT IT COSTS IN DOLLARS				
$$$$	$$$	$$	$	¢
RESTAURANTS				
OVER $30	$20–$30	$12–$20	$8–$12	UNDER $8
HOTELS				
* OVER $350	$250–$350	$150–$250	$80–$150	UNDER $80
** OVER $450	$350–$450	$250–$350	$125–$250	UNDER $125

*EP, BP, CP; **AI, FAP, MAP; Restaurant prices are for a main course at dinner, excluding 10% service charge. Hotel prices are for two people in a double room during high season, excluding 7% BVI tax, 10% service charge, and meal plans (except for all-inclusives).

WHAT TO SEE

Virgin Gorda's most popular attractions are those provided by Mother Nature. Beautiful beaches, crystal clear water, and stellar views are around nearly every bend in the road. That said, remember to get a taste of the island's past at Copper Mine Point.

Numbers in the margin correspond to points of interest on the Virgin Gorda map.

★ Fodor'sChoice **The Baths.** At Virgin Gorda's most celebrated ❸ sight, giant boulders are scattered about the beach and in ☾ the water. Some are almost as large as houses and form remarkable grottoes. Climb between these rocks to swim in the many placid pools. Early morning and late afternoon are the best times to visit if you want to avoid crowds. If it's privacy you crave, follow the shore northward to quieter bays—Spring Bay, the Crawl, Little Trunk, and Valley Trunk—or head south to Devil's Bay. ⊠*Off Tower Rd., The Baths* ☎*284/494–3904* ⊕*www.bvinationalparkstrust. org* ⊠*$3* ☾*Daily dawn–dusk.*

❷ **Coastal Islands.** You can easily reach the quaintly named Fallen Jerusalem Island and the Dog Islands by boat. They're all part of the BVI National Parks Trust, and their seductive beaches and unparalleled snorkeling display the BVI at their beachcombing, hedonistic best. ☎*No phone* ⊠*Free.*

❹ **Copper Mine Point.** Here stand a tall stone shaft silhouetted against the sky and a small stone structure that overlooks the sea. These are the ruins of a copper mine established 400 years ago and worked first by the Spanish, then by the English, until the early 20th century. The route is not well marked, so turn inland near LSL Restaurant and look for the hard-to-see sign pointing the way. ⊠*Copper Mine Rd.* ☎*No phone* ⊕*www.bvinationalparkstrust.org* ⊠*Free.*

GETTING AROUND The ferry service from the public dock in Spanish Town can be a tad erratic. Call ahead to confirm the schedule, get there early to be sure it hasn't changed, and ask at the dock whether you're getting on the right boat. The Thursday and Sunday service between Virgin Gorda and St. John is particularly prone to problems.

❶ **Spanish Town.** Virgin Gorda's peaceful main settlement, on the island's southern wing, is so tiny that it barely qualifies as a town at all. Also known as the Valley, Spanish Town has a marina, some shops, and a couple of car-rental agencies. Just north of town is the ferry slip. At the Virgin Gorda Yacht Harbour you can stroll along the dock and do a little shopping.

❺ Virgin Gorda Peak National Park. There are two trails at this
★ 265-acre park, which contains the island's highest point, at 1,359 feet. Small signs on North Sound Road mark both entrances; sometimes, however, the signs are missing, so keep your eyes open for a set of stairs that disappears into the trees. It's about a 15-minute hike from either entrance up to a small clearing, where you can climb a ladder to the platform of a wooden observation tower and a spectacular 360-degree view. ⊠*North Sound Rd., Gorda Peak* ☎*No phone* ⊕*www.bvinationalparkstrust.org* ☐*Free.*

WHERE TO EAT

Dining out on Virgin Gorda is a mixed bag, with everything from hamburgers to lobster available. Most folks opt to have dinner at or near their hotel to avoid driving on Virgin Gorda's twisting roads at night. The Valley does have a handful of restaurants if you're sleeping close to town.

AMERICAN

$$$–$$$$ ✕ **Restaurant at Leverick Bay.** This bi-level restaurant looks out over North Sound. The fancier upstairs dining room is slightly more expensive, with a menu that includes steaks, lobster, and fresh fish. There's a prime rib special on Saturday night. Below, the bar offers light fare all day—starting with breakfast and moving on to hamburgers, salads, and pizzas until well into the evening. There's a children's menu downstairs. ⊠*Leverick Bay Resort & Marina, Leverick Bay* ☎*284/495–7154* ☐*MC, V.*

$$–$$$$ ✕ **Flying Iguana Restaurant & Bar.** Local art is displayed in
☘ this charming restaurant's comfortable lounge. The open-air dining room looks past the island's tiny airport to the sea. Enjoy classic eggs and bacon for breakfast; for lunch there are sandwiches and juicy hamburgers. The dinner menu includes fresh seafood, grilled chicken, sizzling steaks, and a pasta special. ⊠*Virgin Gorda Airport, The Valley* ☎*284/495–5277* ☐*MC, V.*

$$–$$$$ ✕**LSL Restaurant.** An unpretentious place along the road to the Baths, this small restaurant with pedestrian decor is a local favorite. You can always find fresh fish on the menu, but folks with a taste for other dishes won't be disappointed. Try the veal with mushrooms and herbs in a white wine sauce or the breast of chicken with rum cream and nuts. ✉ *Tower Rd., The Valley* ☎ *284/495–5151* ▭ *MC, V.*

$$–$$$$ ✕**Mine Shaft Café.** Perched on a hilltop that offers a view of spectacular sunsets, this restaurant near Copper Mine Point serves simple yet well-prepared food, including grilled fish, steaks, and baby back ribs. Tuesday night features an all-you-can-eat Caribbean-style barbecue. The monthly full-moon parties draw a big local crowd. ✉ *Copper Mine Point, The Valley* ☎ *284/495–5260* ▭ *MC, V.*

$$–$$$ ✕**Bath & Turtle.** You can sit back and relax at this informal tavern with a friendly staff—although the noise from the television can sometimes be a bit much. Well-stuffed sandwiches, homemade pizzas, pasta dishes, and daily specials like conch soup round out the casual menu. Local musicians perform Wednesday night. ✉ *Virgin Gorda Yacht Harbour, Spanish Town* ☎ *284/495–5239* ▭ *AE, MC, V.*

$–$$ ✕**Fat Virgin's Café.** ☼ This casual beachfront eatery offers a straightforward menu of flying-fish sandwiches, baby back ribs, chicken roti, vegetable pasta, and fresh fish specials for lunch and dinner. Saturday nights there's a special Chinese menu. You can find a good selection of Caribbean beer. ✉ *Biras Creek Resort, North Sound* ☎ *284/495–7052* ▭ *MC, V.*

$–$$ ✕**Top of the Baths.** ☼ At the entrance to the Baths, this popular restaurant starts serving at 8 AM. Tables are on an outdoor terrace or in an open-air pavilion; all have stunning views of the Sir Francis Drake Channel. Hamburgers, coconut chicken sandwiches, and fish-and-chips are among the offerings at lunch. For dessert, the mango raspberry cheesecake is excellent. The Sunday barbecue, served from noon until 3 PM, is an island event. ✉ *The Valley* ☎ *284/495–5497* ▭ *AE, MC, V* ☼ *No dinner.*

CONTINENTAL

$$$$ ✕**Biras Creek Restaurant.** This hilltop restaurant at the Biras Creek Hotel has eye-popping views of North Sound. The four-course prix-fixe menu changes daily and includes several choices per course. For starters, there may be an artichoke, green bean, and wild mushroom salad with a balsamic vinaigrette, or cream of sweet potato soup topped

with potato straws. Entrées may include pan-seared snapper over horseradish pearl pasta. The desserts, including a lemon ricotta cheesecake with a spicy passion fruit sauce, are to die for. Dinner ends with Biras Creek's signature offering of cheese and port. ⊠*Biras Creek Hotel, North Sound* ☎*284/494–3555 or 800/223–1108* ⌂*Reservations essential* ▭*AE, D, MC, V.*

$$$$ ✕**Little Dix Bay Pavilion.** For an elegant evening, you can't do better than this—the candlelight in the open-air pavilion is enchanting, the always-changing menu sophisticated, the service attentive. Superbly prepared seafood, meat, and vegetarian entrées draw locals and visitors alike. Favorites include the pan-seared marinated tuna with sweet chili sautéed spinach, rack of lamb with a garlic puree, and red snapper fillet with fennel served with sweet-potato tempura. The Monday evening buffet shines. ⊠*Little Dix Bay Resort, Spanish Town* ☎*284/495–5555* ⌂*Reservations essential* ▭*AE, D, MC, V.*

ITALIAN

$$$$ ✕**Giorgio's Table.** Gaze up at the stars and listen to the water lap against the shore while dining on homemade ravioli, beef fillet in a brunello wine sauce, or truffle duck ragout served over pappardelle pasta. House specialties include fresh lobster that you choose yourself from a 5,000-gallon seawater pool. There's also a selection of 120 wines kept in a temperature-controlled cellar. Lunch is more casual and includes pizzas and pasta dishes. ⊠*Mahoe Bay* ☎*284/495–5684* ▭*AE, MC, V.*

$$–$$$$ ✕**The Rock Café.** Surprisingly good Italian cuisine is served among the waterfalls and giant boulders that form the famous Baths. For dinner at this open-air eatery, feast on chicken and penne in a tomato-cream sauce, spaghetti with lobster sauce, or fresh red snapper in a butter and caper sauce. For dessert, don't miss the chocolate mousse. ⊠*The Valley* ☎*284/495–5482* ▭*AE, D, MC, V* ⊗*No lunch.*

FOOD STUFF. Virgin Gorda's grocery stores barely equal convenience stores elsewhere. The selection is small and the prices high. Many Virgin Gorda residents head to Tortola or even to St. Thomas to do their shopping. If you're coming here from another island, you might want to bring along one or two items you know you'll need.

SEAFOOD

$$$$ ✕**The Clubhouse.** The Bitter End Yacht Club's open-air
★ waterfront restaurant is a favorite rendezvous for the sailing set, so it's busy day and night. You can find lavish buffets for breakfast, lunch, and dinner, as well as an à la carte
menu. Dinner selections include grilled swordfish or tuna,
local lobster, chopped sirloin, as well as veggie dishes.
✉*Bitter End Yacht Club, North Sound* ☎*284/494–2745*
✍*Reservations essential* ▭*AE, MC, V.*

WHERE TO STAY

While villas are scattered all over Virgin Gorda, hotels are
centered in and around the Valley, Nail Bay, and in the
North Sound area. Except for Leverick Bay Resort, which
is around the point from North Sound, all hotels in North
Sound are reached only by ferry.

HOTELS & INNS

$$$$ ⊞**Biras Creek Resort.** Although Biras Creek is tucked out of
★ the way on the island's North Sound, the get-away-from-it-
all feel is actually the major draw for its well-heeled clientele. Anyway, you're just a five-minute ferry ride from the
dock at Gun Creek. There are a handful of other hotels in
the area, but this resort's gourmet meal plan means you
won't want to leave. A member of the exclusive Relais &
Châteaux family of hotels, Biras Creek offers sophisticated
suites with separate bedroom and living areas, though only
bedrooms have air-conditioning. Guests get around on complimentary bicycles. Rates are per couple, per night, and
include everything but beverages. Pros: luxurious rooms,
professional staff, good dining options. Cons: expensive
rates, isolated location, difficult for people with mobility
problems. ⌂*Box 54, North Sound VG1150* ☎*284/494–
3555 or 800/223–1108* ☏*284/494–3557* ⊕*www.biras.com*
↪*34 suites* ⌂*In-room: safe, refrigerator, no TV (some),
dial-up. In-hotel: 2 restaurants, bar, tennis courts, pool, spa,
beachfront, water sports, bicycles, no elevator, public Internet, public Wi-Fi* ⊙*Closed Sept.* ▭*AE, MC, V* ⦿*FAP.*

★ **Fodor's**Choice ⊞**Bitter End Yacht Club.** Sailing's the thing at this
$$$$ busy hotel and marina in the nautically inclined North
☾ Sound, and since the use of everything from small sailboats
to kayaks to Windsurfers is included in the price, you have

no reason not to get out on the water. If you're serious about taking to the high seas, sign up for lessons at the resort's sailing school. Of course, if you just want to lounge about on the beachfront chaises or on your balcony, that's okay, too. There's a busy social scene, with guests gathering to swap tales at the hotel's bars. Rooms are bright and cheery, with the decor leaning toward tropical colors. You can reach the Bitter End only by a free private ferry. Pros: lots of water sports, good diving opportunities, friendly guests. Cons: expensive rates, isolated location, lots of stairs. *Box 46, North Sound VG1150* 284/494–2746 or 800/872–2392 284/494–4756 *www.beyc.com* 87 rooms *In-room: no a/c (some), no TV. In-hotel: 3 restaurants, bar, pool, beachfront, diving, water sports, no elevator, children's programs (ages 6–18), public Internet, public Wi-Fi* AE, MC, V AI.

$$$$ **Little Dix Bay.** This laid-back luxury resort offers something for everyone, which is why we like it. You can swim, sun, and snorkel on a gorgeous sandy crescent, play tennis or windsurf, or just relax with a good book. The hotel's restaurants serve stellar food, but you're only a five-minute drive from Spanish Town's less expensive restaurants and shopping. Rooms have rattan and wood furniture and a casual feel. The gardens are gorgeous, with lots of lush plantings kept snipped to perfection. Depending on when you visit, your fellow guests will be honeymooners or folks who've spent a week or two in the winter season for years. Pros: convenient location, lovely grounds, near many dining options. Cons: expensive rates, very spread out, insular but not isolated. *Box 70, Little Dix Bay VG1150* 284/495–5555 284/495–5661 *www.littledixbay.com* 98 rooms, 8 suites, 2 villas *In-room: safe, refrigerator, no TV, dial-up, Wi-Fi. In-hotel: 3 restaurants, bars, tennis courts, pool, gym, spa, beachfront, water sports, no elevator, children's programs (ages 3–16), public Internet, public Wi-Fi* AE, MC, V EP.

$$–$$$$ **Nail Bay Resort.** Rambling up the hill above the coast, this resort offers a wide selection of rooms and suites to fit every need. The beach is a short walk away from the units at lower elevations, but if you're staying higher up the hill, you might want to drive to avoid the uphill trek back to your room. You get cooking facilities (at least microwave, fridge, toaster oven, and coffeemaker) no matter how small your room. Part of the road here is in awful condition, but it's being repaved. There's a restaurant and lots of activities, so you won't need to leave unless you

want to. The rooms and apartments have modern rattan furniture, tile floors, and nice views. Pros: full kitchens, lovely beach, close to town. Cons: construction noise, road being repaired, uphill walk from beach. *Box 69, Nail Bay VG1150* ☎284/494–8000 *or* 800/871–3551 📠284/495–5875 ⊕*www.nailbay.com* 🛏4 rooms, 5 suites, 9 villas ♿*In-room: kitchen, VCR. In-hotel: restaurant, bar, tennis court, pool, spa, beachfront, water sports, no elevator, public Internet, public Wi-Fi* ⊟AE, MC, V ⦿EP.

$$–$$$$ 🖼**Saba Rock Resort.** Reachable only by a free ferry or by private yacht, this resort on its own tiny cay isn't for everyone. However, it's good for folks who want to mix and mingle with the sailors who drop anchor for the night. The bar and restaurant are busy with yachters gathering for sundowners, lunch, and dinner. The rooms are spacious, each with a different decor. All have tile floors, rattan or wood furniture, and colorful spreads and drapes. A resort boat will drop you at nearby North Sound resorts if you need a change of pace. Pros: party atmosphere, convenient transportation, good diving nearby. Cons: tiny beach, isolated location, on a very small island. *Box 67, North Sound VG1150* ☎284/495–7711 *or* 284/495–9966 📠284/495–7373 ⊕*www.sabarock.com* 🛏7 1-bedroom suites, 2 2-bedroom suites ♿*In-room: no phone (some), kitchen (some), refrigerator. In-hotel: restaurant, bar, beachfront, water sports, no elevator, public Wi-Fi* ⊟D,MC, V ⦿CP.

$$$ 🖼**Olde Yard Village.** All the condos in this upscale complex have at least partial ocean views. The location, a few minutes' drive from Spanish Town, is ideal: close enough so that you can easily pop out to dinner but far enough to make you feel as if you're more isolated than you really are. You will need a car, though, to make those trips a breeze. The Olde Yard Village will be building new units over the next several years, but construction is a bit removed from the existing accommodations. Every condo is decorated to the owner's taste, but you can count on a comfortable tropical ambience. Pros: close to Spanish Town, lovely pool, recently built units. Cons: no beach, on a busy street, noisy roosters nearby. *Box 26, The Valley VG1150* ☎284/495–5544 *or* 800/653–9273 📠284/495–5986 ⊕*www.oldeyardvillage.com* 🛏29 condos ♿*In-room: kitchen, refrigerator, Wi-Fi. In-hotel: restaurant, 2 lighted tennis courts, bar, pool, gym, spa, no elevator* ⊟AE, MC, V ⦿EP.

$–$$$ 🖼**Leverick Bay Resort & Marina.** With its colorful buildings and bustling marina, Leverick Bay is a good choice. The resort does not have a great beach, but with easy access to various water-sports activities, a tasty on-site restaurant, and comfortable and spacious rooms, it's still appealing. If you prefer an apartment, opt for one of the units stretching up the hillside above the marina. There's a one-week minimum stay in the apartments. All the accommodations have tile floors and pastel accents with a tropical feel. Pros: lively location, good restaurant, small grocery store. Cons: very small beach, no laundry in units, 15-minute drive to town. ⌂*Box 63, Leverick Bay VG1150* ☎*284/495–7421 or 800/848–7081* 🖷*284/495–7367* ⊕*www.leverickbay. com* ⌕*14 rooms, 4 condos* ⌂*In-room: safe, kitchen (some), refrigerator, Wi-Fi. In-hotel: 2 restaurants, bar, tennis court, pool, spa, beachfront, diving, laundry facilities, public Internet* ⊟*AE, MC, V* ⋈*EP.*

$–$$ ▣**Fischer's Cove Beach Hotel.** The rooms are modest, the furniture discount-store style, and the walls thin, but you can't beat the location. Budget travelers should consider this hotel if they want a good beach just steps away. If you plan on staying put, you won't even need a car. Spanish Town's handful of restaurants and shopping at Virgin Gorda Yacht Harbor are an easy 15-minute walk away. For better views, opt for the beachfront rooms. Pros: beachfront location, budget price, good restaurant. Cons: very basic units, thin walls, no a/c in some rooms. ⌂*Box 60, The Valley VG1150* ☎*284/495–5252* 🖷*284/495–5820* ⊕*www.fischerscove.com* ⌕*12 rooms, 8 cottages* ⌂*In-room: no a/c (some), kitchen (some), refrigerator, no TV (some), dial-up. In-hotel: restaurant, beachfront, no elevator* ⊟*AE, MC, V* ⋈*EP.*

VILLAS

Those craving seclusion would do well at a villa. Most have full kitchens and maid service. Prices per week in winter run from around $2,000 for a one- or two-bedroom villa up to $10,000 for a five-room beachfront villa. Rates in summer are substantially less. On Virgin Gorda, a villa in the North Sound area means you can pretty much stay put at night unless you want to make the drive on narrow roads. If you opt for a spot near the Baths, it's an easier drive to town.

BOOKING AGENCIES

The St. Thomas–based **McLaughlin-Anderson Luxury Villas** (⊠*1000 Blackbeard's Hill, Suite 3, Charlotte Amalie, USVI 00802* ☎*340/776–0635 or 800/537–6246* ⊕*www. mclaughlinanderson.com*) represents nearly two dozen properties all over Virgin Gorda. Villas range in size from two bedrooms to six bedrooms and come with many amenities, including full kitchens, pools, and stellar views. The company can hire a chef and stock your kitchen with groceries. A seven-night minimum is required during the winter season.

Tropical Care Services (⊡*Box 1039, The Valley VG1150* ☎*284/495–6493* ⊕*www.tropicalcareservices.com*) manages about a dozen properties stretching from the Baths to the Nail Bay area. Several budget properties are included among the more pricey offerings. Most houses have private pools, and a few are right on the beach. A sister company at the same number, Tropical Nannies, provides babysitting services.

Virgin Gorda Villa Rentals (⊡*Box 63, The Valley VG1150* ☎*284/495–7421 or 800/848–7081* ⊕*www.virgingordabvi. com*) manages more than 40 properties near Leverick Bay Resort and Mahoe Bay, so it's perfect for those who want to be close to activities. Many of the accommodations—from studios to six or more bedrooms—have private swimming pools and air-conditioning, at least in the bedrooms. All have full kitchens, are well maintained, and have spectacular views.

VILLA RESORTS

$–$$$$ ☷**Mango Bay Resort.** Sitting seaside on Virgin Gorda's north coast, this collection of contemporary duplex apartments will make you feel right at home. Each apartment is individually owned, so each has a different decor, but you can count on tile floors and tropical accents. The homes come with floats, kayaks, and snorkeling equipment, so you can find plenty to do when you're tired of lounging in the chaise. Giorgio's Table, a popular Italian restaurant, is a short walk away. Pros: nice beach, homey feel, good restaurant nearby. Cons: construction in area, drab decor, some units have lackluster views. ⊡*Box 1062, Mahoe Bay* ☎*284/495–5672* ☎*284/495–5674* ⊕*www.mangobayresort.com* ⇝*24 condos, 5 villas* ⌂*In-room: kitchen, dial-up. In-hotel: beachfront, no elevator* ▭*MC, V* ⊺⊙*EP.*

$$–$$$ ⊞**Guavaberry Spring Bay Vacation Homes.** Rambling back
★ from the beach, these hexagonal one- and two-bedroom
villas give you all the comforts of home with the striking
boulder-fringed beach just minutes away. The villas are best
for independent travelers who want to be able to cook or
simply head 10 minutes to Spanish Town for a night out.
The popular Baths are a short walk away, and snorkeling
is excellent. The rooms have dark-wood or white walls, tile
floors, and tropical bright spreads and curtains. Not all have
sea views. Pros: short walk to the Baths, easy drive to town,
great beaches nearby. Cons: few amenities, older property, basic decor. ⊡*Box 20, The Valley* ☎*284/495–5227*
🖷*284/495–5283* ⊕*www.guavaberryspringbay.com* ➪*12
1-bedroom units, 6 2-bedroom units, 1 3-bedroom units,
18 villas* ⌂*In-room: no a/c (some), no phone, kitchen, no
TV (some). In-hotel: beachfront, no elevator, public Internet, public Wi-Fi* ☱No credit cards ⑩EP.

BEACHES

Although some of the best beaches are reachable only by
boat, don't worry if you're a landlubber, because you can
find plenty of places to sun and swim. Anybody going to
Virgin Gorda must experience swimming or snorkeling
among its unique boulder formations, which can be visited
at several sites along Lee Road. The most popular is the
Baths, but there are several other similar places nearby that
are easily reached.

The Baths. Featuring a stunning maze of huge granite boulders that extend into the sea, this national park is usually
crowded midday with day-trippers. The snorkeling is good,
and you're likely to see a wide variety of fish, but watch
out for dinghies coming ashore from the numerous sailboats anchored offshore. Public bathrooms and a handful
of bars and shops are close to the water and at the start of
the path that leads to the beach. Lockers are available to
keep belongings safe. ⊠*About 1 mi (1½ km) west of Spanish Town ferry dock on Tower Rd., Spring Bay* ☎*284/494–
3904* ☜*$3* ⊙*Daily dawn–dusk.*

Nail Bay. Head to the island's north tip and you can be
rewarded with a trio of beaches within the Nail Bay Resort
complex that are ideal for snorkeling. Mountain Trunk
Bay is perfect for beginners, and Nail Bay and Long Bay
beaches have coral caverns just offshore. The resort has a

Getting Your Goat

Roaming livestock is a way of life in the tropics, particularly in less developed places like Virgin Gorda. Indeed, residents who leave their car windows open occasionally return to find a freshly laid egg on the front seat. If you have time to sit a spell at places like Virgin Gorda Yacht Harbour, you might see a mother hen followed by a string of little ones.

While crowing roosters can rouse annoyingly early, grazing goats pose traffic hazards. Some have owners, but many of them wander off to forage for food. Be particularly careful when you're driving around bends or over the top of hills. You might find a herd of goats, or maybe a sheep or two, camped out in the middle of the road. Sound your horn and be patient. They'll move in their own time.

And should you happen to see a vendor selling local dishes, the relatives of those goats and chickens are probably bubbling in the pot.

restaurant, which is an uphill walk but perfect for beach breaks. ⊠*Nail Bay Resort, off Plum Tree Bay Rd., Nail Bay* ☎*No phone* ☎*Free* ☉*Daily dawn–dusk.*

★ **Savannah Bay.** For a wonderfully private beach close to Spanish Town, try Savannah Bay. It may not always be completely deserted, but you can find a spot to yourself on this long stretch of soft, white sand. Bring your own mask, fins, and snorkel, as there are no facilities. The view from above is a photographer's delight. ⊠*Off North Sound Rd., ¾ mi (1¼ km) east of Spanish Town ferry dock, Savannah Bay* ☎*No phone* ☎*Free* ☉*Daily dawn–dusk.*

Spring Bay Beach. Just off Tower Road, this national-park beach gets much less traffic than the nearby Baths, and has the similarly large, imposing boulders that create interesting grottoes for swimming. The snorkeling is excellent, and the grounds include swings and picnic tables. ⊠*Off Tower Rd., 1 mi (1½ km) west of Spanish Town ferry dock, Spring Bay* ☎*284/494–3904* ☎*Free* ☉*Daily dawn–dusk.*

SPORTS & THE OUTDOORS

DIVING & SNORKELING

Where you go snorkeling and what company you pick depends on where you're staying. Many hotels have on-site dive outfitters, but if they don't, one won't be far away. If your hotel does have a dive operation, just stroll down to the dock and hop aboard—no need to drive anywhere. The dive companies are all certified by PADI. Costs vary, but count on paying about $75 for a one-tank dive and $95 for a two-tank dive. All dive operators offer introductory courses as well as certification and advanced courses. Should you get an attack of the bends, which can happen when you ascend too rapidly, the nearest decompression chamber is at Roy L. Schneider Regional Medical Center in St. Thomas.

There are some terrific snorkel and dive sites off Virgin Gorda, including areas around the Baths, the North Sound, and the Dogs. The Chimney at Great Dog Island sports a coral archway and canyon covered with a wide variety of sponges. At Joe's Cave, an underwater cavern on West Dog Island, huge groupers, eagle rays, and other colorful fish accompany divers as they swim. At some sites you can see 100 feet down, but divers who don't want to go that deep and snorkelers will find plenty to look at just below the surface.

☼ The **Bitter End Yacht Club** (✉*North Sound* ☎*284/494–2746* ⊕*www.beyc.com*) offers two snorkeling trips a day. **Dive BVI** (✉*Virgin Gorda Yacht Harbour, Spanish Town* ☎*284/495–5513 or 800/848–7078* ✉*Leverick Bay Resort and Marina, Leverick Bay* ☎*284/495–7328* ⊕*www.dive-bvi.com*) offers expert instruction, certification, and day trips. **Sunchaser Scuba** (✉*Bitter End Yacht Club, North Sound* ☎*284/495–9638 or 800/932–4286* ⊕*www.sunchaserscuba.com*) offers resort, advanced, and rescue courses.

GOLF

The 9-hole minigolf course, **Golf Virgin Gorda** (✉*Copper Mine Point, The Valley* ☎*284/495–5260*), is next to the Mine Shaft Café, delightfully nestled between huge granite boulders.

WINDSURFING

☾ The North Sound is a good place to learn to windsurf: it's protected, so you can't be easily blown out to sea. The **Bitter End Yacht Club** (⊠*North Sound* ☎*284/494–2746* ⊕*www. beyc.com*) gives lessons and rents equipment for $60 per hour for nonguests. A half-day Windsurfer rental runs $80 to $100.

SHOPPING

Most boutiques are within hotel complexes or at Virgin Gorda Yacht Harbour. Two of the best are at Biras Creek and Little Dix Bay. Other properties—the Bitter End and Leverick Bay—have small but equally select boutiques.

CLOTHING

Blue Banana (⊠*Virgin Gorda Yacht Harbour, Spanish Town* ☎*284/495–5957*) carries a large selection of gifts, clothing, and accessories. At **Dive BVI** (⊠*Virgin Gorda Yacht Harbour, Spanish Town* ☎*284/495–5513*), you can find books about the islands as well as snorkeling equipment, sportswear, sunglasses, and beach bags. **Fat Virgin's Treasure** (⊠*Biras Creek Hotel, North Sound* ☎*284/495–7054*) sells cool island-style clothing in tropical prints, a large selection of straw sun hats, and unusual gift items like island-made hot sauces, artistic cards, and locally fired pottery. **Margo's Boutique** (⊠*Virgin Gorda Yacht Harbour, Spanish Town* ☎*284/495–5237*) is the place to buy handmade silver, pearl, and shell jewelry. The **Pavilion Gift Shop** (⊠*Little Dix Bay Hotel, Little Dix Bay* ☎*284/495–5555*) has the latest in resort wear for men and women, as well as jewelry, books, housewares, and expensive T-shirts. **Pusser's Company Store** (⊠*Leverick Bay* ☎*284/495–7369*) has a trademark line of sportswear, rum products, and gift items.

FOOD

The **Bitter End Emporium** (⊠*Bitter End Yacht Harbor, North Sound* ☎*284/494–2746*) is the place for such edible treats as local fruits, cheeses, baked goods, and gourmet prepared food to take out. **Buck's Food Market** (⊠*Virgin Gorda Yacht Harbour, Spanish Town* ☎*284/495–5423* ⊠*Gun Creek, North Sound* ☎*284/495–7368*) is the closest the island offers to a full-service supermarket and has everything from an in-store bakery and deli to fresh fish and produce departments. The **Chef's Pantry** (⊠*Leverick Bay* ☎*284/495–7677*) has the fixings for an impromptu party in your villa or boat—fresh seafood, specialty meats, imported cheeses, daily baked breads and pastries, and an impressive wine and spirit selection. The **Wine Cellar & Bakery** (⊠*Virgin Gorda Yacht Harbour, Spanish Town* ☎*284/495–5250*) sells bread, rolls, muffins, cookies, sandwiches, and sodas to go.

GIFTS

Flamboyance (⊠*Virgin Gorda Yacht Harbour, Spanish Town* ☎*284/495–5946*) has a large line of fragrances, including those inspired by tropical flowers. The **Palm Tree Gallery** (⊠*Leverick Bay* ☎*284/495–7479*) sells attractive handcrafted jewelry, paintings, and one-of-a-kind gift items, as well as games and books about the Caribbean. **Reeftique** (⊠*Bitter End Yacht Harbor, North Sound* ☎*284/494–2746*) carries island crafts and jewelry, clothing, and nautical odds and ends with the Bitter End logo.

NIGHTLIFE

Pick up a free copy of the *Limin' Times*—available at most resorts and restaurants—for the most current local entertainment schedule.

During high season, **Bath & Turtle** (⊠*Virgin Gorda Yacht Harbour, Spanish Town* ☎*284/495–5239*), one of the liveliest spots on Virgin Gorda, hosts island bands Wednesday from 8 PM until midnight. Local bands play several nights a week at the **Bitter End Yacht Club** (⊠*North Sound* ☎*284/494–2746*) during the winter season. **Chez Bamboo** (⊠*Across from Virgin Gorda Yacht Harbour, Spanish Town* ☎*284/495–5752*) is the place for live jazz on Monday night and calypso and reggae on Friday night. The bar at **Little Dix Bay** (⊠*Little Dix Bay* ☎*284/495–5555*) presents elegant live entertainment several nights a week in season. The **Mine Shaft Café** (⊠*Copper Mine Point, The Valley* ☎*284/495–5260*) has live bands on Wednesday and Friday. The **Restaurant at Leverick Bay** (⊠*Leverick Bay Resort & Marina, Leverick Bay* ☎*284/495–7154*) hosts live music on Saturday through Wednesday in season. The **Rock Café** (⊠*The Valley* ☎*284/495–5177*) has live bands Friday.

VIRGIN GORDA ESSENTIALS

To research prices, get advice from other travelers, and book travel arrangements, visit www.fodors.com.

TRANSPORTATION

BY AIR

There's no nonstop service from the continental United States to Virgin Gorda. Air Sunshine flies among Virgin Gorda and St. Thomas and San Juan, Puerto Rico. If you have seven or more people in your party, it probably pays to hire a charter plane from St. Thomas or San Juan. Fly BVI is one of the local charter services. If you're traveling to North Sound from St. Thomas, Seaborne Airlines flies from the downtown Charlotte Amalie waterfront on Friday and weekends. If you're coming from Puerto Rico, Seaborne flies from Old San Juan with a connection in St. Thomas.

Airport Transfers Mahogany Rentals & Taxi Service (✉ *Virgin Gorda* ☎ *284/495–5469*).

BY BOAT & FERRY

Ferries connect St. Thomas with Virgin Gorda; they leave from both Charlotte Amalie and Red Hook, but not daily. Ferries also link St. John and Tortola with Virgin Gorda.

Ferries to Virgin Gorda land in Spanish Town. All ferries to Red Hook, St. Thomas, stop in St. John first to clear U.S. customs. Ferry schedules vary by day, and not all companies make daily trips. The BVI Tourist Board Web site *(⇨ see Visitor Information in Virgin Islands Essentials)* has links to all the ferry companies, which are the best up-to-date sources of information for specific routes and schedules.

BY CAR

Virgin Gorda has a small road system, and a single, very steep road links the north and south ends of the island, but if you will probably need a car to get around for at least a few days of your stay unless you plan in staying put at your resort.

Contacts L&S Jeep Rental (✉ *South Valley, Virgin Gorda* ☎ *284/495–5297* ⊕ *www.landsjeeprentals.com*). **Mahogany Rentals & Taxi Service** (✉ *Spanish Town, Virgin Gorda* ☎ *284/495–5469* ⊕ *mahoganyrentals.puzzlepiece.net*). **Speedy's Car Rentals** (✉ *The Valley, Virgin Gorda* ☎ *284/495–5240* ⊕ *www.speedysbvi.com*).

5

BY TAXI

Taxi rates aren't set on Virgin Gorda and are by the trip, not per person, so you should negotiate the fare with your driver before you start your trip. It's cheaper to travel in groups because there's a minimum fare to each destination, which is the same whether you have one, two, or three passengers. The taxi number is also the license plate number. Andy's Taxi & Jeep Rental offers service from one end of Virgin Gorda to the other. Mahogany Rentals & Taxi Service provides taxi service all over Virgin Gorda.

Information **Andy's Taxi & Jeep Rental** (⌧ The Valley, Virgin Gorda ☎ 284/495-5252). **Mahogany Rentals & Taxi Service** (⌧ The Valley, Virgin Gorda ☎ 284/495-5469).

CONTACTS & RESOURCES

BANKS

First Caribbean International is in Virgin Gorda Yacht Harbour. First Bank is across the street from Virgin Gorda Yacht Harbour.

EMERGENCIES

Ambulance, Fire & Police **General emergencies** (☎ 999).

Hospitals & Clinics **Virgin Gorda Government Health Clinic** (⌧ The Valley, Virgin Gorda ☎ 284/495-5337).

Marine Emergencies **VISAR** (☎ 767 from phone or Marine Radio Channel 16).

Pharmacies **Medicure Pharmacy** (⌧ Spanish Town, Virgin Gorda ☎ 284/495-5479). **O'Neal's Drug Store** (⌧ Spanish Town, Virgin Gorda ☎ 284/495-5449).

INTERNET, MAIL & SHIPPING

There's a post office in Spanish Town on Virgin Gorda. For a small fee, Rush It, in Spanish Town, offers most U.S. mail and UPS services (via St. Thomas the next day). If you wish to write to an establishment in the BVI, be sure to include the specific island in the address.

Many hotels have Internet access for their guests. Internet cafés, however, are harder to find.

Contacts **Rush It** (⌧ Spanish Town, Virgin Gorda ☎ 284/495-5821).

SAFETY

Although crime is rare, use common sense: don't leave your camera on the beach while you take a dip or your wallet on a hotel dresser when you go for a walk.

TOUR OPTIONS

Romney Associates/Travel Plan Tours can arrange island tours, boat tours, snorkeling and scuba-diving trips, dolphin swims, and yacht charters from its Virgin Gorda base.

Information **Romney Associates/Travel Plan Tours** (☎284/494–4000).

WEDDINGS

Contacts **BVI Wedding Planners & Consultants** (☎284/494–5306 ⊕*www.bviweddings.com*).

5

In Focus Virgin Islands Essentials

PLANNING TOOLS, EXPERT INSIGHT,
GREAT CONTACTS

There are planners and there are those
who, excuse the pun, fly by the seat
of their pants. We happily place our-
selves among the planners. Our writers and editors try to anticipate all the
issues you may face before and during
any journey, and then they do their
research. This section is the product of
their efforts. Use it to get excited about
your trip to Virgin Islands, to inform your
travel planning, or to guide you on the
road should the seat of your pants start
to feel threadbare.

www.fodors.com/forums

GETTING STARTED

We're proud of our Web site: Fodors.com is a great place to begin any journey. Scan Travel Wire for suggested itineraries, travel deals, restaurant and hotel openings, and other up-to-the-minute info. Check out Booking to research prices and book plane tickets, hotel rooms, rental cars, and vacation packages. Head to Talk for on-the-ground pointers from travelers who frequent our message boards. You can also link to loads of other travel-related resources.

▌RESOURCES

ONLINE TRAVEL TOOLS

Information on the U.S. & British Virgin Islands is just a click away on the islands' respective tourism Web sites. And of course every Caribbean traveler should bookmark the Caribbean Tourism Organization's comprehensive site.

ALL ABOUT THE U.S. & BRITISH VIRGIN ISLANDS

Web Sites **USVI Department of Tourism** (⊕*www.usvitourism.vi*) **BVI Tourism Bureau** (⊕*www.bvitouristboard.com*) **Caribbean Tourism Organization** (⊕*www.doitcaribbean.com*)

Time Zones **Timeanddate.com** (⊕*www.timeanddate.com/worldclock*) can help you figure out the correct time anywhere.

Weather **Accuweather.com** (⊕*www.accuweather.com*) is an independent weather-forecasting service with good coverage of hurricanes. **Weather.com** (⊕*www.weather.com*) is the Web site for the Weather Channel.

VISITOR INFORMATION

Stop by the Tourism Department's local offices for brochures on things to do and places to see. The offices are open only weekdays from 8 to 5, so if you need information on the weekend or on one of the territory's many holidays, you're out of luck. *(For locations, see ⇨ Visitor Information in the Essentials section of each chapter.)* For general information on the islands, contact these tourist offices before you go.

United States Virgin Islands Department of Tourism **USVI Government Tourist Office** (☎*340/774–8784 or 800/372–8784* ⊕*www.usvitourism.vi*).

BVI: British Virgin Islands Tourist Board **BVI Tourist Board** (☎*212/696–0400, 800/835–8530 in New York* ☎*770/874–5951 in Georgia* ☎*213/736–8931 in Los Angeles* ☎*www.bvitourism.com*).

▌ THINGS TO CONSIDER

GEAR

The Virgin Islands are definitely laid-back destinations. If you're staying at a posh resort, you may need some dressier attire, particularly during the winter months. Ties are never required, but jackets for men sometimes are. Sturdy shoes are a must if you plan on hiking, and don't forget to tuck a folding umbrella into your suitcase for those once-in-a-while rain showers. You may need a light sweater or long-sleeve T-shirt for breezy nights (or overly air-conditioned restaurants) or for the ferry ride home after a day in the sun.

Pharmacies, grocery and discount stores—particularly Kmart on St. Thomas and St. Croix— carry a large variety of sundries, but you may not find the brand you want, and most prices are higher. The selection in the BVI, particularly on the out islands, is definitely on the slim side. If you prefer a certain brand of mosquito repellent or baby formula, for example, bring it from home.

There are no prohibitions about bringing any food items to the USVI, but you can't bring meat into the BVI without a $25 agricultural permit. You need to apply in advance at the Agriculture Department.

But we know that frugal folks will still bring some staples from home. Film cans make perfect spice containers, and anything else can go in plastic bags. Double-bag bottled liquids to make sure you don't have leaks and put those in your checked luggage. To bring your favorite cut of meat, freeze it thoroughly, pack it in a cooler with ice packs, and tape the cooler shut with duct tape. Unless the cooler is small enough to fit in the overhead compartment of the airplane, you'll have to check it as luggage.

PASSPORTS

A passport is not required to visit the USVI. There are no immigration procedures upon arriving in St. Thomas or St. Croix, but on your return to the U.S. you will clear immigration and customs before boarding your flight. If you arrive in the USVI by ferry from the BVI, you must also go through customs and immigration procedures.

U.S. citizens must have proof of citizenship (a passport or original birth certificate with raised seal plus a valid photo ID) to enter the BVI, but they must have a valid passport if returning by air (a birth certificate if returning by sea, at this writing). At some point in 2008, it is likely that U.S. citizens will be required to carry a valid passport when visiting the BVI by either air or sea.

In the BVI, you must go through customs and immigration upon arrival. Aside from paying the departure tax, there are no special procedures for departure from the BVI.

Even though passports are not required for travel to or from the USVI, we strongly recommend that you carry proof of citizenship in the form of a birth certificate, as well as a valid photo ID. Even though one is not required, we also recommend that you carry a valid passport when traveling to the U.S. Virgin Islands.

SHOTS & MEDICATIONS

You won't have to worry about diseases like malaria and Lyme disease when visiting the USBVI, but there are occasional outbreaks of dengue fever after long spates of heavy rains increase the mosquito population. The best defense is a liberal application of mosquito repellent. If you're traveling with young children, bring a mosquito net to cover the crib.

■TIP→ **If you travel a lot internationally—particularly to developing nations—refer to the CDC's** *Health Information for International Travel* **(aka Traveler's Health Yellow Book). Info from it is posted on the CDC Web site (wwwn. cdc.gov/travel/default.aspx), or you can buy a copy from your local bookstore for $24.95.**

For more information see Health under On the Ground in the U.S. & British Virgin Islands, below.

Health Warnings National Centers for Disease Control & Prevention (*CDC* ☏*877/394-8747 international travelers' health line* ⊕*www.cdc.gov/travel*). **World Health Organization** (*WHO* ⊕*www.who.int*).

TRIP INSURANCE

What kind of coverage do you honestly need? Do you need trip insurance at all? Take a deep breath and read on.

We believe that comprehensive trip insurance is especially valuable if you're booking a very expensive or complicated trip (particularly to an isolated region) or if you're booking far in advance. Who knows what could happen six months down the road? But whether you get insurance has more to do with how comfortable you are assuming all that risk yourself.

Comprehensive travel policies typically cover trip-cancellation and interruption, letting you cancel or cut your trip short because of a personal emergency, illness, or, in some cases, acts of terrorism in your destination. Such policies also cover evacuation and medical care. Some also cover you for trip delays because of bad weather or mechanical problems as well as for lost or delayed baggage. Another type of coverage to look for is financial default—that is, when your trip is disrupted because a tour operator, airline, or cruise line goes out of business. Generally you must buy this when you book your trip or shortly thereafter, and it's only available to you if your operator isn't on a list of excluded companies.

If you're going abroad, consider buying medical-only coverage at the very least. Neither Medicare nor some private insurers cover medical expenses anywhere outside of the United States besides Mexico and Canada (including time aboard a cruise ship, even if it leaves from a U.S. port). Medical-only policies typically reimburse you for medical care (excluding that related to preexisting conditions) and hospitalization abroad, and provide for evacuation. You still have to pay the bills and await reimbursement from the insurer, though.

Expect comprehensive travel insurance policies to cost about 4% to 7% of the total price of your trip (it's more like 12% if you're over age 70). A medical-only policy may or may not be cheaper than a comprehensive policy. Always read the fine print of your policy to make sure that you're covered for the risks that are of most concern to you. Compare several policies to make sure you're getting the best price and range of coverage available.

TRIP INSURANCE RESOURCES

INSURANCE COMPARISON SITES

Insure My Trip.com (⊕*www.insuremytrip.com*).

Square Mouth.com (⊕*www.quotetravelinsurance.com*).

COMPREHENSIVE TRAVEL INSURERS

Access America (☎*866/807–3982* ⊕*www.accessamerica.com*).

CSA Travel Protection (☎*800/873–9855* ⊕*www.csatravelprotection.com*).

HTH Worldwide (☎*610/254–8700* or *888/243–2358* ⊕*www.hthworldwide.com*).

Travelex Insurance (☎*888/457–4602* ⊕*www.travelex-insurance.com*).

Travel Guard International (☎*715/345–0505* or *800/826–4919* ⊕*www.travelguard.com*).

Travel Insured International (☎*800/243–3174* ⊕*www.travelinsured.com*).

Medical-Only Insurers

International Medical Group (☎*800/628–4664* ⊕*www.imglobal.com*).

International SOS (☎*215/942–8000* or *713/521–7611* ⊕*www.internationalsos.com*).

Wallach & Company (☎*800/237–6615* or *540/687–3166* ⊕*www.wallach.com*).

■TIP→ OK. You know you can save a bundle on trips to warm-weather destinations by traveling during the hurricane season. But there's also a chance that a severe storm will disrupt your plans. The solution? Look for hotels and resorts that offer storm/hurricane guarantees. Although they rarely allow refunds, most guarantees do let you rebook later if a storm strikes.

BOOKING YOUR TRIP

Unless your cousin is a travel agent, you're probably among the millions of people who make most of their travel arrangements online.

But have you ever wondered just what the differences are between an online travel agent (a Web site through which you make reservations instead of going directly to the airline, hotel, or car-rental company), a discounter (a firm that does a high volume of business with a hotel chain or airline and accordingly gets good prices), a wholesaler (one that makes cheap reservations in bulk and then resells them to people like you), and an aggregator (one that compares all the offerings so you don't have to)?

Is it truly better to book directly on an airline or hotel Web site? And when does a real live travel agent come in handy?

ONLINE

You really have to shop around. A travel wholesaler such as Hotels.com or HotelClub.net can be a source of good rates, as can discounters such as Hotwire or Priceline, particularly if you can bid for your hotel room or airfare. Indeed, such sites sometimes have deals that are unavailable elsewhere. They do, however, tend to work only with hotel chains (which makes them just plain useless for getting hotel reservations outside of major cities) or big airlines (so that often leaves out upstarts like jetBlue and some foreign carriers like Air Sunshine).

Also, with discounters and wholesalers you must generally prepay, and everything is non-refundable. And before you fork over the dough, be sure to check the terms and conditions, so you know what a given company will do for you if there's a problem and what you'll have to deal with on your own.

■TIP→ To be absolutely sure everything was processed correctly, confirm reservations made through online travel agents, discounters, and wholesalers directly with your hotel before leaving home.

Booking engines like Expedia, Travelocity, and Orbitz are actually travel agents, albeit high-volume, online ones. And airline travel packagers like American Airlines Vacations and United Vacations—well, they're travel agents, too. But they may still not work with all the world's hotels.

An aggregator site will search many sites and pull the best prices for airfares, hotels, and rental cars from them. Most aggregators compare the major travel-booking sites such as Expedia, Travelocity, and Orbitz; some also look at airline

Web sites, though rarely the sites of smaller budget airlines. Some aggregators also compare other travel products, including complex packages—a good thing, as you can sometimes get the best overall deal by booking an air-and-hotel package.

ONLINE BOOKING RESOURCES

AGGREGATORS

Kayak (⊕www.kayak.com) looks at cruises and vacation packages.

Mobissimo (⊕www.mobissimo.com).

Qixo (⊕www.qixo.com) compares cruises, vacation packages, and even travel insurance.

Sidestep (⊕www.sidestep.com) compares vacation packages and lists travel deals.

Travelgrove (⊕www.travelgrove.com) compares cruises and vacation packages.

BOOKING ENGINES

Cheap Tickets (⊕www.cheaptickets.com) discounter.

Expedia (⊕www.expedia.com) large online agency that charges a booking fee for airline tickets.

Hotwire (⊕www.hotwire.com) discounter.

Luxury Link (⊕www.luxurylink.com) has auctions (surprisingly good deals) as well as offers on the high-end side of travel.

Onetravel.com (⊕www.onetravel.com) discounter for hotels, car rentals, airfares, and packages.

Orbitz (⊕www.orbitz.com) charges a booking fee for airline tickets, but gives a clear breakdown of fees and taxes before you book.

Priceline.com (⊕www.priceline.com)discounter that also allows bidding.

Travel.com (⊕www.travel.com) allows you to compare its rates with those of other booking engines.

Travelocity (⊕www.travelocity.com) charges a booking fee for airline tickets, but promises good problem resolution.

▌ WITH A TRAVEL AGENT

If you use an agent—brick-and-mortar or virtual—you'll usually pay a fee for the service. And know that the service you get from some online agents isn't comprehensive. For example Expedia and Travelocity don't search for prices on budget airlines like Southwest or small foreign carriers. That said, some agents (online or not) *do* have access to fares that are difficult to find otherwise, and the savings can more than make up for any surcharge.

A knowledgeable brick-and-mortar travel agent can be a godsend if you're booking a cruise, a package trip that's not available to you directly, an air pass, or a complicated itinerary including several overseas flights. What's more, travel agents that specialize in a destination may have exclusive access to certain deals and insider information on things such as charter flights. Agents who specialize in types of travelers (senior citizens, gays and lesbians, naturists) or types of trips (cruises, luxury travel, safaris) can also be invaluable.

■TIP→ **Remember that Expedia, Travelocity, and Orbitz are travel agents, not just booking engines. To resolve any problems with a reservation made through these companies, contact them first.**

A top-notch agent planning your cruise may get you a cabin upgrade or arrange to have bottle of champagne chilling in your cabin when you embark. And complain about the surcharges all you like, but when things don't work out the way you'd hoped, it's nice to have an agent to put things right.

If you have the least little bit of computer ability, you can book just about everywhere in the USBVI online. Even the major consolidators now have Web sites that make booking a breeze, and those small, but special bed-and-breakfasts are also online.

Agent Resources American Society of Travel Agents (☎ *703/739–2782* ⊕ *www.travelsense.org*).

▌ ACCOMMODATIONS

Decide whether you want to pay the extra price for a room overlooking the ocean or the pool. At less expensive properties, location may mean a difference in price of only $10 to $20 per night; at luxury resorts, however, it could amount to as much as $100 per night. Also find out how close the proper-

ty is to a beach. At some hotels you can walk barefoot from your room onto the sand; others are across a road or a 10-minute drive away.

Nighttime entertainment is often alfresco in the USBVI, so if you go to bed early or are a light sleeper, ask for a room away from the dance floor. Air-conditioning isn't a necessity on all islands, many of which are cooled by trade winds, but it can be a plus if you enjoy an afternoon snooze or are bothered by humidity. Breezes are best on upper floors, particularly corner rooms. If you like to sleep without air-conditioning, make sure that windows can be opened and have screens; also make sure there are no security issues with leaving your windows open. If you're staying away from the water, make sure the room has a ceiling fan and that it works. In even the most luxurious resorts, there are times when things simply *don't* work; it's a fact of Caribbean life. No matter how diligent the upkeep, humidity and salt air quickly take their toll, and cracked tiles and chipped paint are common everywhere.

The lodgings we list are the cream of the crop in each price category. We always list the facilities that are available, but we don't specify whether they cost extra; when pricing accommodations, always ask what's included and what costs extra. Properties are assigned price categories based on the range between their least and most expensive standard double rooms at high season (excluding holidays).

■TIP➙ **Assume that hotels operate on the European Plan (EP, no meals) unless we specify that they use the Breakfast Plan (BP, with full breakfast), Continental Plan (CP, Continental breakfast), Full American Plan (FAP, all meals), Modified American Plan (MAP, breakfast and dinner) or are all-inclusive (AI, all meals and most activities).**

APARTMENT & VILLA RENTALS

Villas—whether luxurious or modest—are popular lodging options on all the Virgin Islands.

Renting a villa lets you settle in. You can have room to spread out, you can cook any or all of your meals, and you can have all the privacy you desire. Since most villas are in residential neighborhoods, your neighbors probably won't appreciate late-night parties. And you may be disturbed by your neighbor's weekend yard maintenance. That said, there's no better way to experience life in the USBVI.

Many villas are set up specifically for the rental market with bedrooms at opposite ends of the house. This makes them perfect for two couples who want to share an accommodation but still prefer some privacy. Others with more bedrooms are sized right for families. Ask about the villa layout to make sure young children won't have to sleep too far away from their parents. Villas with separate bedroom buildings are probably not a good

idea unless your children are in their teens.

Most villas are owned by people who live somewhere else but hire a local management company to attend to the details. Depending on the island and the rental, the manager will either meet you at the ferry or airport or will give you directions to your villa. Most of the companies offer the same services with the similar degrees of efficiency.

You can book your villa through the numerous agencies that show up on the Internet, but they are usually not based on the island you want to visit. Booking through an island-based manager means that you can talk to a person who knows the villa and can let you know whether it meets your specifications. Your villa manager can also arrange for a maid, a chef, and other staffers to take care of myriad other details that make your vacation go smoothly. They're only a phone call away when something goes wrong or you have a question.

Catered To Vacation Homes focuses on St. John. Vacation St. Croix is based on St. Croix. McLaughlin Anderson has rentals across the USBVI.

Villa Management Companies

Catered To Vacation Homes (✉ Marketplace Suite 206, 5206 Enighed, Cruz Bay, St. John, VI00830 ☎ 340/776–6641 or 800/424–6641 🖷 340/693–8191 ⊕ www.cateredto. com). **McLaughlin Anderson** (🖷 1000 Blackbeard's Hill, Suite

3, Charlotte Amalie, St. Thomas,
VI00802-6739 ☎340/776-0635 or
800/537-6246 ⊕www.mclaugh-
linanderson.com). **Vacation St.
Croix** (✉Box 1150, Christiansted,
St. Croix, VI00821 ☎340/778-0361
or 877/788-0361 ⊕www.
vacationstcroix.com).

**ONLINE BOOKING
RESOURCES**

CONTACTS
At Home Abroad (☎212/421-9165
⊕www.athomeabroadinc.com).

**Vacation Home Rentals World-
wide** (☎201/767-9393 or
800/633-3284 ⊕www.vhrww.com).

Villanet (☎206/417-3444 or
800/964-1891 ⊕www.rentavilla.com).

Villas & Apartments Abroad
(☎212/213-6435 or 800/433-3020
⊕www.vaanyc.com).

Villas International (☎415/499-
9490 or 800/221-2260 ⊕www.
villasintl.com).

Villas of Distinction (☎707/778-
1800 or 800/289-0900 ⊕www.
villasofdistinction.com).

Wimco (☎800/449-1553 ⊕www.
wimco.com).

▌AIRLINE TICKETS

Most domestic airline tickets are
electronic; international tickets may be either electronic or
paper. With an e-ticket the only
thing you receive is an e-mailed
receipt citing your itinerary and
reservation and ticket numbers.

The greatest advantage of an
e-ticket is that if you lose your
receipt, you can simply print out

another copy or ask the airline
to do it for you at check-in. You
usually pay a surcharge (up to
$50) to get a paper ticket, if you
can get one at all.

The sole advantage of a paper
ticket is that it may be easier to
endorse over to another airline
if your flight is canceled and the
airline with which you booked
can't accommodate you on
another flight.

▌RENTAL CARS

When you reserve a car, ask
about cancellation penalties,
taxes, drop-off charges (if you're
planning to pick up the car in
one city and leave it in another), and surcharges (for being
under or over a certain age, for
additional drivers, or for driving
across state or country borders
or beyond a specific distance
from your point of rental). All
these things can add substantially to your costs. Request car
seats and extras such as GPS
when you book.

Rates are sometimes—but not always—better if you book in advance or reserve through a rental agency's Web site. There are other reasons to book ahead, though: for popular destinations, during busy times of the year, or to ensure that you get certain types of cars (vans, SUVs, exotic sports cars).

■ TIP→ **Make sure that a confirmed reservation guarantees you a car. Agencies sometimes overbook, particularly for busy weekends and holiday periods.**

Unless you plan to spend all your days at a resort or plan to take taxis everywhere, you'll need a rental car at least for a few days. While driving is on the left, you'll drive an American-style car with the steering wheel on the left. Traffic doesn't move all that fast in most USBVI locations, so driving on the left is not that difficult to master.

If you're staying on St. Thomas or St. Croix and don't plan to venture far off the main roads, you won't need a four-wheel-drive vehicle. On St. John and in the BVI, a four-wheel-drive vehicle is useful to get up steep roads when it rains. Many rental homes in St. John and the BVI are on unpaved roads, so a four-wheel-drive vehicle with high clearance may be a necessity if you rent a villa. While rental agencies don't usually prohibit access to certain roads, use common sense. If the road looks too bad, turn around.

Most car rental agencies won't rent to anyone under age 25 or over age 75.

Some car rental agencies offer infant car seats for about $5 a day, but check and check again right before you leave for your trip to make sure one will be available. Their use isn't compulsory in the USBVI, but they are always a good idea if you have small children. You might consider bringing your own car seat from home.

Book your rental car well in advance during the winter season. Vehicles are particularly scarce around the busy President's Day holiday. If you don't reserve, you might find yourself with wheels. Prices will be higher during the winter season.

You usually won't find any long lines when picking up your car or dropping it off. If your rental agency is away from the airport or ferry terminal, you'll have to allot extra time to get to there. Ask when you pick up your car how much time you should allot for returning it.

Rates range from $50 a day ($300 a week) for an economy car with air-conditioning, automatic transmission, and unlimited mileage; you may pay as much as $80 a day ($400 a week) for a four-wheel-drive vehicle. Both the USVI and the BVI have major companies (with airport locations) as well as numerous local companies (near the airports, in hotels, and in the main towns), which are sometimes cheaper.

Most provide pick-up service; some ask that you take a taxi to their headquarters.

A driver's license from the U.S. or other countries is fine in the USVI, but in the BVI you'll have to buy a temporary driver's license for $10.

CAR RENTAL RESOURCES

LOCAL AGENCIES
Dependable Car Rental on St. Thomas (☎ 340/774–2253 or 800/522–3076 ⊕ www. dependablecar.com).

Itgo Car Rental on Tortola (☎ 284/494–2639).

Judi of Croix (☎ 340/773–2123 or 877/903–2123 ⊕ www. judiofcroix.com).

L&S Jeep Rental on Virgin Gorda (☎ 284/495–5297).

St. John Car Rental (☎ 340/776–6103 ⊕ www.stjohncarrental.com).

MAJOR AGENCIES
Alamo (☎ 800/522–9696 ⊕ www. alamo.com).

Avis (☎ 800/331–1084 ⊕ www. avis.com).

Budget (☎ 800/472–3325 ⊕ www. budget.com).

Hertz (☎ 800/654–3001 ⊕ www. hertz.com).

National Car Rental (☎ 800/227–7368 ⊕ www.nationalcar.com).

CAR-RENTAL INSURANCE
Everyone who rents a car wonders whether the insurance that the rental companies offer is worth the expense. No one—including us—has a simple answer. It all depends on how much regular insurance you have, how comfortable you are with risk, and whether money is an issue.

If you own a car, your personal auto insurance may cover a rental to some degree, though not all policies protect you abroad; always read your policy's fine print. If you don't have auto insurance, then seriously consider buying the collision- or loss-damage waiver (CDW or LDW) from the car-rental company, which eliminates your liability for damage to the car. Some credit cards offer CDW coverage, but it's usually supplemental to your own insurance and rarely covers SUVs, minivans, luxury models, and the like. If your coverage is secondary, you may still be liable for loss-of-use costs from the car-rental company. But no credit-card insurance is valid unless you use that card for *all* transactions, from reserving to paying the final bill. All companies exclude car rental in some countries, so be sure to find out about the destination to which you are traveling.

■TIP→ **Diners Club offers primary CDW coverage on all rentals reserved and paid for with the card. This means that Diners Club's company—not your own car insurance—pays in case of an accident. It doesn't mean your car-insurance company won't raise your rates once it discovers you had an accident.**

Some countries require you to purchase CDW coverage or require car-rental companies to include it in quoted rates. Ask your rental company about issues like these in your destination. In most cases it's cheaper to add a supplemental CDW plan to your comprehensive travel-insurance policy (⇨ *Trip Insurance under Things to Consider in Getting Started, above*) than to purchase it from a rental company. That said, you don't want to pay for a supplement if you're required to buy insurance from the rental company.

■TIP→ You can decline the insurance from the rental company and purchase it through a third-party provider such as Travel Guard (www.travelguard.com)—$9 per day for $35,000 of coverage. That's sometimes just under half the price of the CDW offered by some car-rental companies.

▌ VACATION PACKAGES

Packages *are not* guided excursions. Packages combine airfare, accommodations, and perhaps a rental car or other extras (theater tickets, guided excursions, boat trips, reserved entry to popular museums, transit passes), but they let you do your own thing. During busy periods packages may be your only option, as flights and rooms may be sold out otherwise.

Packages will definitely save you time. They can also save you money, particularly in peak seasons, but—and this is a really big

"but"—you should price each part of the package separately to be sure. And be aware that prices advertised on Web sites and in newspapers rarely include service charges or taxes, which can up your costs by hundreds of dollars.

■TIP→ Some packages and cruises are sold only through travel agents. Don't always assume that you can get the best deal by booking everything yourself.

A package trip that includes airfare, hotel, and some extras probably saves you money, but you're often limited to the larger properties. That quirky, off-the-beaten path spot, particularly in the British Virgin Islands, probably doesn't work with the airlines or package companies.

Of the major U.S. airline packagers, only American Airlines Vacations offers packages in both the U.S. and British Virgin Islands. US Airways Vacations and Delta Vacations offer trips on all three U.S. Virgin Islands; Continental Vacations offers only St. Thomas.

You'll usually find the best deals on packages in the slower summer season, when hoteliers have lots of vacant rooms. Check with your travel agent, online, airlines, or in the pages of your local major newspaper for the best deals. The best packages for the USVI can often be found through Liberty/GoGo Travel, Travel Impressions, and Apple Vacations. For the BVI, Liberty/GoGo Travel, Apple Vacations, and Classic Custom Vacations offer packages. They often tout last-minute specials, so late planning may save you money.

Online travel agencies such as Orbitz, Expedia, and Travelocity, also offer packages to the Virgin Islands.

Airline Vacation Packagers

American Airlines Vacations (☎ *800/321-2121* ⊕ *www. aavacations.com*). **Continental Airlines Vacations** (☎ *800/301-3800* ⊕ *www.covacations.com*). **Delta Vacations** (☎ *800/654-6559* ⊕ *www. deltavacations.com*). **US Airways Vacations** (☎ *800/422-3861* ⊕ *www.usairwaysvacations.com*).

Large Agency Packagers

Apple Vacations (☎ *800/517-2000* ⊕ *www.applevacations.com*). **Classic Custom Vacations** (☎ *800/635-1333* ⊕ *www.classicvacations. com*). **Liberty Travel** (☎ *888/271-1584* ⊕ *www.libertytravel.com*). **Travel Impressions** (⊕ *www. travelimpressions.com*).

Online Agency Packagers

Cheap Tickets (⊕ *www.cheaptickets.com*). **Expedia** (⊕ *www.expedia.com*). **Orbitz** (⊕ *www.orbitz.com*). **Priceline** (⊕ *www.priceline.com*). **Travelocity** (⊕ *www.travelocity.com*).

Organizations

American Society of Travel Agents (*ASTA* ☎ *703/739-2782 or 800/275-2782* ⊕ *www. astanet.com*). **United States Tour Operators Association** (*USTOA* ☎ *212/599-6599* ⊕ *www.ustoa. com*).

■ TIP→ Local tourism boards can provide information about lesser-known and small-niche operators that sell packages to only a few destinations.

TRANSPORTATION

Both ferries and flights travel between the Virgin Islands; a ferry usually takes longer, but it's more scenic and usually cheaper.

▌ BY AIR

The nonstop flight from New York to St. Thomas or San Juan takes about 4 hours; from Miami to St. Thomas or San Juan it's about 3 hours.

Reconfirming your flights on interisland carriers is still a good idea, particularly when you're traveling to the smallest islands. You may be subjected to a carrier's whims: if no other passengers are booked on your flight, you may be asked to take another flight later in the day, or your plane may make unscheduled stops to pick up more passengers or cargo. It's all part of the excitement—and unpredictability—of travel in the Caribbean. In addition, regional carriers use small aircraft with limited baggage space, and they often impose weight restrictions; travel light, or you could be subject to outrageous surcharges or delays in getting very large or heavy luggage, which may have to follow on another flight.

Airlines & Airports Airline and Airport Links.com (⊕*www. airlineandairportlinks.com*) has links to many of the world's airlines and airports.

Airline Security Issues Transportation Security Administration (⊕*www.tsa.gov*) has answers for almost every question that might come up.

AIRPORTS

The major airports are Terrence B. Lettsome International Airport on Beef Island, Tortola, Cyril E. King Airport on St. Thomas, and Henry Rohlsen Airport on St. Croix. There's a small airport (so small that it doesn't have a phone number) on Virgin Gorda.

Airport Information Terrence B. Lettsome International Airport

TRAVEL TIMES FROM ST. THOMAS	BY AIR	FERRY FROM CHARLOTTE AMALIE	FERRY FROM RED HOOK
St. John	N/A	45 minutes	20 minutes
West End, Tortola	N/A	45 minutes	20 minutes
Road Town, Tortola	15 minutes	1 hour	45 minutes
Virgin Gorda	15 minutes	1 1/2 hours	2 hours
St. Croix	30 minutes	1 1/2 hours	N/A

(☎284/495–2525). **Cyril E. King Airport** (☎340/774–5100). **Henry Rohlsen Airport** (☎340/778–1012).

FLIGHTS

There are nonstop and connecting flights, usually through San Juan, Puerto Rico, from the United States mainland to St. Thomas and St. Croix, with connecting ferry service from St. Thomas to St. John. There are no nonstop flights to the BVI from the United States; you must connect in San Juan or St. Thomas for the short hop over to Tortola or Virgin Gorda.

American Airlines and its subsidiary, American Eagle, are the biggest carriers to the Virgin Islands, with several nonstop flights a day from New York and Miami to St. Thomas and several connecting flights through San Juan. American also flies nonstop to St. Croix from Miami. The frequency of flights is seasonal.

Continental flies nonstop daily to St. Thomas from Newark, and US Airways has nonstop flights from Philadelphia and Charlotte, NC. Spirit Airlines flies nonstop everyday from Fort Lauderdale. Delta flies nonstop from Atlanta. In high season Northwest Airlines has a Saturday flight from Detroit. United also flies nonstop from Chicago and Washington, D.C.

Although connecting through San Juan is your best bet for getting to Tortola or Virgin Gorda, you can also fly from St. Thomas

and St. Croix to Tortola and Virgin Gorda on Air Sunshine.

Some islands in the British Virgin Islands are accessible only by small planes operated by local or regional carriers. International carriers will sometimes book those flights for you as part of your overall travel arrangements, or you can book directly with the local carrier.

Airline Contacts **American Airlines/American Eagle** (☎800/433–7300 ⊕www.aa.com). **Continental Airlines** (☎800/231–0856 ⊕www.continental.com). **Delta Airlines** (☎800/221–1212 ⊕www.delta.com). **jetBlue** (☎800/538–2583 ⊕www.jetblue.com). **Northwest Airlines** (☎800/225–2525 ⊕www.nwa.com). **Spirit Airlines** (☎800/772–7117 ⊕www.spiritair.com). **United Airlines** (☎800/864–8331 ⊕www.united.com). **US Airways** (☎800/622–1015 ⊕www.usairways.com).

Interisland Carriers **Air Sunshine** (☎800/327–8900, 800/435–8900 in Florida ⊕www.airsunshine.com). **Cape Air** (☎800/352–0714 ⊕www.flycapeair.com). **Fly BVI** (☎284/495–1747 ⊕www.fly-bvi.com).**LIAT** (☎888/844–5428 ⊕www.liatairline.com). **Seaborne** (☎340/773–6442 ⊕www.seaborneairlines.com).

▌BY BOAT

Ferries travel between St. Thomas and St. John. You can also travel by ferry from both St. Thomas and St. John to the British Virgin Islands, and between the British Virgin Islands themselves. The companies run regularly scheduled trips, departing from the Charlotte Amalie or Red Hook on St. Thomas; Cruz Bay, St. John; Gallows Bay, St. Croix; West End, Road Town, or Beef Island on Tortola; The Valley or North Sound on Virgin Gorda; and Jost Van Dyke. Schedules change, so check with your hotel or villa manager to find out the latest. The ferry companies are all regulated by the U.S. Coast Guard, and prices are about the same, so there's no point in trying to organize your schedule to take one company's ferries rather than another's. Just show up at the dock to buy your ticket on the next ferry departing for your destination. If it all seems confusing—and it can be very confusing for travel to or around the BVI—just ask a local who's also buying a ticket. They know the ropes.

While you might save a few dollars flying into St. Thomas if you're headed to the BVI, it's much easier to connect through San Juan for a flight to Tortola or Virgin Gorda. If you're headed to St. John or to points like North Sound, Virgin Gorda, or Jost Van Dyke, you'll have to hop a ferry regardless. If you're splitting your vacation between the U.S. and British Virgin Islands, ferries are the perfect way to get from one to another. You'll also get a bonus—views of the many small islands that dot the ferry route.

Dohm's Water Taxi runs from St. Thomas to St. John and any point in the BVI. You'll avoid the often crowded ferries, the crew will handle your luggage, and you'll arrive at your destination feeling relaxed; however, you'll pay significantly more for the convenience.

Ferry Contacts **Dohm's Water Taxi** (*340/775-6501*). **Inter-Island Boat Service** (☎ *340/776-6597 in St. Thomas, 284/495-4166 in Tortola*). **Native Son** (☎ *340/774-8685 in St. Thomas, 284/495-4617 in Tortola,* ⊕ *www.nativesonbvi. com*). **New Horizon Ferry Service** (☎ *284/495-9477* ⊕ *www. jostvandykeferry.com*). **North Sound Express** (☎ *284/495-2138*). **Peter Island Ferry** (☎ *284/495-2000* ⊕ *www.peterisland.com*). **Reefer** (☎ *340/776-8500 Ext. 6814* ⊕ *www. marriottfrenchmansreef.com*). **Smith's Ferry** (☎ *340/775-729 2in St. Thomas, 284/495-4495 in Tortola* ⊕ *www.smithsferry.com*). **Speedy's Ferries** (☎ *284/495-5240* ⊕ *www. speedysbvi.com*). **Tortola Fast Ferry** (☎ *284/494-2323* ⊕ *www.tortola-fastferry.com*).

❙ BY CAR

A car gives you mobility. You'll be able to spend an hour browsing at that cozy out-of-the-way shop instead of the 10 minutes allotted by your tour guide. You can beach-hop without searching for a ride, and you can sample that restaurant you've heard so much about that's half an hour (and an expensive taxi ride) away. On parts of some of the islands, you may need to rent a four-wheel-drive vehicle to really get out and about. Paved roads are generally good, but you may encounter a pothole or two (or three). Except for one divided highway on St. Croix, roads are narrow, and in hilly locations, twist and turn with the hill's contours. The roads on the north side of Tortola are particularly serpentine, with scary drop-offs that will send you plummeting down the hillside if you miss the turn. Drive slowly. Many villas in St. John and the BVI are on unpaved roads. A four-wheel drive could be a necessity if it rains. A higher clearance vehicle will help get safely over the rocks that may litter the road.

GASOLINE

Except in St. Croix, gas is up to $1 to $2 more per gallon than in the U.S. USVI stations sell gas by the gallon; BVI stations sell it by the liter or the gallon, depending on the station. Most stations accept major credit cards, but don't count on that. Some stations have a pump-it-yourself policy, but it's still easy to find ones with attendants. There's no need to tip unless they change a tire or do some other quick mechanical chore. You'll have to ask for a handwritten receipt if you're not paying by credit card. On smaller islands, stations may be closed on Sunday.

PARKING

Parking can be tight in towns across the USBVI. Workers grab up the street parking, sometimes arriving several hours early to get prime spaces. It's particularly difficult to find parking in Cruz Bay, St. John. There are free public lots scattered around town, but they're usually filled by folks taking the ferry to St. Thomas. Instead, your rental car company probably will allow you to park in their lot. Charlotte Amalie, St. Thomas, has a paid parking lot next to Fort Christian. A machine takes your money—$1 for the first hour and $5 for all day. In Christiansted, St. Croix, you'll find a public parking lot on Strand Street. Since the booth isn't staffed, there's no charge. There's also a public lot near Fort Christianvaern, but that lot is locked at 4:30 PM. It costs $1 for the first hour, and $6 for all day. Tortola has several free parking lots near the waterfront. In Virgin Gorda, there's a free lot at Virgin Gorda Yacht Harbor. There are no parking meters anywhere in the USBVI. Even if you're desperate for a parking space in the USVI, don't park in a handicapped space without a sticker—unless you want to pay a $1,000 fine.

ROAD CONDITIONS

Island roads are often narrow, winding, and hilly. Those in mountainous regions that experience heavy tropical rains are also potholed and poorly maintained. Streets in towns are narrow, a legacy of the days when islanders used horse-drawn carts. Drive with extreme caution, especially if you venture out at night. You won't see guardrails on every curve, although the drops can be frighteningly steep. And pedestrians and livestock often share the roadway with vehicles.

You'll face rush hour traffic in St. Thomas (especially in Charlotte Amalie); in St. Croix (especially in Christiansted and on Centerline Road); and in Tortola (especially around Road Town). All the larger towns have one-way streets. Although they're marked, the signs may be obscured by overhanging branches and other obstacles.

Drivers are prone to stopping in the road to chat with a passerby, to let a passenger out, or to buy a newspaper from a vendor. Pay attention when entering curves because you might find a stopped car on the other side.

ROADSIDE EMERGENCIES
To reach police, fire, or ambulance, dial 911 in the USVI and 999 in the BVI. There are no emergency-service companies such as AAA in the USBVI. Before driving off into the countryside, check your rental car for tire-changing equipment, including a spare tire in good condition.

RULES OF THE ROAD
Driving in the Virgin Islands can be tricky. Traffic moves on the left in *both* the USVI and BVI. Almost all cars are American, which means the driver sits on the side of the car next to the road's edge, a position that makes some people nervous.

Buckle up before you turn the key. Police in the USVI are notorious for giving $25 tickets to unbelted drivers and front-seat passengers. The police are a bit lax about driving under the influence, but why risk it? Take a taxi or appoint a designated driver when you're out on the town.

Traffic moves at about 10 mph in town; on major highways you can fly along at 50 mph. On other roads, the speed limit may be less. Main roads in the USVI carry route numbers, but they are not always marked, and locals may not know them. (Be prepared for such directions as, "Turn left at the big tree.") Few USVI secondary roads have signs; BVI roads aren't very well marked either.

ON THE GROUND

■ ADDRESSES

"Whimsical" might best describe USBVI addresses. Street names change for no apparent reason, and most buildings have no numbers. Streets in the main towns generally have names, though they may not have signs. Once you get out into the country on all islands, street names are rare. Areas are often known by their old plantation or estate names; for example, Estate Emmaus in St. John is found in what's now the heart of Coral Bay. Sometimes the estate names appear on maps, and sometimes they don't. The smaller the island, the less chance there is of a location having a specific street address. Addresses throughout this guide may include cross streets, landmarks, and other directionals. But to find your destination, you might have to ask a local—and be prepared for such directions as, "Go past the gas station, then take a right at the fish market. Stay on that road past the church and take a left after the palm tree."

■ COMMUNICATIONS

INTERNET

Many hotels now offer high-speed or dial-up Internet service. In most cases, Internet service is complimentary, but some resorts do charge a fee. Some provide computers in their lobbies if you've left your computer at home. You'll also find a few restaurants, bars, and businesses that offer Internet service for a fee. Specific coverage of Internet cafés can be found in the individual destination chapters.

Contacts **Cybercafes** (⊕*www. cybercafes.com*) lists over 4,000 Internet cafés worldwide.

PHONES

The good news is that you can now make a direct-dial telephone call from virtually any point on earth. The bad news? You can't always do so cheaply. Calling from a hotel is almost always the most expensive option; hotels usually add huge surcharges to all calls, particularly international ones. In some countries you can phone from call centers or even the post office. Calling cards usually keep costs to a minimum, but only if you purchase them locally. And then there are mobile phones (⇨*following*), which are sometimes more prevalent—particularly in the developing world—than landlines; as expensive as mobile phone calls can be, they're still usually a much cheaper option than calling from your hotel.

Phone service to and from the Virgin Islands is up-to-date and efficient. Phone cards are used throughout the islands for long-distance and international calling; you can buy them (in several denominations) at many retail shops and convenience stores. They must be used in special card phones, which are also widely available.

CALLING WITHIN THE USBVI

Local calls from USBVI pay phones run 25¢, although some privately owned phones are now charging 35¢. Calls from the USVI to the BVI and vice versa are charged as international toll calls. In the USVI and BVI, you dial just as if you were anywhere else in the U.S.

The area code for the USVI is 340; for the BVI, 284.

In the USVI, dial 913 to reach the operator. In the BVI, dial 119. In both locations, dial 0 for advice on how to place your call.

CALLING OUTSIDE THE USBVI

The country code for the United States is 1.

Calling the United States and Canada from the USBVI is just like making a long distance call within those countries: dial 1, plus the area code. To reach Europe, Australia, and New Zealand, dial 011 followed by the country code and the number.

If you're using a U.S.-based calling card, the U.S. access number should be on the back of the card. If you're using a local calling card, the access number will be on the back of your calling card.

MOBILE PHONES

If you have a multiband phone (some countries use different frequencies than what's used in the United States) and your service provider uses the world-standard GSM network (as do T-Mobile, AT&T, and Verizon), you can probably use your phone abroad. Roaming fees can be steep, however: 99¢ a minute is considered reasonable. And overseas you normally pay the toll charges for incoming calls. Internationally, it's almost always cheaper to send a text message than to make a call, since text messages have a very low set fee (often less than 5¢).

There are no cell phone rental companies in the USBVI. There are a few places that sell cell phones, but they price is much higher than in the U.S. Cell phones from most U.S. companies work in most parts of the USVI if you have a roaming feature. If you're on St. John's north coast, you may have some difficulties; you may find yourself connected to BoatPhone, a Tortola service. If you're on the south side of Tortola and in Spanish Town on Virgin Gorda, you may be able to connect to AT&T and Sprint, but other locations in the BVI have sporadic service.

Contacts Cellular Abroad (☎800/287–5072 ⊕www.cellular-abroad.com) rents and sells GMS phones and sells SIM cards that work in many countries. **Mobal** (☎888/888–9162 ⊕www.mobal-rental.com) rents mobiles and sells GSM phones (starting at $49) that will operate in 140 countries. Per-call rates vary throughout the world. **Planet Fone** (☎888/988–4777 ⊕www.planetfone.com) rents cell phones, but the per-minute rates are expensive.

Information AT&T (☎340/777–7777). **Sprint** (☎340/715–5400)

▌ CUSTOMS & DUTIES

You're always allowed to bring goods of a certain value back home without having to pay any duty or import tax. But there's a limit on the amount of tobacco and liquor you can bring back duty-free, and some countries have separate limits for perfumes; for exact figures, check with your customs department. The values of so-called "duty-free" goods are included in these amounts. When you shop abroad, save all your receipts, as customs inspectors may ask to see them as well as the items you purchased. If the total value of your goods is more than the duty-free limit, you'll have to pay a tax (most often a flat percentage) on the value of everything beyond that limit.

As long as you're not bringing in meat, passing through BVI customs is usually a breeze. If you want to bring that special cut of steak from home, you'll need a $25 agriculture permit, but it's not worth the effort since you can buy meat all over the BVI. You don't clear customs entering the USVI if you're coming from the U.S. You can't take fruits and vegetables out of either the USVI

or BVI, so eat up that apple on the way to the airport. You may travel with your pets to the USBVI without any special shots or paperwork.

U.S. Information U.S. **Customs & Border Protection** (⊕www.cbp.gov).

▌ ELECTRICITY

The USBVI use the same current as the U.S. mainland—110 volts. European appliances will require adaptors. Since power fluctuations occasionally occur, bring a heavy-duty surge protector (available at hardware stores) if you plan to use your computer.

Contacts Steve Kropla's **Help for World Travelers** (⊕www.kropla.com) has information on electrical and telephone plugs around the world. **Walkabout Travel Gear** (⊕www.walkabouttravelgear.com) has a good coverage of electricity under "adapters."

ETIQUETTE

When passing strangers on the street, say good morning, good afternoon, or good evening. It's considered polite. When meeting new people, Virgin Islanders usually shake hands. (No kissy-kissy here.) It's particularly important to take the time to greet shop-keepers and other service personnel, as you'll get much better service if you do. Any interaction should start with some kind of pleasantry, whether you're doing business or not; it's considered rude if you don't. It's also important to try not to come on too strong; too much assertiveness is considered rude in any interaction, even when you are making a valid complaint. Take a deep breath and smile.

Cover up when you're not at the beach; Virgin Islanders are modest folks. How to dress when you're out on the town depends on where you're going. Heading down to that beach-front bar? Shorts and T-shirts are fine. If you're planning to dance the night away at the resort's nightclub, you'll want to wear something nicer. Some resorts have a dress code, so check before you pack so you have the right clothes.

GAY & LESBIAN TRAVEL

Gay and lesbian travelers are generally welcome in the USB-VI, but some unfriendly attitudes still exist. Ask at your hotel for advice on places to go. St. Thomas has a thriving gay community, and you'll be made very welcome. St. Croix has gay-friendly resorts perfect for couples as well as singles.

HEALTH

The most common types of illnesses are caused by contaminated food and water. If you have problems, mild cases of traveler's diarrhea may respond to Imodium (known generically as loperamide) or Pepto-Bismol. Be sure to drink plenty of fluids; if you can't keep fluids down, seek medical help immediately.

Mosquito-borne illnesses are also a problem in the Caribbean; always use an insect repellant to protect yourself in the Virgin Islands.

Condoms can help prevent most sexually transmitted diseases, but they aren't absolutely reliable and their quality varies from country to country. Speak with your physician and/or check the CDC or World Health Organization Web sites for health alerts, particularly if you're pregnant, traveling with children, or have a chronic illness.

SPECIFIC ISSUES IN THE U.S. & BRITISH VIRGIN ISLANDS

Water in the USBVI is generally safe to drink. Mosquitoes can be a problem here, particularly after a spate of showers. Insect repellent is readily available, but you may want to bring something from home because it is more expensive in the Virgin Islands. Dengue fever is a particular concern in the Virgin Islands because of widespread outbreaks in nearby Puerto Rico in 2007.

Less dangerous, but certainly a nuisance, are the little pests from the sand-flea family known as no-see-ums. You don't realize you're being had for dinner until it's too late, and these bites itch, and itch, and itch. No-see-ums start getting hungry around 3 PM and are out in force by sunset. They're always more numerous in shady and wooded areas (such as the campgrounds on St. John). Take a towel along for sitting on the beach, and keep reapplying insect repellent.

Beware of the manchineel tree, which grows near the beach and has green applelike fruit that is poisonous and bark and leaves that burn the skin.

Even if you've never been sunburned in your life, believe the warnings and use sunscreen in the USBVI. If you're dark-skinned, start with at least an SPF of 15 and keep it on. If you're fair-skinned, use a sunscreen with a higher SPF and stay out of the sun during midday. Rays are most intense between 11 and 2, so move under a sea grape tree (although you can still burn here) or, better yet, take a shady lunch break. You can also burn in this part of the world when it's cloudy, so putting sunscreen on every day no matter what the weather is the best strategy.

OVER-THE-COUNTER REMEDIES
Over-the-counter-medications like aspirin, Tylenol, and Mylanta are readily available in the USBVI. Kmart on St. Thomas and St. Croix have cheaper prices, but you can find a big selection of these products at grocery and drug stores across the USBVI. You can find less of a selection (and considerably higher prices) on the smaller islands.

HOURS OF OPERATION

Bank hours are generally Monday through Thursday 9 to 3 and Friday 9 to 5; a handful open Saturday (9 to noon). Walk-up windows open at 8:30 on weekdays. Hours may vary slightly from branch to branch and island to island, but they are generally weekdays 7:30 or 8 to 4 or 5:30 and Saturday 7:30 or 8 to noon or 2:30.

Shops, especially those in the heavily touristed areas, are open Monday to Saturday 9 to 5. Those near the cruise ships may also be open on Sunday.

HOLIDAYS
In addition to the U.S. federal holidays, locals in the USVI celebrate Three Kings Day (Jan. 6); Transfer Day (commemorates Denmark's 1917 sale of the territory to the United States, Mar. 31); Holy Thursday and Good Friday; Emancipation Day (when slavery was abolished in the Danish West Indies in 1848, July 3); Columbus Day and USVI–Puerto Rico Friendship Day (always on

Columbus Day weekend); and Liberty Day (honoring David Hamilton Jackson, who secured freedom of the press and assembly from King Christian X of Denmark, Nov. 1).

Although the government closes down for 23 days a year, most of these holidays have no effect on shopping hours. Unless there's a cruise-ship arrival, expect most stores to close for Christmas and a few other holidays in the slower summer months.

The following public holidays are celebrated in the BVI: New Year's Day, Commonwealth Day (Mar. 14), Good Friday (Fri. before Easter), Easter Sunday (usually Mar. or Apr.), Easter Monday (day after Easter), Whit Monday (1st Mon. in May), Sovereign's Birthday (June 16), Territory Day (July 1), BVI August Festival Days (usually 1st 2 wks in Aug.), St. Ursula's Day (Oct. 21), Christmas, and Boxing Day (day after Christmas).

▌MAIL

Airmail between the USBVI and cities in the United States or Canada takes 7 to 14 days; surface mail can take 4 to 6 weeks. For island-specific information on post office locations, postal rates, and opening hours, *see* Mail & Shipping *in* the Essentials sections of individual island chapters.

SHIPPING PACKAGES

Courier services (such as Airborne, DHL, Federal Express, UPS, and others) operate in the USBVI, although not every company serves each island. "Overnight" service is more likely to take two or more days, because of the limited number of flights on which packages can be shipped. Service to St. John and the smaller of the British Virgin Islands can take even longer.

▌MONEY

The U.S. dollar is the currency on both the USVI and BVI.

Prices throughout this guide are given for adults. Reduced admission fees for senior citizens are hard to come by in the USBVI.

ATMS & BANKS

Your own bank will probably charge a fee for using ATMs abroad; the foreign bank you use may also charge a fee. Nevertheless, you'll usually get a better rate of exchange at an ATM than you will at a currency-exchange office or even when changing money in a bank. And extracting funds as you need them is a safer option than carrying around a large amount of cash.

▐ TIP➜ **PIN numbers with more than four digits are not recognized at ATMs in many countries. If yours has five or more, remember to change it before you leave.**

You can find ATMs at most banks in the USBVI. The ATMs at FirstBank and Scotia Banks, the only two in St. John, sometimes run out of cash on long holiday weekends.

CREDIT CARDS

Throughout this guide, the following abbreviations are used: **AE**, American Express; **D**, Discover; **DC**, Diners Club; **MC**, MasterCard; and **V**, Visa.

It's a good idea to inform your credit-card company before you travel, especially if you're going abroad and don't travel internationally very often. Otherwise, the credit-card company might put a hold on your card owing to unusual activity—not a good thing halfway through your trip. Record all your credit-card numbers—as well as the phone numbers to call if your cards are lost or stolen—in a safe place, so you're prepared should something go wrong. Both MasterCard and Visa have general numbers you can call (collect if you're abroad) if your card is lost, but you're better off calling the number of your issuing bank, since MasterCard and Visa usually just transfer you to your bank; your bank's number is usually printed on your card.

Major credit cards are widely accepted at hotels, restaurants, shops, car-rental agencies, other service providers, and ATM machines throughout the Caribbean. The only places that might not accept them are open-air markets or tiny shops in out-of-the-way villages. Villa renters should be forewarned that some managers may not accept credit cards.

Reporting Lost Cards American Express (☎800/992–3404 in U.S., 336/393–1111 collect from abroad ⊕ www.americanexpress.com). **Diners Club** (☎800/234–6377 in U.S., 303/799–1504 collect from abroad ⊕ www.dinersclub.com). **Discover** (☎800/347–2683 in U.S., 801/902–3100 collect from abroad ⊕ www.discovercard.com). **MasterCard** (☎800/622–7747 in U.S., 636/722–7111 collect from abroad ⊕ www.mastercard.com). **Visa** (☎800/847–2911 in U.S., 410/581–9994 collect from abroad ⊕ www.visa.com).

TRAVELER'S CHECKS & CARDS

Some consider this the currency of the caveman, and it's true that fewer establishments accept traveler's checks these days. Nevertheless, they're a cheap and secure way to carry extra money, particularly on trips to urban areas. Both Citibank (under the Visa brand) and American Express issue traveler's checks in the United States, but Amex is better known and more widely accepted; you can also avoid hefty surcharges by cashing Amex checks at Amex offices. Whatever you do, keep track of all the serial numbers in case the checks are lost or stolen.

American Express now offers a stored-value card called a Travelers Cheque Card, which you can use wherever American Express credit cards are accepted, including ATMs. The card can carry a minimum of $300 and a maximum of $2,700, and it's a very safe way to carry your funds. Although you can get replacement funds in 24 hours if your card is lost or stolen, it doesn't really strike us as a very good deal. In addition to a high initial cost ($14.95 to set up the card, plus $5 each time you "reload"), you still have to pay a 2% fee for each purchase in a foreign currency (similar to that of any credit card). Further, each time you use the card in an ATM you pay a transaction fee of $2.50 on top of the 2% transaction fee for the conversion—add it all up and it can be considerably more than you would pay when simply using your own ATM card. Regular traveler's checks are just as secure and cost less.

Contacts **American Express** (☎ 888/412–6945 in U.S., 801/945–9450 collect outside of U.S. to add value or speak to customer service ⊕ www.americanexpress.com).

▌ SAFETY

In the USVI, ask hotel staff members about the wisdom of venturing off the beaten path. Although it may seem like a nice night for a stroll back to your hotel from that downtown restaurant, it's better to take a taxi than face an incident. Although local police go to great lengths to stop it, crime does occur. The BVI has seen less crime than its neighbors to the west, but again, better safe than sorry.

Follow the same precautions that you would anywhere. Look around before using the ATM. Keep tabs on your pocketbook; put it on your lap—not the back of your chair—in restaurants.

Stow valuable jewelry or other items in the hotel safe when you leave your room; hotel and villa burglaries do occur infrequently. Deserted beaches on St. John and the BVI are usually safe, but think twice about stopping at that luscious strand of lonely sand on St. Croix and St. Thomas. Hotel or public beaches are your best bets. Never leave your belongings unattended at the beach or on the seats of your rental car. Be sure to lock the doors on your rental villa or hotel room. Break-ins can happen across the USBVI, so it's better to be safe than sorry.

■ TIP → Distribute your cash, credit cards, IDs, and other valuables between a deep front pocket, an inside jacket or vest pocket, and a hidden money pouch. Don't reach for the money pouch once you're in public.

▌ TAXES

There's no sales tax in the USVI, but there's an 8% hotel-room tax; most hotels also add a 10% service charge to the bill. The St. John Accommodations Council members ask that hotel and villa guests voluntarily pay a $1 per day surcharge to help fund school and community projects and other good works. Many hotels add additional energy surcharges and the like, so please ask about any additional charges, but these are not government-imposed taxes.

In the BVI, the departure tax is $5 per person by boat and $20 per person by plane. There's a separate booth at the airport and ferry terminals to collect this tax, which must be paid in cash in U.S. currency. Most hotels in the BVI add a service charge ranging from 5% to 18% to the bill. A few restaurants and some shops tack on an additional 10% charge if you use a credit card. There's no sales tax in the BVI. However, there's a 7% government tax on hotel rooms.

TIME

The USBVI are in the Atlantic Standard Time zone, which is one hour later than Eastern Standard or four hours earlier than GMT. During daylight saving time, between April and October, Atlantic Standard is the same time as Eastern Daylight Time.

TIPPING

Many hotels in the USVI add a 10% to 15% service charge to cover the services of your maid and other staff. However, some hotels use part of that money to fund their operations, passing on only a portion of it to the staff. Check with your maid or bellhop to determine the hotel's policy. If you discover you need to tip, give bellhops and porters 50¢ to $1 per bag and maids $1 or $2 per day. Special errands or requests of hotel staff always require an additional tip. At restaurants bartenders and waiters expect a 10%–15% tip, but always check your tab to see whether service is included. Taxi drivers in the USVI get a 15% tip.

In the BVI, tip porters and bellhops $1 per bag. Sometimes a service charge of 10% is included on restaurant bills; it's customary to leave another 5% if you liked the service. If no charge is added, 15% is the norm. Cabbies normally aren't tipped because most own their cabs; add 10% to 15% if they exceed their duties.

INDEX

ABOUT OUR WRITERS

St. Thomas–based writer and dietitian **Carol M. Bareuther**, works part-time for the government of the U.S. Virgin Islands. In her other life as a writer, she writes for local, regional, and international publications on the topics of food, travel, and water sports. She's the author of two books, *Sports Fishing in the Virgin Islands* and *Virgin Islands Cooking*. She is the mother of Nikki and Rian, as well as the longtime partner of photographer Dean Barnes. She covered St. Thomas, Anegada, and Jost Van Dyke for this edition, and she contributed the essays on island cuisine and chartering a yacht.

Long-time St. John resident **Lynda Lohr** lives above Coral Bay with her significant other and two chubby cats. She moved to St. John in 1984 for a bit of adventure; she's still there and still enjoying the adventure. The editor of *Island News*, a newsletter for people with a serious interest in the Virgin Islands, she also writes for numerous national, regional, and local publications as well as travel Web sites. On her rare days off, she swims at Great Maho Bay and hikes the island's numerous trails. For this edition, she covered St. John, St. Croix, Tortola, Virgin Gorda, and many of the smaller islands. She was also responsible for Essentials and the essay on diving.